WAITING FOR AN ARMY TO DIE

By the same author

Grass Roots: An Anti-Nuclear Source Book

Fred A. Wilcox

WAITING FOR AN ARMY TO DIE

THE TRAGEDY OF AGENT ORANGE

Random House · New York

All rights reserved under International and Pan-American Copyright Conventions.
Published in the United States by Random House, Inc., New York, and
simultaneously in Canada by Random House of Canada Limited, Toronto.
Paperback edition published simultaneously by Vintage Books.

Library of Congress Cataloging in Publication Data
Wilcox, Fred.
Waiting for an army to die.
1. Veterans—Diseases—United States. 2. Agent
Orange—War use. 3. Agent Orange—Toxicology.
4. Vietnamese Conflict, 1961–1975—Chemical warfare.
I. Title.
UB369.W54 1983   363.1'79   82-42791
ISBN 0-394-52797-6

Manufactured in the United States of America
98765432
First Edition

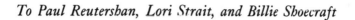

To Paul Reutershan, Lori Strait, and Billie Shoecraft

I wish to thank John and Deborah Green for providing me with valuable research material and moral support, and for the work they have done on behalf of Vietnam veterans; my agent, Glen Hartley, for his advice and intelligent criticism; and Lisa Kiddon, for her considerable assistance. I also wish to express my admiration for all of the men and women who contribute so much of their time and energy to helping Agent Orange victims.

CONTENTS

	Introduction	ix
1	Ketchup and Water	3
2	The Doomed Platoon	16
3	Seals and River Rats	31
4	A Maimed Generation	44
5	Dying Down Under	59
6	Stonewall	79
7	When You Can't Sue the Government That Kills You	98
8	Casualty Report	114
9	Humans, Rats, and Lesser Beings	126
10	The Vietnamization of America	147
11	Vietnam Veterans Are America's Future	175
	Appendix	183
	Bibliography	207
	Notes	209
	Index	215

INTRODUCTION

In the spring of 1978, a twenty-eight-year old Vietnam veteran who appeared on the *Today* show shocked many of the program's viewers by announcing: "I died in Vietnam, but I didn't even know it." As a helicopter crew chief responsible for transporting supplies to the 20th Engineering Brigade, Paul Reutershan flew almost daily through clouds of herbicides being discharged from C123 cargo planes. He observed the dark swaths cut into the jungle by the spraying, watched the mangrove forests turn brown, sicken and die, but didn't really worry about his own health. Agent Orange, according to the Army, was "relatively nontoxic to humans and animals." On December 14, 1978, Reutershan succumbed to the cancer that had destroyed much of his colon, liver, and abdomen.

In the months before he died, Reutershan founded Agent Orange Victims International, and spent all of his waning energies trying to inform the American people about his belief that his cancer was the result of his exposure to a herbicide called Agent Orange. But the VA denied, and still denies, any connection between exposure to Agent Orange and the many illnesses Vietnam veterans suffer. Just three weeks before he died, however, Reutershan did receive a disability check from the VA. "He was too weak to even sign it," his sister told reporters. Two days after his death, Paul's mother received a letter from the Veterans Administration requesting that the check be returned.

Agent Orange, named after the color-coded stripe that was painted around the fifty-five-gallon barrels in which it was stored, is a fifty-fifty combination of two commercial herbicides, 2,4-D (n-butyl-2,4-dichlorophenoxyacetate) and 2,4,5-T (n-butyl-2,4,5-trichlorophenoxyacetate). It was first developed by the U.S. Army as an instrument of chemical warfare at Fort Detrick, Maryland. Following a warning by the National Academy of Sciences concerning the potential dangers of biological warfare to the United States, the U.S. Army began experimenting with a number of substances to "regulate" or destroy the growth of plant life. By 1959, the first large-scale aerial tests of herbicides for military defoliation were being conducted at Ft. Drum, New York. These tests were so successful that in 1961 Defense Secretary McNamara suggested that further testing be done on jungle vegetation in Vietnam. In 1962 the Department of Defense commenced a program of systematically defoliating millions of acres of Vietnamese forests and croplands. By the time the program was called to a halt in 1971, herbicides had destroyed an estimated 4.5 million acres of Vietnamese countryside.*

Sprayed undiluted, Agent Orange proved highly successful in killing broad-leaved vegetation and by 1965 became the most widely used herbicide in the defoliation campaign.† By 1970, 11.2 million gallons of Agent Orange had been dumped on the vegetation and people of Vietnam, destroying some areas so completely that it may take decades for the natural vegetation to fully return. Far from being harmless to animals and man, herbicide Orange

---

*According to Agent Orange Victims International, "Schedules of the herbicide spraying missions were recorded on HERBS tapes, a computerized record of time, place, geographic location of beginning, end, and flight line of the mission, amount of herbicide and the military purpose of the operation. The tapes cover the period from August, 1965, to February, 1971." However, even with the computerized documentation of the HERBS tapes, estimates vary on just how many acres of Vietnam were defoliated.

†In addition to Agent Orange the United States sprayed approximately 1.1 million gallons of Agent Blue and 5.1 million gallons of Agent White on Vietnam. For a description of these herbicides see pp. 186–190 of the appendix.

contained TCDD-dioxin, a substance so toxic that Dr. Jacqueline Verrett of the Food and Drug Administration calls it "100,000 times more potent than thalidomide as a cause of birth defects in some species."[1]

In response to the veterans' claims that their exposure to Agent Orange is causing them serious health problems, the Veterans Administration insists that too little is known about the effects of dioxin on human health to justify such claims. But in testimony before the New York State Temporary Commission on Dioxin Exposure, Dr. Steven Stellman, assistant vice president for epidemiology of the American Cancer Society, stated:

> The biological effects of the ingredients of Agent Orange have been studied in experimental animals for more than fifteen years. And animal experiments are used to test toxic properties of chemicals, because it is unethical to test them deliberately on people . . . Dioxin is embryotoxic; that is, it kills embryos in pregnant rodents; and teratogenic; that is, causes birth defects in several strains of rats and mice.

Dr. Stellman is just one of the many scientists who have concluded that dioxin is teratogenic and carcinogenic when given to laboratory animals. Many of the symptoms from which veterans suffer, including chloracne, a severe skin rash similar to teenage acne; cancer; and multiple birth defects in their offspring, correspond to the effects of dioxin on experimental animals.

As diabolical as the defoliation campaign may seem years after the last C_{123} dumped its cargo on the Vietnamese countryside, to the pilots who flew those missions it was a means of saving American lives and hastening an end to a war that, year after year, politicians insisted was "nearly won." Destroying the enemy's cover, the military argued, would greatly reduce his opportunity to ambush American forces, and would force him into the open where, these theorists believed, he would be decimated by American firepower. Destroying foodstuffs that might aide hostile forces would erode the enemy's morale and diminish his fighting ability.

Whether the use of herbicides was a violation of the Geneva Protocol of 1925, which proposed a ban on chemical warfare, will undoubtedly be debated by historians and scholars for many years. To the military it was just one tactic that a conventional army might use to defeat insurgents "fighting in their own backyard."

To those Americans who survived mines, ambushes, booby traps, and firefights, the supreme irony is to discover, as Paul Reutershan did, that your own government may have killed you. Worse yet, when Reutershan and many other sick and dying veterans tried to force the Department of Defense and Veterans Administration to take some responsibility for their suffering, they were met with intense resistance. While head of the VA, Max Cleland insisted that there was simply no evidence linking Agent Orange to the types of ailments about which the veterans were complaining. Many claims for service-connected disability were routinely denied, and veterans seeking help from VA hospitals were often given inadequate, sometimes hostile, treatment and diagnosed as suffering from a variety of psychosomatic symptoms. Informed that their service records had been lost or burned, veterans were discouraged from looking further into the source of their illness. But the intimidation and bureaucratic stonewalling seem only to have strengthened the veterans' resolve to force their government and the manufacturers of herbicides to admit responsibility for the tragedy that has befallen Vietnam veterans and their families.

While advocates for Vietnam veterans keep the pressure on the Veterans Administration and Congress, lawsuits on behalf of the veterans are pending against several manufacturers of herbicides, including Dow Chemical, Monsanto, Diamond Shamrock, and Hooker Chemicals. Establishing legal responsibility for the contamination of several million men and women, however, may prove to be a formidable task. Dow, for example, argues that what information it had on the hazardous effects of Agent Orange was given to the Department of Defense; therefore, Dow insists, liability for how the product was used lies with the government. The question of just who knew what about the dangers of spraying toxic herbicides over long periods of time on areas inhabited by human beings and animals will be clarified, one hopes, during the litigation over this issue. But it is already tragically clear that chemical companies developed, manufactured, and sold a product containing significant quantities of dioxin to the Department of Defense, which then used it for chemical warfare.

According to Dow Chemical, critics of herbicide use are engaged in a "witch hunt" reminiscent of the McCarthy era, with chemicals replacing politicians on the environmental fanatic's black list. To Dow, the complaints of veterans who are dying of cancer, Vietnamese women whose children have been born horribly deformed, and women in the U.S. who have suffered miscarriages or given birth to stillborn children following the use of dioxin-contaminated herbicides near their homes are "without scientific foundation." But listening to the testimony of veterans and their wives at hearings held by the New York State Temporary Commission on Dioxin Exposure I was overwhelmed by the extent of this tragedy; my research into the Agent Orange issue had simply not prepared me for what I heard.

For their chloracne, one of the indisputable symptoms of dioxin exposure, veterans testified that VA doctors recommended "salves" and "powders" and, in many cases, visits to a staff psychiatrist, implying that their rash was symptomatic of what the VA calls "war neurosis." One woman testified that her husband, who was exposed to Agent Orange in Vietnam, had suffered from a number of ailments for several years. "But recently," she told a hushed auditorium, "he cleaned all of the useless medication the VA had prescribed from the cabinet. He just became psychotic, and last August he took his own life." Commenting on the Agent Orange physical examination touted by the VA as an expression of its concern for Vietnam veterans, a former Marine called it "a fraud, a fake, an exercise in stupidity." The "physical," said those who testified, is at best cursory, with little or no attempt on the VA's part to contact veterans with the results of their "examination." Describing the sudden weight loss that many Vietnam veterans seem to suffer, one veteran told the commission: "I had lost eighteen pounds in three days. I was vomiting, couldn't hold water. I was dehydrated, and called the VA's dietician to ask what I should do. She said, 'Suck on candy, and take liquids at room temperature.' " Summing up the veterans' feelings, a former helicopter pilot said: "To tell you the truth I wouldn't trust the VA with a hangnail!"

In the process of writing *Waiting for an Army to Die*, I have traveled thousands of miles, poured through stacks of documents, and spoken with hundreds of people about Agent Orange. I have interviewed scientists who have spent years researching the effects of dioxin on laboratory animals; veterans who are suffering from one or more of the symptoms associated with dioxin exposure; veterans' wives who have suffered repeated miscarriages or given birth to children with multiple birth defects; women living near Alsea, Oregon, whose complaints were instrumental in getting the EPA to suspend certain domestic uses of 2,4,5-T; lawyers for veterans who are suing the chemical companies; and many others. I have concluded that in a very real sense we are all Vietnamese to the chemical companies, who feel their annual profits are more important than the health of human beings. America, like Vietnam during the war years, is a testing ground for the chemical companies and their vested interests. We have allowed ourselves to be used as guinea pigs, permitted our land and water to be poisoned, and accepted the notion that the average citizen is powerless to stop the ecological devastation of our nation and our world. Fortunately, the men and women who fought in Vietnam have refused to accept this notion of powerlessness, and I greatly admire their courage and fortitude.

In writing about Agent Orange I do not wish to create yet another stereotype of Vietnam veterans. More than one hundred thousand veterans have undergone the VA's "Agent Orange examination" while thousands more have applied for service-connected disability due to their exposure to Agent Orange. But this does not mean that all veterans are sick, dying, or have fathered children with birth defects. When I use the term "veteran," I am referring specifically to those men and women who served in Vietnam and who believe they were exposed to toxic chemicals. Some veterans are bitter at having served in a war they consider a "waste," while others would willingly return to Southeast Asia if called upon by their government (the majority of men who served in Vietnam volunteered for duty there). And just as there is no unanimity among veterans about the war, they often disagree on how best to go about convincing the government to take their complaints seriously. Regardless of how they feel about Vietnam, and in spite of their political differences, all of the veterans with whom I spoke share a common desire. They wish to see those veterans who are too sick to work or who are dying from cancer compensated for their illnesses, and they want the Veterans Administration to show good faith regarding the health and welfare of Vietnam veterans.

This book, I hope, will clarify matters for those who are confused or bewildered by contradictory reports on the hazards of using herbicides contaminated with dioxin. In future years, scientists will undoubtedly continue to debate the effects of dioxin on human health, lawyers will fight for compensation for victims of dioxin poisoning, and politicians will, on occasion, acknowledge that a serious problem exists. Meanwhile, the suffering continues. Thousands of Vietnam veterans are frustrated, angry, disillusioned. They simply cannot wait for another two, five, or ten years for help. By that time far too many will have died from the effects of the substance that many scientists, including Professor Matthew Meselson of Harvard, a dioxin expert, call "the most toxic small molecule known to man."

WAITING
FOR
AN ARMY
TO DIE

1

KETCHUP
AND WATER

(BIEN HOA, SOUTH VIETNAM, 1966) The twin-engine C123 Provider transports are loaded, the booms on their wings checked. There is no real damage to any of the craft from the hits they took the day before, and the crews are checking the coordinates, air speed, and other details of the day's mission. They will be airborne before daybreak, flying south, then east, and after circling at high altitudes they will descend in tight formation to spread thousands of gallons of Agent Orange over a target approximately 8.5 miles long, with each plane covering a swath about 250 feet wide. Within the dense mangrove forests are colonies of Viet Cong who have struck at the surrounding countryside for years, only to vanish into an impenetrable stronghold. But the men who participate in Operation Ranch Hand are not always told what lies beneath the foilage, or what they are spraying. Their assignment is to strip away the enemy's cover, flushing him into the open where, tacticians believe, he will be destroyed by American and South Vietnamese ground forces. Until 1970, when the Air Force suspends use of Agent Orange in Vietnam, the Ranch Hand team will fly hundreds of missions, destroying thousands, then millions, of acres of mangrove forests, jungle, and crops.

Because of navigational difficulties, and the possibility of losing crew members when a plane is shot down, night flights have been ruled out. The slow-moving planes, skimming in broad daylight just 150 feet above the trees, make tempting targets to enemy gunners. The planes move in patterns similar to those one makes when mowing the lawn, forward and back until a predetermined area has been fully covered. Although a mission can be completed in three to five minutes, the Ranch Handers take many hits, making them among the most decorated veterans of the Vietnam War.

Sometimes the C123s spray around the perimeters of base camps, where shirtless men carrying tanks of herbicides on their backs now and then playfully spray one another, or Huey helicopters mounted with spray booms work and rework approaches to the base. Some of the troops complain of headaches that last for hours, even days, and skin rashes that cover their arms, necks, and faces. But no one collapses or dies following his exposure to Agent Orange, and the defoliated Maginot Line between base camp and jungle might mean the difference between life and death. The defoliation campaign, though a topic of casual conversation among the troops, is accepted as just one part of the overall effort to defeat the enemy.

"I really didn't know what they were spraying," explains John Green, who served as a medic in Vietnam. "Some people thought it was for mosquitoes, but I never really gave it much thought. I do remember walking through defoliated zones. Everything was dead. The trees had literally grown to death, because that's how Agent Orange works—it accelerates growth in a plant's cells until finally the plant or tree dies. Did we drink the water? Of course we did. Where we were there was nothing else to drink. If we found a bomb crater full of water we just scooped it out and drank it, no matter how brown or scummy it looked. Some of our food was undoubtedly sprayed with Agent Orange. But how were we to know? The army told us the stuff was harmless. And we were told it was supposed to be saving our lives. The 'strategists' had this idea that the enemy moved in neat little patterns, like a highway grid or something. You eliminate the pattern and you shut the man off, he can't move anymore. But that, unfortunately, was nonsense. If they shut off one of his trails, he just found another. It was his country, and he really knew how to compensate."

Because of the frequency with which men and equipment were moved from one location to another, some veterans are not certain where they were at any given time. But they do remember being doused with herbicides or walking through defoliated moonscapes. They remember that even before they left Vietnam, their bodies were covered with rashes; they felt dizzy, nauseous, and suffered from migraine headaches, stomach cramps, and black depressions. The rashes were considered just another variety of "jungle rot" by medical personnel, while other symptoms of dioxin exposure were dismissed as the result of stress brought on by the war. Some soldiers realized that their problems had something to do with the spraying, but there was little they could do to stop it or to protect themselves from further poisoning. They had not been issued protective gear, had no idea when or where a spray mission might occur, and lived in the same clothing for days, even weeks, while in the field. If they survived twelve months they would be home free. They had little reason to believe otherwise.

One of the men who believed he had escaped serious injury in Vietnam now lives near Syracuse, New York, just fifty miles from where the first large-scale tests of herbicides for military use took place. On the walls of the small rented house where Ray Clark lives with his wife and five children, there are no medals framed in glass, no photographs of smiling young men in battle dress, no captured enemy weapons or flags. Unlike veterans of World War II, who are fond of displaying the booty of a victorious army, Vietnam veterans seldom reserve a room—or even one wall—of their home for a shrine to the glories of war. And, though he once walked point as a minesweeper in Vietnam, one of the most dangerous assignments of the war, Ray Clark, with his pipe and sorrowful blue eyes, reminds one more of a history professor than of Hollywood's gung-ho Marine. While recuperating from battle fatigue Clark learned that his battalion had been nearly wiped out when their newly arrived M16s misfired during a battle. Six years later, at the age of twenty-eight, he would discover that he was suffering from bladder cancer.

Before our interview, I had phoned to ask directions to the Clarks' home and, as I passed dilapidated trailers and patchwork houses with smoke curling from crooked little chimneys, I thought about the many veterans I knew who had grown up in impoverished areas like this. It was here that, during the sixties and early seventies, military recruiters scoured the high schools looking for adolescents willing to be turned into Marines, Green Berets, Rangers, and grunts. And it was here that the military, offering young men the chance to become authentic heroes, easily filled their monthly quotas, sending hundreds of thousands to fight in a country about which the majority of Americans knew virtually nothing. Passing through the village near the Clarks' house, I half expected to see a monument to those who fought, and died, in Vietnam.

When Clark returned home there were no parades, no crowds, no politicians handing out keys to "grateful cities." If they survived their tour of duty, Vietnam veterans boarded "freedom birds" at Tan Son Nhut Airport and were whisked through the twilight zone to San Francisco, where they were often met by antiwar demonstrators. Then they flew home to cities that were bitterly divided over the war, or took a bus that deposited them at 3:00 A.M. on the deserted streets of their hometown. Others hitchhiked home and, when a car stopped to offer them a lift, wondered whether they should keep quiet, or perhaps even lie, about where they had spent the past twelve months. While still in Vietnam they had heard that many Americans were angry about the war—angry, strangely enough, at them. They would discover that their arrival in California was a portent of things to come. "I got sick of the stereotypes," Clark explains. "The movies, books, radio, newspapers had us typed as baby killers, psychos, drug addicts. I just didn't want to walk down the street and have someone say, 'Hey, there goes Ray Clark. He takes drugs, kills babies, rapes women. He's really weird, man.' "

Ray married, found a job, and started school. He didn't want to talk about the war, and most of all he just wanted to be left alone to raise his children and live a "normal" life. "I joined the American Legion once," Clark says. "And all they wanted to do was parade around saying, 'We fought a good war. We fought a good old war, didn't we.' Well, we didn't fight a good war. We lost. We lost fifty-four thousand men for absolutely nothing." Then he found that before he would celebrate his thirtieth birthday, he might die of a form of cancer that rarely kills anyone under fifty. The fighting hadn't killed him, but something with which he had come into contact in the jungles of Vietnam just might.

In his aversion to war stories and his desire to put the war behind him, Ray Clark is typical of most Vietnam veterans. But unlike many veterans, he does not have to work at forgetting his combat experiences. Because, except for arriving in and returning from Vietnam, Clark has little conscious recollection of his experiences there. With his wife's help, and by talking to other veterans, he has managed to piece together fragments of the period he spent in Vietnam, but there are still gaps, the picture remains incomplete. "He would talk in his sleep," Mrs. Clark explains, "or not really talk, but mutter, and he wouldn't sleep. He would go into a kind of agitated state or trance, talking all night and, in the morning, remembering little, if anything, he said." Like all of the veterans with whom I've talked, Clark has never received a letter from the Department of Defense or Veterans Administration advising him that he might have spent time in a region sprayed with Agent Orange. But by talking with Vietnam veterans who served in the same region as he did, and who remember being sprayed with Agent Orange, walking through defoliated areas, and drinking water contaminated with herbicides, Ray has verified his suspicion that he was exposed to deadly chemicals. Only after becoming involved with Agent Orange Victims International, however, did Clark learn about the many symptoms of dioxin exposure, one of which is *loss of memory.*

Although he can remember little about his combat experiences, Ray Clark's recollection of his nearly ten-year battle with the Veterans Administration is vivid. As the youngest patient to be treated for bladder cancer at a VA hospital, he has fought bureaucratic stonewalling, indifference, and incompetence. Even when VA doctors finally admitted that Clark had bladder cancer and decided to operate, his family was not told the cancer could be controlled. "They told me," Clark says, "to get my insurance in order. That's about all." It was only after his mother-in-law obtained a booklet from the American Cancer Society that Ray's family discovered his cancer was not terminal.

Leafing through a stack of letters from the Veterans Administration, congressmen, and the Department of Defense, Clark sips coffee and answers my questions slowly, carefully, and at times with the irritation of having gone over the same painful ground too often. Mrs. Clark joins us at the kitchen table, but her involvement with politics has made her skeptical, even slightly bitter. Recalling a press conference at which Senator Moynihan was to appear with her husband and other Vietnam veterans, she explains that the senator arrived more than an hour late and, placing his hands on Clark's chest, made an inane comment about Agent Orange. Except for the senator's entourage, no one laughed. "He was lucky," Mrs. Clark says, "that one of the veterans standing nearby didn't hit him."

In the beginning she believed that her idealism, indeed her fervor, would inspire local and national leaders to take action on behalf of Vietnam veterans and their families. But she has discovered that promises are not always kept, headlines do not necessarily mean progress, and unless it can be quantified by a government agency or verified by a panel of experts, human suffering does not inspire bureaucracies to action. Vietnam veterans, she now believes, might be one more commodity in a throwaway society. "They were used over there, and now they're being used here," Mrs. Clark says. Her husband nods, but declines to elaborate.

"I served in Vietnam from 1966 through 1967," Clark explains, glancing at his wife for what I first mistook to be confirmation, but later realized was simply an open display of trust and love for the woman who, like so many wives of Vietnam veterans, had seen him through the long, difficult, post-Vietnam adjustment period. "And in 1972 I developed cancer of the bladder. I also have a heart problem, which is a common problem among Nam veterans. When I first went into the VA hospital for a checkup, the doctors kept asking me if I had ever worked in a chemical plant, or if I had been exposed to radiation. And I had to say no to these questions because I worked in an appliance store before I went in the service, and as far as I know I was never exposed to any chemicals. And of course doctors were surprised at my age, because this type of cancer usually affects men between sixty and eighty years of age. We also discovered, going back through my records, that VA doctors had kept my heart murmur a secret from my family and myself. Suddenly I found myself in the hospital, with monitors all over me, and they announce: 'Ray, you've got a heart problem.' I was in intensive care for a week. Before that they had told me nothing about it."

Describing his frustration with the Veterans Administration, Clark reveals a familar pattern that has both angered and embittered Vietnam veterans. "Their attitude," one veteran told me, "is 'Hear no evil, speak no evil, see no evil.' In other words, what *they* don't know can't hurt *us!*" Even before a veteran enters the hospital he may be aware of what his symptoms mean, only to be informed by staff doctors that "It's all in your head." So many veterans have heard this from the VA that it would take a massive outreach and publicity campaign to change the negative attitudes many veterans have toward the bureaucracy in Washington and the majority of regional VA hospitals.

"In the beginning, when I first started urinating blood," Clark continues, "they insisted I was putting ketchup and water in the specimen jars. They said I was doing something to myself so I could receive disability, and that the problem was all in my mind. They also scheduled me for an appointment with the staff psychiatrist because they said my illness was self-inflicted. I would get really upset with them and say, 'Look, when I start urinating blood I'll just fill a test tube and bring it in so you can see for yourself I'm not lying.' So I brought it in and the doctor looked at it and said, 'Oh sure, Ray, that's ketchup and water.' Or,

'C'mon, Ray, that's just ketchup and urine and you know it.'

"They tested me for everything *but* bladder cancer. They gave me a brain scan, shot dye into my kidneys, announced that I was suffering from a nervous breakdown, and even tested me for epilepsy. They did every test you could possibly do, except the one that would determine if I had bladder cancer. After a month and a half of testing they finally said, 'Okay, we're going to look inside your bladder.' So they looked inside, and of course they saw the cancer. They told me to go home and get my affairs in order and to come in for the operation, which I did. I've been going in every three months for treatment since then."

At the Veterans Administration hospital in Syracuse, New York, veterans who went in for what had been advertised as an "Agent Orange examination" were given a routine physical by a physician's assistant.

"The funny thing is that they were always asking me if I had been in Vietnam," Clark says, pouring another cup of coffee and shaking his head as though he can not quite believe what he is saying. "And they kept wanting to know if I had been exposed to chemicals. But they never mentioned Agent Orange or dioxin. I never even heard of Agent Orange until I discovered Agent Orange Victims International. After I read an article about a veteran who was dying of a rare form of cancer, I wrote to my congressman asking if he knew anything about this issue. A few days later my wife answered the phone, and it was the congressman, or one of his aides, wanting to know just how much we knew about this 'Agent Orange.' They actually thought we knew an espionage agent by that name, and they wanted to find out just who this fellow was, and what we knew about him. Rather than a herbicide that is killing Vietnam veterans, they thought we were talking about a spy. The Veterans Administration was little help, because either they knew nothing about Agent Orange, or what they did know they were not about to tell Vietnam veterans.

"After my operation I filed a claim for service-connected disability. I went to a Veterans Administration counselor and told him what I wanted to do, but he didn't know anything about

Agent Orange—absolutely nothing. I actually had to bring in the paperwork and show him how to fill it out. About a month after I filed my claim I received a form letter from the VA stating that 'there is no evidence supporting a connection between Agent Orange exposure and any disease, except for chloracne.' They didn't send any documents or articles about Agent Orange, just their statement that 'these are the facts.' And when I did write asking for documentation on Agent Orange, they said their information had all been consumed in a fire. Then of course we received the next good laugh in the mail when they wrote that they had lost all of my service records while I was overseas. How could they just lose all our records? I did receive some information, some records, but they still don't have any of my records from Vietnam, or my first two years in the military. But I've corresponded with enough veterans who were in the area I was in and who were exposed to Agent Orange, and they can verify that we were exposed."*

One of the early ploys which the Veterans Administration used to avoid paying service-connected disability to victims of Agent Orange was to argue that veterans could not really prove they were exposed to herbicides in Vietnam. The Department of Defense also used this argument to discredit veterans' claims of cancer and birth defects due to exposure to Agent Orange. In testimony before the Committee on Veterans' Affairs, United States Senate, Major General William S. Augerson, at the time deputy assistant secretary of defense, argued against a retrospective epidemiological study of Vietnam veterans. Because there

---

*According to Vietnam Veterans of America, "The General Accounting Office studied Marines in Northern I Corps from 1966 to 1969, and comparing troop placements with the records of where and when Agent Orange was sprayed, found that nearly 6,000 Marines were within one-third of a mile of the spraying of Agent Orange on the day of the spraying missions. Another 10,600 were within nine-tenths of a mile on the day of the spraying. The total equals 8 percent of all Marines in the area during the three years studied. The General Accounting Office study not only verifies that veterans were exposed, but strongly suggests that many more veterans were exposed than anyone had previously been able to prove" (*Vietnam Veterans of America Newsletter*, March/April 1980).

"are generally no data exposure concentrations and exposure times," said Augerson, the results of such a study would be "highly unreliable." Given the existence of HERBS tapes that constitute a computerized record of the time, date, place, and amount of herbicide sprayed, the major general's statement would appear at best based upon bureaucratic rhetoric. And had he attended any of the hearings that are being held throughout the country on the problems and perils of dioxin exposure, he would have heard hundreds of veterans testify that they were exposed to Agent Orange in Vietnam. For example, a veteran who had served with the First Aircraft, Air Mobile, told the New York State Temporary Commission on Dioxin Exposure: "After the LZ [landing zone] was sprayed, we walked around the perimeters, strung barbed wire all around it. Then we sat down, the helicopters flew in, and this stuff was blowing all over the place. Most of us drank out of bomb craters, showered in bomb craters. All the guys know about that. That's the only time we could wash up. And all that water was polluted with Agent Orange."

Clark spreads the form letters denying him service-connected disability payments for his bladder cancer on the table, and waits while I examine them. They are succinct, designed to make the reader feel hopeless, as though appealing the decision would be folly. There is no "Thank you for serving your country." Or "We are sorry you are suffering and only hope that, once further research is done into this matter, we can be of help." Nothing to soften the blow. Just flat denial. In one letter, however, the VA does elaborate on its reasons for rejecting Clark's request for disability. The letter reveals that while undergoing an examination Clark once fainted and that this has led the VA to conclude that he just might have a "hysterical personality." That he might have lost consciousness because his body was reacting to a serious assault from cancer seems not to have occurred to the Veterans Administration. "They think we're all nuts," said one veteran. "And if they can prove that, then they don't really have to help us. And they claim we're just looking for pity or a fast buck."

"But even if the VA hospitals were really interested in helping veterans of what they insist on calling the 'Vietnam era'—they refuse to call it a war—they couldn't do it because they don't have the facilities or the staff," Clark says, tossing the rejection letters into a folder. "They couldn't do it because last year the Syracuse VA Hospital lost half of its staff and millions of dollars in funding, and it's just one part of a rapidly deteriorating system. They don't have any facilities for testing you for exposure to toxic chemicals, and even if Congress orders them to treat us with respect, to give so-called Agent Orange examinations, the VA hospitals will continue to attract incompetent staff, and it would take a monumental effort for them to get veterans to trust the VA again. But assuming they make that effort and manage to get the veterans whom they've alienated to return for tests, they would have to do 2.9 million fat biopsies at a cost of billions of dollars. Given our rank on the 'fiscal priority list' it is unlikely that the tests will ever be run."

Like nearly all of the men and women who served in Vietnam, Ray Clark was in top physical condition when he entered the service; and like every veteran with whom I've spoken or heard testify at state-sponsored hearings into dioxin exposure, he can recall little if any illness before he went to Vietnam. Before the war, veterans say, they never suffered from skin rashes, weakness of limbs, nervous disorders, liver disease, heart murmurs, cancer, loss of libido. Ten years after their return from Asia, they are aging with frightening rapidity, afraid for themselves, their children, and their childrens' children. And in their attempts to find answers, to explain the tragedy that has befallen them and their children, they search through their family trees to discern if there might be a pattern of cancer or birth defects in their lineage. Quite often they discover, as Ray Clark and his wife discovered, that no pattern exists.

"When I got out of high school I was in perfect health, and there is no history of cancer in my family. And what amazes me is that out of the millions of men who went to Vietnam, a sizable percentage now have health problems. Most of these men are in the thirty-five-year-old age bracket, the prime of life, and yet their problems are severe, and quite often rare from a medical point of view. Ed Juteau, vice president of Agent Orange Victims International, died of lymphatic cancer, and after his death the VA cut off payments to his wife and son because the VA claims he died of 'kidney failure.' In the past few years I've met veterans with cancer of the colon, testicular cancer, liver dysfunction, heart ailments, veterans whose children were born with as many as sixteen birth defects. And yet for so long no one was willing to do studies to determine just what is causing all these problems. They've studied rats, mice, rabbits, chickens, and monkeys, and found that dioxin gives them cancer, causes their death, deforms and kills their offspring. But all this doesn't apply to us. Well, no one has ever shown that dioxin *didn't* poison us. And we know that shortly after they began spraying Agent Orange in Vietnam the chemical companies sent a letter to the government advising them that there could be health problems from the herbicide. But of course the government doesn't want to admit that the stuff they were spraying on people was 2,000 percent—almost twenty times —more contaminated by dioxin than the domestic 2,4,5-T that was banned in 1979 by the Environmental Protection Agency. Some of the stuff sprayed on Nam was 47,000 percent more contaminated. And they sprayed it over and over on the same areas. What the government doesn't want to admit is that it is responsible for killing its own troops."

Clark explains that he has dropped out of most of the lawsuits in which he had been a plaintiff following his operation for bladder cancer. And since the Veterans Administration has never notified eligible claimants of favorable changes in benefit rules, it is unlikely that he will hear from the VA again, even if he is ruled eligible for disability payments.

"I don't need the money," he says. "Money isn't going to do me any good. What I really want to see is the money used to create a government agency, or should I say a governing agency, that would stop them from experimenting with radiation and herbicides. I don't care about winning a million dollars. My health, which is the most important thing a person can have, is gone now. It's all in my past. I just don't want the same thing to happen to my children that has happened to me. I volunteered for the military, and through some quirk of fate I got sent to Vietnam, but once I got there I didn't have any choice about being subjected to herbicides and other dangerous chemicals. And I resent that. I want the system changed so that we're not guinea pigs, and so we don't let the government, or anyone else, do this again. Every time I walk into the Veterans Hospital in Syracuse, I see this quote from President Lincoln: WE SHALL TAKE CARE OF THE WIDOWS AND CHILDREN OF THOSE WHO SERVED. Well, they're not. They have completely forgotten about us. I think they're just waiting for all of us to die, and then someone can say, 'Oh dear, maybe we did make a mistake with this Agent Orange.' At the rate things are going they won't have to wait very long."

Clark walks me to my car and we shake hands. Three of his five children are playing on a nearby swing set and we talk for a moment about our children and how much they mean to us. On the drive home I think about what has brought Ray Clark, a former Marine, and me, a former antiwar activist, together. In the sixties we might have met in a bar and argued, perhaps even fought, over the war. But now we have spent a rainy afternoon discussing the aftermath of chemical warfare. Clark's cancer, in remission for nearly five years, has reappeared, and every three months he must visit the VA hospital where a tube is inserted into his urethra to search for new signs of damage to his bladder.

Not long before our interview, two dead owls were discovered a short distance from the Clarks' home, and state officials said it was possible they had eaten fish or small animals contaminated with dioxin from Lake Ontario. "Lately," Mrs. Clark said, unfolding a map of the United States shortly before I left, "we've been looking for a safe place to move. But the more we looked, the more we realized there really is no place to hide."

2

THE DOOMED PLATOON

Growing up in New York City, Ron DeBoer played in an abandoned tenement that was frightening and, he thought, very dark. But years later, hunkered down in the jungle with members of the 17th Air Cavalry, he discovered a shade of darkness so impenetrable that he felt suspended in a void, a black hole into which, unless he was extremely careful, he might vanish. Staring into the dark and praying for sunrise, DeBoer realized that nothing he might experience during the next twelve months would be more terrifying than that first night in the bush.

From April 1968 to April 1969, DeBoer and his unit searched for and engaged in combat with enemy units in the Central Highlands of South Vietnam, sometimes walking through areas that appeared to have been bombed with such intensity that the earth was scorched, entire sides of mountains burned away. But the men in his platoon saw no bomb craters, and thought it odd that such a devastating air strike would fail to turn the jungle into a crazy quilt of water-filled pockmarks. Filling their canteens with water from pools or streams in the defoliated zone, they would pass on, leaving the mystery behind; in the scheme of things at the time, it really didn't seem that important.

For months DeBoer suffered from splitting headaches that he attributed to stress. His skin, as well as that of nearly every member of his unit, was massively discolored from what they called the "creeping crud." Some of the men had chloracne on their necks and shoulders, which DeBoer recalls as being "really hideous"; but they had been told nothing about the nature of the spraying around their base camps, never observed a formation of C123s saturating the side of a mountain with herbicides, and attributed any skin problems they might have to infrequent bathing or to the ferocious heat.

Ron DeBoer survived his twelve-month tour of duty and returned to New York City, where he spent the next ten years putting the war behind him and pursuing, he says, the "Great American Dream." He started his own construction company and soon owned a suburban home complete with two-car garage, patio, and swimming pool. Sometimes he thought about the men he had known who didn't make it back, but he disdained war stories and made no effort to explain what the war had been like for him; he knew he could not substitute words for experience. The past, he told himself, was the past. Let it be. And even when he first began feeling ill, when the lump in his groin began swell and he suspected it wouldn't go away, he dismissed the articles his wife was clipping from the paper about a herbicide that had been sprayed, quite possibly, upon the area of Vietnam where he had served.

But the lump in his scrotum did not go away, and DeBoer's wife, Linda, persisted in her attempts to get him to take seriously the stories about dioxin and Agent Orange that were appearing with increasing frequency in periodicals and newspapers. One of the articles was about a scientific experiment in which mice given minute doses of dioxin developed testicular cancer, a disease so rare that it affects only 6 out of every 100,000 white males between the ages of eighteen and twenty-four. DeBoer was only twenty-eight at the time, but doctors told him that the lump in his scrotum was malignant, and that if he wanted to live, they would have to operate. Bewildered, confused, angry, hardly able to believe that he had survived twelve months of guerrilla warfare only to succumb to a disease that hardly ever attacked men his age, DeBoer phoned a local attorney to ask if he knew of other Vietnam veterans who were suffering from testicular cancer.

"I had seen Victor Yannacone's name in the newspaper, and so I called him up. And he told me that he had other Vietnam veterans with testicular cancer and that there definitely tended to be a correlation between our exposure to dioxin and these types of cancers. Yannacone also said that he was going ahead with a lawsuit he had filed on behalf of Vietnam veterans, although at that time I think there were only twenty plaintiffs and I was one of them."

Yannacone inspired DeBoer to begin his own intensive research into the effects of dioxin on animals and humans, and the more he read the more convinced he became that his illness was symptomatic of dioxin exposure. Why, he wondered, had the men in his platoon not been warned against drinking water and eating food that had been sprayed with herbicides containing this deadly substance? Did the government really know that the defoliants they were spraying contained a carcinogen and teratogen that would remain in the soil and water for years? Had anyone checked the thousands of barrels of Agent Orange that were shipped each year to Vietnam to determine just how much dioxin they contained? Did Dow Chemical warn the Department of Defense that men and women working in a plant where 2,4,5-T was produced had suffered from chloracne? Why was the government insisting that no problem existed when he was sick and might even be dying from an extremely rare form of cancer? What constituted a problem? Every day he seemed to hear about other veterans who were suffering from serious ailments, and who suspected that their own government might have poisoned them.

DeBoer's skepticism soon gave way to anger, and his reluctance to revive memories of his combat experiences was swept aside by a passionate desire to discover just what had happened to him and the members of his platoon. Eventually he founded Agent Orange Victims of New York, launching a speaking tour that would take him into American Legion and VFW halls, high schools, and colleges throughout New York state. But he also wanted to talk to all of the members of his unit to see if they, too, were suffering from symptoms of dioxin exposure.

DeBoer soon realized that he couldn't count on the Department of Defense or the Veterans Administration for help in locating members of the unit he would one day dub "The Doomed Platoon." The DOD maintained that very few veterans had been exposed to herbicides in Vietnam, while informing those who requested their service records that many of the military's records had been lost in the chaotic evacuation of Saigon, or destroyed in a fire in St. Louis, Missouri. Already skeptical of the VA, DeBoer concluded that asking the government for help, even in what appeared to be a rather simple matter, was an exercise in futility. Instead, he decided to become a sleuth, an amateur Sherlock Holmes trying to track down not the perpetrator of a murder but the possible victims of chemical warfare. If he could find one of the men in his platoon, he felt certain that he might be able to locate all twenty.

Recalling a conversation with a member of his unit who had said he intended to become a police officer in civilian life, DeBoer tried to remember if the man with whom he had spent a year of his life dodging ambushes, cursing the heat, going on R&R, bragging about sexual conquests both knew were more fiction than fact, counting first the months then the days and finally the hours until they left "the Nam" for good—if the man with whom he had spent that first terrifying night in the jungle had ever really told him where he planned to settle down after the war. But since he was playing Holmes and knew that quite often this distinguished investigator would break a case with a hunch that seemed foolhardy to his associates, DeBoer decided to gamble. He went to Number One Police Plaza in Manhattan, where he inquired after a police officer named Kevin ————.* To his amazement he was told that Kevin did work for the New York City police department, but because he was a narcotics agent the department was not at liberty to give his number or address to anyone. They did

*Name withheld by request.

agree to leave a message for Kevin, asking him to call Ron DeBoer.

DeBoer waited near the telephone that night, excited but not at all certain this break would lead much further. It had been more than ten years since he and Kevin boarded their "Freedom Bird" to the states, and they had not kept in touch. In the intervening years many veterans, wanting only to forget their combat experiences and bitter over the way they had been treated since returning from Asia, had gone more or less underground, and DeBoer knew that it would not be easy to ferret them out. But the phone rang and "Lo and behold it was Kevin. And he was really excited to hear from me, and just couldn't believe that I would go to all that trouble to find him. We talked for some time and I asked him how he was feeling, and whether or not he was having any problems. He said that his health was fine, although something about the way he said it made me suspect that he might not be telling me the whole truth. But what he did say was that his first child was born dead, and his son was born with a deformed penis. So I had the cancer and Kevin had this tragedy strike in his life. But at the time I just thought, Well, this is a coincidence. Still, I really wanted to talk to more of the guys in my platoon. By this time I had read too much about dioxin and its effects, talked to Victor Yannacone at length, and gone through my own turmoil over my testicular cancer. I felt that I just couldn't be satisfied until I had talked with every one of the men I had served with."

Kevin gave DeBoer the address of a member of their platoon who was working as a postman in a small Pennsylvania town, and DeBoer soon tracked him down. "Just like Kevin he couldn't believe that I would be looking him up after all these years. And he tells me he's doing fine, that he has no problems; but when I asked him how his children were, he said that his daughter had been born with a deformed leg and his son was born with PKU, which is a form of mental retardation. But what interested me the most was that neither one of these veterans have any family history of birth defects. They don't know what caused these things. But I knew, and I still know, what it was—they had been exposed to dioxin.

"So here I was now and it was just around Christmas time, and I had cancer, Kevin had a child born dead and another with a birth defect, and Hoffman had two children born with birth defects, so it was just like batting a thousand. I couldn't stop now. I wanted to talk with every member of my platoon just as soon as I could, because I had already gone beyond the coincidence stage in my investigation. The case wasn't ironclad yet, but it was getting tighter."

Hoffman gave DeBoer the telephone number of Al Boyd, a platoon member living in California who also worked for the post office. Boyd was married, but he and his wife had decided not to have children. However, when DeBoer asked him about his health, Boyd answered that "he had all kinds of health problems. All kinds. At thirty-three he is suffering from hypertension, severe hypertension. He has to be on medication for it. He has a constant nervous upset stomach and they don't know what the hell his problem is. He's been hospitalized with hepatitis. He has liver problems. Just about anything you can name. And the guy told me, he says, 'Ron, I'm thirty-three years old and I feel like I'm sixty.' "

From California the trail doubled back to Denver, Colorado, to a veteran who told DeBoer he was divorced, had not been feeling well for the past few years, and that something had happened that he simply could not understand. Before he went to Vietnam, he told DeBoer, he had enjoyed the taste of beer and had actually prided himself on the amount he was able to consume during a night out with his drinking buddies. But now, he lamented, he could not drink even one can of beer without getting violent headaches, feeling dizzy, and even passing out. His intolerance for alcohol had become "total," and he wondered what had happened to his body, whether he had picked up some exotic disease in Vietnam. That his liver might have contained traces of dioxin had not occurred to him. Neither the VA nor the Department of Defense had sent him a letter advising him that he and members of the 17th Air Cavalry had been exposed to the most toxic man-made substance in the world, and that it might be beneficial to him if he submitted to a complete physical examination. Like DeBoer just a year or two before, the man knew little about the defoliation campaign in Southeast Asia and could not understand why, when just a few years before he had felt ready to compete in the Olympics, his body seemed now to betray him.

One of the most peculiar responses to DeBoer's inquiries, yet one that he would come to understand during his work with the New York State Temporary Commission on Dioxin Exposure, came during a conversation he had with the sixth member of his platoon. The man and his wife were on the phone, and, says DeBoer, the veteran's wife seemed very interested in his questions and seemed to want more information about how exposure to Agent Orange might have affected her husband. But the man became extremely defensive, even angry, and dismissed DeBoer by announcing that there "is nothin' wrong with me and nothin' wrong with my family. Goodbye. I hope you guys make out all right, but don't call me, I'll call you." DeBoer never heard from him again, and he was unable to uncover any other leads.

"So I was able to locate only six men out of the twenty that were in the platoon, and what I found was that five out of the six had hard-core Agent Orange problems: dead children, deformed children, cancer, gastritis, hypertension, liver problems, and other serious health problems. From then on I knew that there was something that made us different from the rest of the country. I was totally convinced of that then, and I'm totally convinced of it now. And the fact that the Veterans Administration has gone out of its way to drag its feet in coming to terms with conducting a true epidemiological study of the 2.5 million men and women who served in Vietnam, comparing them to 2.5 million people who did not go to Vietnam but were in the service, is indicative of just how serious the problem may be. Why haven't we been compared to noncombat veterans to see if in fact we are sicker, our children are born with more birth defects, we suffer from a higher rate of cancer? We know that there are people who can do this study, that it wouldn't even be all that difficult to do. But instead the VA prefers to insult us by dragging its feet and then finally coming up with a prototype for a study that is perforated with inconsistencies, just a waste of the taxpayers' money. So once again we have found that Vietnam combat veterans just can't trust the VA.

"The VA continues to hang its hat on its Ranch Hand study," says DeBoer "but I think that it's because many of the men who are involved in that study are still on active duty.* They're pilots, career Air Force personnel, and these individuals are not going to step forward with an array of health problems because they'll get kicked right out of the military, or be grounded and lose their flight pay. So there are many reasons why the Ranch Hand study will fail to provide the kind of information we need. You've got to remember that the men being examined, the pilots who flew the C123s for example, did not drink water or eat food contaminated with dioxin, like the grunts did week after week. When those pilots returned to base they showered every night, instead of living in the same clothes for days or even weeks. So instead of insisting on examining members of the Ranch Hand units, why doesn't the government take a look at A Troop, Seventh Squadron 17th Air Cavalry, and compare us to another infantry platoon that was stationed in Germany? What is the VA afraid of? One has to wonder.

"I mean, look, I found six of the men in my unit on my own, and I attempted to get the other fourteen names. But I couldn't

*Between 1962 and 1970 approximately 1,200 men served as pilots and ground crew members with the U.S. Air Force's Operation Ranch Hand. Because many of these men were exposed to herbicides, either by handling barrels in which they were stored or from mists that blew into the cockpit and fuselage of the C123s, the Air Force has commenced a study to determine if their health has been affected. According to Lieutenant Colonel Philip Brown (USAF) the study will continue through the year 2002 and will involve three phases. In the first phase the Air Force will examine the records of deceased Ranch Hand personnel to determine the cause of death. This, says Brown, will continue for the next twenty years. The second or "questionnaire phase" involves sending a representative from Lou Harris and Associates into each Ranch Hander's home with a questionnaire in hand. "We're interested in knowing what happened to them since Vietnam, what kind of offspring they've fathered, and we also ask the spouse about her experience so we can address the fertility or reproductive history of these people." The third phase of the study involves asking former Ranch Handers to undergo a physical examination at the Kelsey-Seybold Clinic where, Brown says, they will undergo a thorough physical and neuropsychiatric examination.

get them, because they said that I would have to file a Freedom of Information Act to get the names of the guys that I fought with in Vietnam. I could hardly believe it. The VA wouldn't give me any help. Then I talked with my congressman and he said that there are many guys trying to locate the men they served with. It's just like everything else where Vietnam veterans are concerned. The VA and DOD just aren't going to give us any help. But I plan on doing it on my own. I'm going to keep on investigating until I know what happened to every one of the men in that unit."

Because he was fully covered by medical insurance, DeBoer did not have to go through what he calls the "VA atrocity," and in spite of the fact that the private doctors who first examined him knew nothing about dioxin and little if anything about Agent Orange, he received "superb medical care." As the years passed and he returned for postoperative checkups, some of the physicians became interested in the issue and would ask DeBoer what he knew about the symptomology of dioxin exposure. They were amazed, he says, when he told them that among the plaintiffs in the class action suit were at least *one hundred cases* of testicular cancer. "They just couldn't believe it. It really seemed almost beyond their comprehension that we could have that many testicular cancers in our population of Vietnam veterans."

By 1982 the number would grow into the hundreds, a figure that, given the average age of Vietnam veterans and their health records before they were sent to Vietnam, clearly demonstrates the disastrous effects that exposure to dioxin can have on human health. Given the rate at which testicular cancers have been discovered among Vietnam veterans it seems highly likely that even more cases will be added to the class action suit before Yannacone and his consortium of attorneys face the war contractors in a court of law.

Despite the physical, emotional, and financial problems DeBoer's illness caused him and his family, he decided that he must do whatever he could to educate the American public to the hazards of dioxin, and to convince people that the ailments of

Vietnam veterans are both real and devastating. Soon he was deluged with offers to speak, and he accepted nearly all of them, becoming, he soon realized, a full-time Agent Orange activist. Invited to attend hearings in Albany on the hazards of toxic substances in the workplace, DeBoer went because "I pretty much considered myself to be Exhibit A as to what can happen to people who are exposed to toxic substances, and I wanted to say something about the men in my platoon who had told me about the problems they were experiencing from their exposure to dioxin." Although the state assembly committee that was sponsoring the hearings realized that the problem of dioxin exposure was national in scope, with its roots in Washington rather than Albany, the committee concluded that a state commission on dioxin exposure should be established to examine the possibility that large numbers of Vietnam veterans (of which New York has 600,000) and nonveteran residents of the state may have been exposed to dioxin. The majority of the New York State Temporary Commission on Dioxin Exposure's members would be combat veterans and, because of his work on behalf of veterans and research into the effects of dioxin on laboratory animals and human beings, DeBoer was asked to become a member.

The commissioners agreed to hold a series of hearings, inviting members of the public to express their concerns about the effect dioxin might be having on their health. The commissioners were instructed not to reach conclusions, pass judgments, or make any specific rulings during the course of these hearings. Their job was simply to listen. Thus began what seemed, at times, a tragedy without end. On occasion, says DeBoer, even the stenographers wept as they listened to a young widow describe her husband's death from cancer, a Vietnam veteran speak lovingly and with anger about his deformed daughter or son, or a woman explain that in spite of her love for her husband and desire to bear children she was frightened of giving birth to a "thalidomide baby." While he admits that he was sometimes disappointed that more veterans didn't appear at the hearings, DeBoer can "understand that nobody wants to come to a hearing and be told that you've been exposed to dioxin. Nobody really wants to come to a meeting and see their contemporaries sick, genuinely suffering, and nobody wants to come out and look at deformed children."

Ron DeBoer and I are sitting on a park bench near City Hall in lower Manhattan. Across from us an elderly man admonishes the pigeons to be more considerate. He tells them they are not so "smart as they think" and warns them that their "uppity ways" are going to bring them to an unhappy end. Bells chime, taxis jockey for position at a red light, honking like angry geese and hurling down Broadway in ragged formation. Office workers stroll through the park and bask in the sun beside a small reflection pool. The Vietnam War has been over for eight years. *Coming Home, The Deer Hunter,* and *Apocalypse Now* have come and gone. Novels, documentaries, books of poetry, new journalistic accounts of the war have been written, produced, reviewed, awarded prizes, enshrined as classics, or dismissed as failed attempts to portray what some people feel may be unportrayable. But DeBoer, an aspiring film scriptwriter, feels the most devastating film is yet to be made. "When they make a movie out of this Agent Orange thing, and believe me they will make a movie out of it, it'll make *Apocalypse Now* look like a Walt Disney flick."

This is said without a trace of bitterness or anger, just the matter-of-fact manner of a man who knows that the government he served has lied to him and his fellow veterans for many years. As a member of the New York State Temporary Commission on Dioxin Exposure he has talked with hundreds, perhaps even thousands, of Vietnam veterans throughout the nation. And he has heard time and again that the use of defoliants was not confined to remote areas of Vietnam, that base camp perimeters were routinely sprayed, and C_{123}s sometimes jettisoned their thousand-gallon loads near or directly on areas occupied by American servicemen. From General Accounting Office reports he discovered that his unit had been deployed in defoliated areas; and from HERBS tapes (which do *not* include information about Navy Seabee, Army Engineer, Marine Corps Engineer, South Vietnamese, Australian, or CIA use of defoliants in Vietnam) he found that the year he spent in Vietnam had been one of the peak years for the military's use of defoliants.

"There can be no question that the Department of Defense and the Veterans Administration perpetuated a fraud on the American public by insisting for a good solid eighteen months when I first became involved in this issue that we were *not* exposed, we were *not* at risk of exposure, and American ground forces were not in areas that had been sprayed. And then, thanks to Senator Percy's efforts to get the General Accounting Office to examine the DOD's records, we find out that not only were we in areas that had been defoliated, but that some of these areas had been sprayed directly on several occasions with herbicides that were hundreds of times more contaminated with TCDD-dioxin than the strongest herbicide used domestically in the U.S.

"Yet it took us forever to get any information from the Veterans Administration and the Department of Defense. We've had so little cooperation from the people who were involved in administrating the war. Every step along the way we've had to file a Freedom of Information Act claim to get information. It's been like pulling teeth since day one to get any information out of the Veterans Administration. But why do they behave this way? I still don't quite understand it. I've met with them, and it seems rather obvious to me that the heavy lobbying of Dow, Monsanto, Diamond Shamrock, and Uniroyal have an influence on the government's decisions. As an individual, and as a Vietnam veteran, I can only think that when they all get together in the friendly back room or by the poolside and they dip their well-manicured fingers into the caviar jar, the conversation is 'How are we going to keep these young guys who have in fact been poisoned by dioxin from collecting what's justly theirs?' And the way they decide to do that is *through the bureaucracy:* Just keep putting up the barrier of no cause and effect, no correlation, and never do the tests that might prove we're right. When you do spend over a hundred thousand dollars to design a study, just make sure that it's like the UCLA epidemiological protocol, that it's doctored up and utterly useless. That way you can stall progress for another two, five, ten years. No, I think it's dollars, *big* money, and that's what's really behind all this. We Vietnam veterans have been given a price tag, and the tag seems to be too high for the government to afford."

In Vietnam DeBoer did not feel that he was fighting for the state of New York, California, or Ohio. He and his fellow soldiers were there "as Americans, not as representatives of our individual states." Thus he finds it difficult to understand "why the court-house door is being closed to us now. In eighteen states veterans are time-barred by the statute of limitations from arguing for compensation from the war contractors once the class action suit has been heard, and, we assume, won. And this is probably the most terrible, the most tragic thing that has happened to the Vietnam veterans. It's the ultimate slap in the face to a people who were fighting tyranny and communism, or so they were told, to come home and be informed—and this may well include hundreds of thousands of men—that 'No, you are not going to have your day in court. Yes, your brother veteran in California will be able to have *his* day in court, but you who live in any of the eighteen states where you are time-barred will not have your day.' "

Ron DeBoer was nineteen when he went to Vietnam. Today he is thirty-four. The organization that he founded three years ago no longer exists, and now he wants nothing more than to write about what it felt like to be a nineteen-year-old kid in Vietnam, to spend that first terrifying night in the jungle, to see the dead and the wounded, and to survive. But he has not given up the hope that his "brother veterans will be accorded the dignity and compassion to which they are entitled," even though he knows that, in spite of cosmetic proclamations, rhetorical flourishes, and public relations scams, very little has changed at VA headquarters. The Agent Orange examination is still a game of Pin the Tail on the Donkey, useless and humiliating to the eighty thousand veterans who, distressed over their own deteriorating health and concerned that their future children might be born with myriad birth defects, have sought help at VA clinics. The anger and shock that followed his discovery that he had testicular cancer and that propelled him to work nonstop for three years on behalf of other Agent Orange victims has been replaced by stoicism.

"There's nothing left anymore that these people can do that will affect me on an individual basis—you know, get me upset. They are beyond scruples. They are beyond decency. They will do anything. They will sit there and cover up, and they will tell you that there was absolutely no spraying in Laos, no spraying in Cambodia. And just as soon as we file a Freedom of Information Act they will admit that 'Yes, we sprayed there. Yes, we lied all along.' All the war contractors present this façade of true patriotism, but I've been saying 'Profit before patriotism' for three years. They knew, or they damn well should have known, that their herbicide was contaminated with dioxin. As a matter of fact, *their* scientists knew years before anyone else just how toxic this substance was. And I really wouldn't be that concerned with Dow's credibility or sincerity if we had only dumped a couple hundred thousand gallons of Agent Orange on Vietnam, but when you consider *eleven million gallons* there is no one who can tell me that at some time Dow's scientists didn't sit down and ask, 'Now wait a minute, just what the hell are they doing with all this stuff?' We're talking about *three hundred and sixty-eight pounds of dioxin!* A substance that kills laboratory animals in *parts per billion*, which is really only a microscopic dose.

"I'm familiar with all their arguments. We all are. That dioxin breaks down in sunlight. Well, sure it does if you place it on a petri dish in a laboratory, but in Vietnam it got into the muck, the water, and in the jungle where there was no sunlight. And Matthew Meselson [Harvard University] found it in fish that had been caught several kilometers from where we had sprayed, so it was dispersed into the food chain, and into *our* bodies."

DeBoer believes that eventually "justice will be done to the Vietnam veterans and their families who have suffered because of their exposure to dioxin," but he admits that he is not altogether certain what he means when he uses the word "justice."

"I've asked myself that question so many times, and I know that there will be no victory in a traditional sense. This thing will never end with a victory party or people waving some sort of banners or something like that. But I think there will be an accounting for corporate irresponsibility, for chemical warfare, for the cover-ups. People are going to be exposed for what they were, and for what they are, and that's all I'm hoping will happen. That's all I'm looking for, because what do you say to a thirty-year-old widow? What do you say to a kid born with a missing arm or leg, a cleft palate, or duplicate sex organs? What are you going to say to that kid? That I won, that Ron DeBoer and all the other people, the Ryans and the McCarthys and the Mullers and everybody else involved won? What did we really do for you? We didn't really do anything except get involved in something which we believed in, and something which, when you've had cancer and you think you might be dying and you look at all your brother veterans and see their problems, there really isn't much choice but to get into it.

"But I can tell you this: without a doubt the number of people who have come forward with problems this far, as astronomical as it may seem, is only the tip of the iceberg. There are so many more out there. So many guys who were superficially wounded in Nam but who refused medical treatment, those guys who saw death and dying and considered themselves lucky and now they look back on it all and if they are sick they just say, 'What's a little pain, or numbness in the legs, or violent headaches? I'm alive, aren't I? So I'll just hang in there and live with it.' But most of all they just want to leave the whole Vietnam experience in the closet where they feel it belongs. They just don't want to be stereotyped any further. They want to believe that they survived the war, and I ask you, can you really blame them? We may be the first army in history that has had to keep fighting for our lives *after* the war is over."

3

SEALS AND
RIVER RATS

The wind is from the south, but bitter, sweeping across the deserted platform in great bone-chilling gusts. Opposite the Long Island Rail Road station is a tavern that once might have been a warehouse—squat, battered, uninviting.

The voice over the phone says, "Just stand by the escalator and face the direction you came from. Look for a blue '66 Chevrolet." I pace between the station and the escalator to the elevated platform. The man who arrives a few moments later wears a black beret, and introduces himself as a former "river rat."

When he was still in high school, Bobby Sutton joined the Naval Reserve, was later assigned to a precommissioning detail in Newport, Rhode Island, and eventually spent a year on the U.S.S. *Wainwright* off the coast of Haiphong.

"We were a kind of 'radar picket'—that is, *positive identification radar* air zone," Sutton explains. "We controlled all the aircraft in the Gulf of Tonkin. They had to come up on our air frequency or they'd get blown out of the sky. Fortunately we didn't have any combat, just long hours." Sutton finished his tour of duty and, after only fifty-six days as a civilian, reenlisted. "I was then on the U.S.S. *Newell*, and I would see these little green boats being tested off one of the main piers at Pearl Harbor. And believe me I felt safe on the fantail of that ship. 'Damn!' I said, 'I know where they're goin'. I'm glad I'm on this ship.' And lo and behold, just three weeks later I had my orders for training at Mare Island and Coronado, California, at the naval inshore operations training center and was assigned to Rivron 9."

Assigned to a "zippo monitor," or flamethrower boat, Sutton cruised the rivers and streams of the Mekong Delta, burning off "dead brush or half-living foliage" to expose enemy bunkers and ambush sites. Sutton estimates that there were over 50,000 miles of rivers and streams in the Mekong Delta, many of them "laced with bunkers, underground hospitals, VC R&R areas, and spider holes. Did I know some of the areas we were burning had been sprayed with herbicides?" Sutton demands. "Absolutely not. I never even heard of Agent Orange until late 1978, even though I've been sick since 1976."

On the door to Sutton's basement apartment, where he lives with his wife, Patty, his twenty-one-pound tabby cat, and hundreds of articles, books, scientific papers, government documents, and tapes on the defoliation campaign and the health effects of herbicides, is a sign: THIS PROPERTY PROTECTED BY AN ARMED VIETNAM VETERAN.

"I've spent the past two and a half years researching this problem," says Sutton, leading me into his living room, "and they don't like me very much at the VA because I tend to be very outspoken about this thing. I just won't put up with any more of their bullshit. See, I don't have much education. In fact, when I write to the VA now I put down that I'm a *research analyst,* which is what I am, really. But they don't wanna hear about it because they just don't wanna admit that our government might have killed its own troops."

We return to the dining room table, and Sutton puts water on the stove for tea. Pointing to one of the many documents stacked and strewn about the table, he says, "This information isn't top secret, just look at it. I got this stuff from *them,* from the very people who deny that we are sick. They deny that we're sick and dying, but their own literature describes the teratogenic and carcinogenic effects of the stuff we were exposed to in Nam." Opening one of his photo albums, Sutton points to a picture of the zippo monitor on which he served. In the photograph a small craft —Sutton explains the zippos were about fifty-seven feet long— is spraying a riverbank with fire. Another photograph shows two zippo monitors cruising the Mekong Delta, one just a few hundred yards behind the other. Between the two craft a mortar shell has landed, sending up a geyser. Beneath the photograph a caption reads: "This one missed. The next one didn't."

Sutton talks in short bursts of rage, in monologues replete with technical references to the harmful effects of herbicides. The effort seems to exhaust him, and he closes his eyes, stroking the enormous cat that reclines atop the dining room table's clutter. Regaining his composure, Sutton announces that in a few moments a "Seal" and his wife will be arriving. "I thought you might want to talk to him," Sutton says, "because he's sick too, and he can tell you that we're not just makin' this whole thing up."

Joe Naples and his wife Charlotte arrive, and Sutton explains that he and Naples have been living just a few blocks apart for years and only recently discovered that they had spent time on the same boat in the Mekong Delta. Mrs. Naples says that she doesn't really wish to talk, preferring to give her husband support and, when necessary, prompting him with details about the years he has spent fighting the debilitating effects of herbicides on his health. "It's not unusual," Sutton explains, referring to Naples' temporary memory lapses. "You'll talk to a lot of vets who have this problem. It's just part of the effect of dioxin on the central nervous system. I sometimes forget what I'm saying or doing, too."

Naples, who spent three years in Vietnam as a Navy Seal, but "more in the bush than on a boat," removes his leather jacket and, shoving the sleeves of his sweater to his elbows, exposes tattooed forearms heavily scarred by chloracne and "punch biopsies." The biopsies, Naples explains, were taken by VA doctors to determine whether or not his fatty tissue contains traces of dioxin. He has had the rashes for many years and when they spread to his arms and legs and the sores broke, covering his skin with a "pussy glaze," he went to the Veterans Administration for help.

"All that's left here," says Naples, pointing to his left forearm, "is scar tissue. They took a skin biopsy, and after about a month I went back to Northport Hospital [Long Island, New York]. The biopsy had been sent to the Bronx to be analyzed and Northport was trying to get the results from there. And the two doctors that were taking care of me in Northport were really honest; they were very interested in it, and one of them called me into her office. So I asked her about the results of the biopsy; and she said she hadn't gotten any results on the biopsy, and that they couldn't get the slides. So I says, 'How come?' And she says, 'Joe, there are just three things that possibly could have happened to them slides. One, somebody took the slides and wants to study them some more. Two, they were on their way here in the mail and got lost. Or three, they were conveniently lost, dropped through a hole in the floor.' And she says, 'If you want my opinion it was probably the last one. I just feel that this is what happened.' "

Angered over having undergone minor surgery, only to be told that he might never find out the results of lab tests performed on the dime-sized pieces of skin removed from his arms, Naples went to Victor Yannacone, attorney for Vietnam veterans in their suit against the VA for gross negligence, to see if the slides could be subpoenaed. But Yannacone told Naples this wasn't possible, that the slides had obviously disappeared and little could be done to find them. The rash continued to spread over Naples' forearms, thighs, calves, stomach, and face, making him so uncomfortable at times that he couldn't sleep. And when the Manhattan VA called to say that doctors there would like to take a look at his lesions, Naples thought perhaps he might get help after all.

"They called us in," says Naples, "and on the day we got there, all of a sudden the doctor was called away. So we went home. And they call us back a second time and we went in to see the doctor, and she was friendly, really responding to us, genuinely interested in the rashes. And then she said, 'Oh, I've got to make a phone call. I'm gonna try to call the Bronx VA to find out just what happened to those slides.' She went out of the room for a few minutes, came back in and announced: 'Okay, Joe, we've found out what we needed to know, you can go home now, we don't have to do anything more.' I had hand-carried my records to Manhattan, signed a release of information form so they could get whatever they needed, and I said, 'What about this release of information form I signed?' And she said, 'No, when your lesions come back up you come and see me then.' And since then we haven't heard anything more about it. The thing was, she was really warm, friendly, *till she made that phone call,* and then all of a sudden it was *zap, gone,* just get outta here."

While Joe Naples and Bobby Sutton talk, I think about the many times I have seen men like them leaving a steel mill in Gary, Indiana, an auto assembly plant in Detroit, or a coal mine in West Virginia, lunch box under the left arm. And in how many neighborhood bars we have sat together on a Saturday afternoon, chugging shots and sipping beer while watching reruns of sporting events. But for Naples and Sutton, that was before Vietnam. Because of the slow debilitating effects of dioxin and phenoxyacetic acid, they find it difficult to work, and the damage to their livers rules out drinking.

"I thought the stuff they were spraying was insect repellent," says Naples, "and of course some of it was. But I didn't know nothin' about herbicides at the time. When I first got to Dong Tam, there was a lot of vegetation. But by the time I left, the mangrove forest that had been there was so burnt out we ended up playin' softball on it. And I hear from Bobby that when he got there the place was almost like a desert."

"Listen," Sutton says, "when a place is so fertile that you can take a piss and ten minutes later something will grow there, you know somethin's wrong when it turns to muck, just dirt." Opening one of his photo albums, Sutton points to a picture of something that resembles a brown sheet of construction paper superimposed on a tiny pool table, leaving only a thin green margin. "There it is," he says, pointing to the brown sheet, "that's the softball field Joe's talkin' about. One time it was jungle, but that's the way it looked in 1969."

"Before I entered the service," Naples continues, pulling his sleeves carefully over his forearms, as though by covering the chloracne he can stop the rash from spreading or anesthetize the terrible itching and burning, "I lettered in almost every sport in high school. I was on the wrestling team, played Triple A baseball, and had no physical problems whatsoever. But for the past ten, maybe twelve years, I've had these rashes that have gotten progressively worse. I'm losing my balance. I'm dizzy, I've got constant headaches. My eyes are sensitive to light, and I'd just say my health has been goin' downhill most of the time. As time goes by, it just gets worse."

Charlotte Naples nods painfully in agreement after each statement, massaging her husband's arms and occasionally whispering encouragement. During his three-year tour of duty, Naples was "mostly involved in reconnaissance, setting up ambushes, intercepting gun runners and tax collectors." He was wounded three times—once in the neck by a .30-caliber machine gun—and was with "the very first group, or one of the first," to enter Cambodia in 1966, four years before the war "officially" spread to that country. He was in his teens when he went to war; but now, though he has not yet celebrated his thirty-fifth birthday, he feels like an old man, confused, bewildered, angry at the nation that seems to want to punish him for the thirty-six months he spent in combat.

"If I might interject," says Sutton, obviously in pain and impatient to talk about his long struggle to get the VA to recognize his many ailments as genuine and service-connected. "It's really ironic, because I would say that Joe and I have about 95 percent of the same symptoms, only he doesn't vomit after meals like I do. I've had the headaches, abnormal electroencephalograms, chronic diarrhea, a Class I enlarged prostate gland, my sperm looks like tapioca pudding, and after four years of trying, my wife and I lost our first child after a half-term pregnancy, which really set both of us back. My knees buckle from under me, and I have photosensitivity of the eyes, that's why I have to wear sunglasses. I suffer from peripheral neuropathies. The VA says I don't have them, but they've issued this device to kill the pain they say I don't have," lifting his shirt and pointing to a small box from which several wires protrude. "The box is supposed to send electrical impulses which will block the pain messages to my brain; that's why I have these electrodes attached to my lower back and thighs. But I ache all over, really. I get pains that come right out of left field, the left-field bleachers, and it hurts, that's all.

"And another thing, they try to treat us like psychos at the VA. You're automatically a drug addict, baby burner, or maniac. Every time anybody goes in it's the same questions: 'What kind of drugs are you takin',' and 'You're an alcoholic, aren't you?' Hell, Joe can't drink. I can't drink. A lot of vets can't even take one beer without fallin' on their ass. One beer, man, and I'm just done."

Naples nods, shakes his head sadly, and, lighting a cigarette, adds, "When I went into the clinic with my lesions they asked me if I wanted to see a psychiatrist. And I said, 'Sure, why not?' But it wasn't because of the lesions. I wanted to see him because I was gettin' the nightmares and flashbacks. But the first thing they ask you is, 'You're an alcoholic, aren't you?' Any Nam vet that has been in contact with herbicides will tell you that you can't drink. You have a headache that will last for three days, and it starts *while* you are drinkin'; I mean you're actually hung over after just a few sips of beer. And you'll vomit your intestines out, for christsake. I take a drink of beer now and I'm just gone. Before even a half of a can goes down the headache is there, it just starts pounding."

"Dioxin," Sutton explains, "collects in the fatty tissues of your liver, and you can't filter out the poisons. It also affects the DNA process. When a baby is forming in the womb and the genes are splitting to form the phalanges, the facial muscles, the different organs, just one molecule of dioxin can take the place of a normal gene splay. And that's where you get polygenetic birth defects, the same as the Vietnamese people are having."

In spite of the treatment he has received from the VA, Naples, who augments the family income by training attack Doberman pinschers, finds a certain grim humor in the VA's incompetence. "I went in for a compensation hearing and this doctor had me sit down and he says, 'Joe, can I see the flamethrower burns?' I says, 'What flamethrower burns?' He says, 'You were burned by a flamethrower, that's what those things on your arms are, aren't they?' I says, 'No, I was never burned by a flamethrower; these are rashes that have been comin' up for the past fourteen years, and every year they intensify. And this is the worst they've ever been!' 'Oh well,' he says, 'I thought they were flamethrower burns.' "

Naples laughs and, after a brief conference with his wife, continues. "Then they tried to tell me it was from the tattoos, the color from the tattoos was causin' my chloracne. On my legs? I don't have tattoos on my legs. And then," laughing, "I go down the hall to see this next doctor and I tell him about the headaches, the stomach cramps, and everything, and he says, and this is exactly what he said, he says, 'Joe, the headaches are just tension. And we consider you a "breather" or a "sigher." ' That's what he said I was, that was his entire diagnosis."

"And I'm considered an air swallower," Sutton announces with a touch of pride. "But see, it's true that some of us have difficulty getting air into our lungs or oxygen to our blood. So the VA calls people like Joe who may need to take an extra breath now and then 'breathers' or 'sighers.' "

In the beginning, says Sutton, the VA tried to tell him that he could not have been exposed to toxic herbicides because he served with the Navy in Vietnam. "Yeah, they'll take my service records and say, 'But you were in the Navy, you couldn't have been exposed.' But look," opening his photo album to a page of zippo monitors, "you see how close we were to the riverbank. Our flamethrowers were pressurized at two thousand pounds per square inch and could reach the length of a football field, but sometimes we were as close to the bank as we are right now from that fence," pointing to the fence that surrounds his backyard, a distance of no more than thirty feet. "So when the wind was from the wrong direction it came right back in our face, you got it, you got the smoke. And you've got to remember too that when plants and wood take up Agent Orange and it is burned, you can get more dioxin. And we were always in and out of the water, taking baths, and even swimming in places where there was obviously run-off from the defoliated banks. We had one of those fifty-five-gallon herbicide drums on our boat too, and we cut it in half, painted it green, and used it for a shower. Now what was in that drum I wouldn't know, and some of the guys even used those drums to store watermelons in, or for barbecues, or God knows what all."

According to the Department of Defense, U.S. military personnel didn't enter a sprayed zone until six weeks after it had been saturated with herbicides, but Naples and Sutton hotly dispute this. "Six weeks," says Naples, "that's ridiculous. We would be dropped off at an ambush site and spend hours actually lying in the stuff. It would actually be comin' down on us. Whether they knew we were in there or not I'll never know. I spent a lot of time on my stomach in Nam, and in and out of water that would have contained the stuff either from direct spray or run-off. You'd bathe in a bomb crater, so you'd be drinkin' it, you'd be takin' a bath in it, you'd wash your clothes in it. You'd get the rice and sweet potatoes in the field that had been sprayed with this stuff, but we didn't know that. I also saw guys pile empty barrels around their bunkers, and if the bunker took a hit, they would get sprayed with whatever was left of the stuff inside those barrels."

"You see," Sutton explains, "we know now that they weren't just defoliating the jungle to destroy the enemy's ambush sites. They were also trying to destroy his *food* supplies so that he would be forced into the open. Hindsight may be terrible sight, but it's better than no sight at all. And we also know from Dow Chemical's own statistics that the year I was there was the year they sprayed the most Agent Orange on Vietnam. But I think, Joe, that we should also be concerned with Agent Blue, because that's what they were usin' a lot of in the delta to kill off the rice crop. It's a carcinogen, and some of the Australian veterans who were in the Mekong area have been suffering the effects of it. Between Blue and Orange they really had us by the short hairs, didn't they."

Naples glances about the room as though this were all a disappointing film for which the manager would give him a refund.

The humor of a few moments earlier has left him, and he speaks even more slowly. "My wife and I went up there to Northport to check on the tumor registry. We were looking for a registry number, and they said they had no such thing at that hospital, no such registry. But Bobby had showed me this door, and it stuck in my mind. I could have sworn I seen that sign somewhere before: TUMOR REGISTRY. And my wife remembered it too. And sure enough, we're walkin' through the halls, and behind ETA on the first floor there's a door with a big sign, TUMOR REGISTRY. And yet they insist that there's no such thing."

Sutton shuffles a stack of papers, closes his photo albums, and says, "Right before you, you have literature on an international level. Now if they know in Amsterdam, Australia, Canada, Czechoslovakia, Hungary, Russia, Sweden, as well as the United States, that dioxin makes people sick, kills people, is carcinogenic and teratogenic, then why doesn't the VA know it? Why doesn't our government admit it? If I, with a high school education, can find this out, if I can take the data you see here and put it in its proper perspective, then the VA sure as hell can. They know. They *know*, but they don't want to admit it because it's gonna cost them a lot of money. *Money*, that's what it's really all about. You know, when Joe was in the hospital the nurses wouldn't even touch his chloracne. They thought it was contagious, so they left him alone. He had to change his own bandages, take care of himself—right there in the hospital. Did you ever hear of anyone in a civilian hospital changing his own dressings?"

Pain and exhaustion fill the room like a fog. We have been talking for nearly three hours, and it appears we can go no further; the interview is over.

Sutton, holding back tears, breaks the silence. "Listen, I used to be a very patriotic person. Like Joe, I was on my second enlistment. I loved going to sea, loved my rate; I took great pride in it. I had planned on making the service a career. We still hold to a lot of values that our peers have thrown away a long time ago, but how long can we be patient? I'm nobody's asshole. And I've just about fuckin' had it. Sometimes it seems like you have to do somethin' bloody and gory to get attention, and by God we're capable of it. But we've seen enough of that. I've got a conscience. I don't want to hurt my fellow Americans. I don't really want to hurt anybody, but so help me God there may come a day when . . .

"You know, when I came back I was a union steamfitter. I was strong. I could do as good a day's work as anyone. But my muscles are just giving out. I can't do that kind of work no more. I can't work at all now. The old Archie Bunkers say, 'It's a great system, fellas, the price is right, don't complain, I got this and I got that, and it only took me thirty-five years . . .' Well, we're not gonna be here thirty-five years from now. Some of us ain't gonna be around three to five years from now. We're going to succumb to the bioaccumulation of toxic chemicals in our bodies."

Naples mentions the difficulty he has had in acquiring records to substantiate his argument that he was exposed to herbicides while serving in Vietnam. To secure service-connected disability he needs records that appear to be nonexistent. "They have the records from the time I left Coronado, California, and beginning again when I returned to the Brooklyn Navy Yard. But the three years in Vietnam are totally gone. And I'm not the only Nam vet who has had this problem. We just can't get those records."

Sutton stands beside the dining room table, working to control his anger. "Supposedly, under the Freedom of Information Act we should be allowed to get those records, but they tell you the old familiar theme that the records were destroyed in a fire in St. Louis, Missouri. But even Dow's attorney, Leonard Rivkin himself, said that was a very minimal fire and the records are not missing. I mean, where else are you going to find a guy in his early thirties dying from not just one, but two, three, four blasts of cancer? And some of these cancers are inoperable. Why did the VA destroy all the cancer registry numbers of all the Vietnam veterans? Why was that? Do they have something to hide? You're goddamn right they do!"

The tabby cat appears to be deep in thought or perhaps meditating on the vicissitudes and (because he has lived more than a decade) the pleasures of a long life. I have missed the four o'clock train to Brooklyn and wonder whether or not my car will still be

there when I return. The sky is turning subway gray, with patches of blue and pink graffiti here and there.

"Ask not what your country can do for you, but what you can
do for your country," Sutton says flatly. "Yeah, I listened to that
bullshit when I was about seventeen years old. Oh, you remember. It sunk in. My father was in World War II, and my father-in-
law was a prisoner of war, and Joe's father fought in World War
II also. I guess we wanted to be just like daddy. I think this is more
than a disgrace. We didn't disgrace this nation, and I think it's
disgusting that our policymakers are doing this to a segment of
society that did nothing more than answer the call to arms when
it was asked."

Mrs. Naples, who until now has whispered quiet encouragement to her husband, is suddenly angry. "There is constant clicking on our phone, like a tape rewind. And an echo, and Joe here,
he's seen government cars taking pictures of our house with tele-
scopic lenses."

"I've had the hang-ups," Joe confirms, "got cut off mid-sen-
tence. I won't say who or why. I know who, and I hope you get
it in the book and they get a gander at it. It seems like ever since
this thing has started to build and I got involved in it, all this other
craziness has started to happen, the tapping of the phone, the
pictures from government cars, and all this other nonsense."

Sutton's wife returns from work with two bags of cat food and
a stack of xeroxed copies of a recent article about the discovery
of a government memorandum that says Agent Blue, used for
rice-crop destruction in Vietnam, has been clinically shown to be
a human carcinogen.* The memo's author, the date it was sent,
and the person to whom it was written have been masked out, and
Leonard Rivkin, attorney for Dow Chemical, is quoted as accus-
ing the government of engaging in a "cover-up" on the Agent
Orange issue. Sutton scrutinizes the article for a moment and
then, ushering Joe Naples and me to the door, announces: "I got
news for those bastards. It's just a matter of time. We're gonna

---

*"U.S. Cover-Up in Defoliant Suit Charged," *Newsday*, February 18, 1982.

win this thing. We ain't gonna wait forever. We're gonna win it either on their terms or on ours, and you can just take that any way you want. We're sick, we're dying, and they keep on playing games with our fucking lives. That just can't go on forever."

Naples offers me a ride to the station, and on the way he talks about his two sons, one of whom was born with webbed toes and suffers from sleep disturbances, seizures, learning disabilities, hyperactivity, and brain damage. "He's only seven years old," Naples says, "and wears coke-bottle glasses, has an abnormal EEG, and wakes in the night screaming. His mom and me, we'll go in the room and we can't stop him; he just keeps it up. And when he does wake up if we ask him what was wrong he'll say, 'I dunno.' He'll be doing something, like writing with his pen, and he'll put it down, go over to get a drink, and forget what he did with the pen. His concentration just blows. He can't keep his mind on anything. We took him down for an EEG and the doctor said, 'This boy's got many, many problems.' And yet there's nothing in my family or my wife's family about anyone having psychiatric problems or anything like this. Our oldest boy stopped breathin' when my wife brought him home, and she brought him back with mouth-to-mouth resuscitation. He was in the hospital in oxygen for a month, then we brought him home and within an hour he stopped breathin' again, and the second time he had to be in oxygen for three months. You know, we suffered from this stuff they sprayed in Nam, and it's bad, and now our kids are gonna suffer from it, and God only knows, how far down the line is this stuff gonna carry through?

"Not long ago my oldest boy was askin' about the war. He wants to hear about it. But there's only so much I can tell him. And one time he said, 'If I get called, I'm not goin'!' So I says, 'If you get called, you'll go, I'll see to it.' But just recently he asked again and we got talkin' and I said, if they don't settle this thing, I'll be the first to take you to Canada. I'll lock and load if I have to. But I'm not gonna let what happened to me happen to my son."

4

A MAIMED GENERATION

Driving home from the hospital, Sandy and Jerry Strait are exceptionally happy. The sky is blue and cloudless, and the grass sparkles from an early morning rain. Adjusting the tiny bundle on her lap so that she can see her daughter's sleeping face, Sandy taps her foot in time with the song on the radio. Just five more minutes and they will be home, so they have to make a decision. Before they can turn off the car's engine, their four-year-old will be tugging at the door, demanding to hold her new "sissy." She will want to carry her seven-pound, six-ounce sibling across the living room to her rocking chair and rock "our baby" to sleep. After a brief discussion the Straits agree that no harm can result from allowing Heather to play mother. After all, just seventy-two hours earlier an obstetrician had called their new daughter "a perfect, beautiful baby."

Glancing at her husband, Sandy notices that he has regained the twenty pounds he lost shortly before she learned she was pregnant. How much better things are now than four years ago when Heather was born. Jerry had been back from Vietnam only a year; they were living in a cramped house and had little money and no hospitalization insurance. When their daughter was only nine weeks old, Sandy had been forced to return to work, but this time, she tells friends and relatives, things will be different. She will be there when her baby utters her first words or takes her first wobbly steps. Having decided that this will be their last child, Sandy just wants to coddle, pamper, even spoil her baby for as long as she can. Pulling into the drive the Straits laugh. Clad in a pink sunsuit Heather races across the yard, her arms held high and her hands spread-eagled.

July and August pass quickly, giving way to a luxurious Indian summer that ends, as Midwestern falls often do, in a sudden, vicious blizzard. Heather can hardly wait for Christmas, demanding to know if her little sister will be talking or walking by then, and if she will want to see Santa Claus or watch the elves making toys in the window of a downtown department store. On Christmas day Sandy's mother arrives with presents and, while her daughter prepares dinner, she goes into the living room to tend to her new grandchild. But as she watches her granddaughter exercise, Sandy's mother notices something peculiar. Reaching into the crib she lifts first Lori's right foot, then her left. The left heel of her pajamas is frayed, nearly worn through, while the right is perfectly intact. "Have you noticed," she asks her daughter later that evening, "that Lori favors her left leg and hardly moves her right?"

Irritated by her mother's remarks, Sandy responds that the child is just naturally quiet and cannot be expected to develop at the same speed as her older sister. Yes, she admits, Lori is not yet able to sit up, rolling sideways when propped on the couch and crying until someone picks her up again. But why rush things the way they had with Heather?

Shortly after Christmas Sandy tells the doctor about her mother's observation, but he shows little concern. Lori, he explains, is simply experiencing a "delay in her development." Demonstrating an eight-week series of exercises the Straits can use to strengthen their daughter's limbs, the physician says they should see some improvement shortly thereafter. For the next month Sandy and Jerry exercise their daughter's limbs several times each day, but without results. By seven months Lori still can not roll over or sit up, and they are worried. Sandy calls the doctor's office and demands an appointment for the next day.

Something is wrong with her baby, she says, and she wants to know exactly what it is.

Wrapping Lori in several layers of blankets, Sandy drives through a snowstorm and watches with a mixture of optimism and dread as the pediatrician taps Lori's limbs with a small rubber hammer. Circling the table on which Lori lies smiling and gurgling, the doctor shakes his head sadly, pats his tiny patient on the head once or twice, and tells Sandy he has some bad news. Her daughter, he says, is suffering from cerebral palsy. It will not shorten her life; however, it will pose special . . .

Sandy is no longer listening. Like someone who jogs five miles to their physician's office for a routine checkup, only to be told they will be dead within six months, Sandy sees but does not hear the doctor.

During the following weeks Lori develops seizures, and the Straits admit her to a hospital for further tests. The seizures occur less frequently, then stop altogether when she is given phenobarbital. After ten days the Straits are told they can take their baby home. But as they walk toward the elevator, they are stopped by a physician who explains that their daughter is suffering from a debilitating nerve disease for which there is no cure. In the final stages of the disease the patient becomes deaf, blind, and then dies. He cannot be certain how long medication will help their daughter, but at least for now the seizures have stopped. The only thing he can recommend for Lori is that they take her home and love her. If the seizures reoccur, they should call him at once.

Two weeks later, Lori has another seizure and is rushed to the emergency ward. Exhausted, frustrated, and angry, the Straits begin to wonder if medical science will ever provide a satisfactory explanation for their daughter's problems. Does she suffer from cerebral palsy, or is she dying from a disease of the nervous system? Might it be possible, Sandy wonders, waving a small piece of colored cloth in front of her daughter to check her eyesight, that Lori will defy the doctor's prognosis and grow up to be a healthy and intelligent child.

One morning Sandy notices that a small crowd has gathered

near her daughter's door. Surrounded by nurses and interns, Lori's doctor appears to be giving a lecture. As she approaches, Sandy observes that one of the nurses is holding Lori "like a new puppy that all the kids wanted to see." The neurologist motions for Sandy, the nurse, and an intern to follow him down the hall where he pauses in front of a linen closet. Removing a flashlight from the pocket of his smock, he clicks it on and off several times and, satisfied that it works, orders everyone into the closet. Snapping off the overhead light the doctor presses his flashlight to the right side of Lori's head and holds it there for a moment before announcing: "This is what healthy brain tissue looks like. The light, as you can see, makes only a faint red glow. That is because it cannot penetrate the brain tissue's denseness." Moving the light to the left side of Lori's tiny head, he continues: "And this is what it looks like when there is no brain tissue. You see the pink glow? Where the light penetrates? Your daughter was born with half of her brain missing." Turning on the overhead light and pocketing his flashlight, the doctor orders the nurse to return Lori to her room. At the moment, he tells Sandy, he does not have time to discuss her daughter's prognosis in depth, but he will be glad to clarify matters later. Then he leaves.

Pacing the hospital room with Lori in her arms, Sandy asks herself questions. How common is Lori's birth defect? Why, when there is no history of birth defects in her own or Jerry's family, has this happened? And how, providing her daughter lives, will she ever tell her that she was born with the left half of her brain missing? When the neurologist returns he advises Mrs. Strait to stop worrying about how she might tell Lori about her birth defect. He has seen only one case like her daughter's, and that was a nine-month-old boy who could not follow light with his eyes and never developed beyond that point. Their daughter, says the neurologist, will never develop physically or mentally. In essence, Lori is a hopeless case.

A few days later, Sandy brings Lori home from the hospital. But Lori does not lose her hearing or eyesight, nor does she lapse into a coma and die. At the Polk County Easter Seals Center, in

Des Moines, the Straits talk with a physical therapist who does not agree with their doctor's pessimistic predictions. Instead, he says, they must take their baby home, remove her clothing, and lay her on the cold floor so she will be uncomfortable enough to want to roll over. If Lori is to develop, they must resist the inclination to make her comfortable; their daughter, says the therapist, simply cannot be allowed to be content. For the next twenty-four months the Straits spend hours each day rolling their daughter on a beach ball so her toes and fingers will touch the floor to simulate crawling, watching her flail about on the kitchen floor and resisting the temptation to help her as she struggles.

After ten months Lori can roll over and she follows her mother about the room this way, rolling from room to room, her mother says, "like a baby seal." After eighteen months Lori can sit up without support and is able to say "Mama," and by two years she is walking, though with a sideways gait because her right leg is still weak. By putting peanut butter behind Lori's teeth and encouraging her to move her tongue toward the treat, a speech therapist teaches Lori how to form sounds, then words. By the age of three she has progressed to the point where she is enrolled in a nursery school for handicapped children; her mother kisses Lori goodbye, pinning a small notebook to her daughter's collar so the teacher can write down some of the day's events. Before the year is over, Lori's memory has so improved that the notebook is no longer necessary. She is now able to recall some of the things that happen during the school day.

While his daughter continues to make miraculous progress, Jerry Strait is beginning to experience symptoms that, like Lori's birth defect, seem mysterious in origin. Nine years after his return from Vietnam, an irritating rash is spreading across his face and scalp, and there are times when his head aches so badly that he is overcome with nausea. But it does not occur to him that his symptoms or Lori's birth defect might be related to his tour of duty in Vietnam, all but a few days of which he spent in the bush. The Department of Defense has not advised him that he spent more than three hundred days in the most heavily sprayed region of Vietnam or that the food he ate and water he drank may have been contaminated by dioxin.

One evening Strait is preparing for bed when his mother calls to ask if he has read the newspaper article about "something called Agent Orange." She also wants to know if he recalls having been exposed to herbicides. As he reads, Strait is surprised not only by the statements some veterans are making, but by how much he seems to have forgotten since his return home. Examining a photograph of a C123 spraying herbicides, Strait wonders why he has given so little thought to the cysts that spread across his body in Vietnam, clinging to his back, legs, and arms like leeches; or the headaches, dizziness, rashes, and stomach cramps that he and others in his platoon had attributed to the heat. Closing his eyes and leaning back on the couch, Strait remembers the A Shau Valley in 1969. The trees are leafless, rotting, and from a distance appear petrified. The ground is littered with decaying jungle birds; on the surface of a slow-moving stream, clusters of dead fish shimmer like giant buttons. A new arrival "in country" remarks that the scene is spooky, but Strait only shrugs. For him, after several months in the bush, the defoliated area is no more spooky than the corner drugstore in his hometown. Leaving the area, the men walk downstream for thirty minutes before pausing to fill their canteens and helmets with cool water. Some of the men drop in purifying tablets, others do not.* After satiating their thirst they splash the remaining water over their necks and faces and then move on.

According to the news article, the VA is offering "Agent Orange examinations" and Strait decides to visit the VA medical clinic. There he is given a four-page questionnaire asking for the *time, date, place,* and *amount* of his exposure to Agent Orange. Strait finds the questions peculiar and perplexing. In Vietnam he paid little attention to the spraying, and ten years later it seems ludicrous that he should be asked to remember such details. Al-

---

*Years later Strait will learn that using army-issue purifying tablets to cleanse water contaminated with dioxin is like trying to neutralize a vat of cyanide with an aspirin.

though he can vividly recall being in defoliated zones, he did not keep a log of his entry and exit from such areas. "We were fighting a war," says Strait, "not conducting an archeological expedition. It just never really occurred to us that it mattered." Nor was it the Army's policy to tell its troops how recently an area had been sprayed or how much dioxin they might ingest if they drank water or ate food contaminated with Agent Orange. How much was he exposed? That's precisely what Strait wants the VA to tell him.

An hour passes before a physician enters the examining room and, after "poking and prodding" Strait for a few minutes, he explains that he has "received special training in these Agent Orange cases" and can assure the former paratrooper that "Agent Orange and dioxin have never hurt anyone, are not hurting and never will hurt anyone." After briefly examining Straight's completed questionnaire, the physician informs him that his headaches are "obviously due to war-related stress" and recommends that he pay a visit to the clinic's psychologist. A consultation with the hospital's dietician, says the doctor, will undoubtedly help Strait's skin rash.

Strait is surprised, even angry. What word has he used, he asks himself, that the man doesn't understand? Did he not just explain that he is working at a steady job, does not drink excessively or take drugs, and does not feel he is suffering from "post-Vietnam syndrome." Realizing that his efforts to persuade Strait to see a psychiatrist are futile, the doctor says that he will make an appointment for him to see a dermatologist. Meanwhile, he tells Strait, "My advice to you is that you go home and stop worrying about all this Agent Orange stuff."

During the following weeks the Straits wait anxiously for the results of Jerry's blood and urine analysis; but when weeks, months, and finally a year pass without notice from the clinic, they conclude that they will never hear from the VA again. Two years and three months later, Sandy is astonished to discover a pamphlet in the mail from the VA's Washington headquarters. "We could hardly believe our eyes after all this time," she explains. "On the outside it said, 'WORRIED ABOUT AGENT ORANGE?' And on the inside there is a picture of Max Cleland and he is saying, 'Oh heavens, don't worry about anything like that. Agent Orange never did anybody any real harm.' I guess they think we're pretty dumb, because Jerry and I know that Cleland has not been the VA's director for some time. Why they're still sending his picture around is a mystery to me."

Although no one knows—because no government agency has bothered to count—how many children fathered by Vietnam veterans have suffered birth defects similar to those seen in the offspring of female laboratory animals exposed to dioxin, everyone agrees that this is one of the most volatile aspects of the Agent Orange issue. To parents of children like Lori Strait, the question of whether dioxin damages the chromosomes or sperm cells of exposed males should have been answered "before one drop" of Agent Orange was used in Vietnam. Yet two decades after the first defoliation mission was flown, there is still no unanimity among scientists on whether TCDD acts as a mutagen in male laboratory animals or in human beings. Citing a study of male mice treated with Agent Orange, the VA continues to argue in its public relations pamphlets that "there is no medical evidence that exposure to Agent Orange has caused birth defects in the children of Vietnam veterans."[1] But according to attorneys for Vietnam veterans involved in the class action suit, "At least 2,000 children may be born with catastrophic deformities due to the chemical poisons their fathers carried home from the war."[2] In addition, the VA's pamphlets fail to mention that TCDD-dioxin is a depressant of spermatogenesis in male rats, and causes mutations in salmonella and drosophila.[3]

Evidence of the possible mutagenic effects of TCDD on exposed males is not limited to bacteria or laboratory rats. In Vietnam, Dr. Ton That Tung and his colleagues have been studying the possible effects of dioxin on North Vietnamese soldiers exposed to herbicides while serving in the South. Among the birth defects Dr. Tung and his colleagues have observed are cleft lips, absence of nose, shortened limbs, absence of nose and eyes, malformed ears, clubfeet, absence of forearm, hydrocephaly (water on the brain) and anencephaly (a condition in which all or a major part of the brain is missing), and a variety of heart problems.

Because Dr. Tung was aware that laboratory research had already proven dioxin teratogenic and fetotoxic in rats and mice, he was careful to inquire whether the wives of former North Vietnamese soldiers had been exposed to herbicides. Through interviews with the veterans and their families, Tung's research teams learned that *none of the women* who had given birth to deformed children had been exposed to herbicides; yet in one district where the researchers found a total of nine birth defects out of two hundred and thirty-three births, all nine of the deformed children were fathered by veterans. In another district, where veterans comprised only a small percentage of the population, Dr. Tung found that half of the deformed children born during a four-year period were fathered by veterans. Six out of the thirty children born with defects were anencephalic, and all six were fathered by veterans.

Statistically, writes Dr. Tung, his findings are extraordinary: In the region he was studying there should have been "one anencephalia in every 2,777 births, whereas we have one anencephalia per 197.7 births among veterans from the south. Furthermore, we must emphasize the great number of cardiac deformities: 15 cases out of 43 defects: i.e. 34.8 percent of the defects. The involvement of the neural tube seems to be in agreement with the studies of Barbara Field, who proved that in Australia there is a linear relationship between the rising rate of *spina bifida* [a condition where the spine is improperly fused] in newborns in the *first generation* and the rate of 2,4,5-T utilized each year." Dr. Tung has also found that the wives of exposed veterans have an abnormally high rate of miscarriages, premature births, and stillbirths, while an unusual number of the veterans suffer from sterility. The fathers of deformed children, writes Dr. Tung, exhibited "signs of direct contact with herbicidal sprays in South Vietnam." Concluding his paper, he states: "By comparing reproductive outcomes of Vietnamese soldiers exposed to Agent Orange and those who were not exposed, there appears to be an excess of birth defects in children of the exposed veterans. This suggests that dioxin may act as a mutagen and thus would represent the first example of teratogenic damage due to male exposure in humans."[4]

In 1967, Arthur W. Galston, a professor of botany at Yale, tried to warn the U.S. against the continued unbridled use of herbicides in Vietnam. "We are too ignorant of the interplay of forces in ecological problems to know how far-reaching and how lasting will be the changes in ecology brought about by the widespread spraying of herbicides. The changes may include immediate harm to people in sprayed areas . . ."[5]

Galston's warning turned out to be prophetic. Just two years later, reports of birth defects in the offspring of Vietnamese women began appearing in Saigon newspapers, but the U.S. government dismissed the peasants' complaints as communist propaganda, arguing that there was no scientific proof that Agent Orange harmed human beings. Today the government's response, through the Veterans Administration, remains essentially unchanged, in spite of the fact that Vietnam veterans have fathered hundreds and perhaps even thousands of seriously deformed children. At the New York State Temporary Commission on Dioxin Exposure hearings, a veteran testified that "before my son was ten and a half months old he had to have two operations because he had bilateral inguinal hernia, which means his scrotum didn't close, and his intestine was where his scrotum was, and his scrotum was the size of a grapefruit. He also has deformed feet . . . My oldest daughter has a heart murmur and a bad heart. Once she becomes active, you can see her heart beat through her chest as though the chest cavity is not even there, as though you were looking at the heart."

Before Vietnam, said the veteran, he had "never even had an aspirin," but since his return he has been given more than a hundred medications for skin rashes, stomach problems, urine in his blood, and inflamed kidneys. The VA, he testified, has written him off as a "hypochondriac."

At the same hearings a Vietnam veteran's wife made the following statement: "I am married to a Vietnam veteran who was a combat veteran in 1967 and 1968. We have two sons, a four-year-old and one who is four months. Our first son was born with his bladder on the outside of the body, a sprung pelvis, a double hernia, a split penis, and a perforated anus. The doctors are attempting to reconstruct the bladder and his penis. He has had five operations, and is due for a sixth operation in the fall. There is no way of telling how many more operations he will have to suffer through before the reconstruction is successful. The question of his being able to father his own children cannot be answered until he reaches puberty.

"We have met other Vietnam veterans and their families. We have met their children. We have seen and heard about the deformities, limb and bone deformities, heart defects, dwarfism, and other diseases for which there is no diagnosis . . . There are hundreds of children with basically the same problem, but in groups: so many bifidas, so many bone deformities, urological, neurological. But it is in groups of hundreds, not ones or twos."

Another tragic aspect of having been exposed to Agent Orange, say veterans, is the fear they experience while waiting for their children to be born. What for centuries has traditionally been a time for rejoicing is all too often a period of prolonged anxiety and nervous tension for veterans and their wives. Many veterans, of course, have fathered perfectly healthy children, and those who worry that sensationalist journalism might encourage veterans or their wives to resort to sterilization have a valid point. But while the VA accuses the media of overreacting, it does not hire a competent staff of geneticists to counsel veterans, fails to do extensive testing of veterans' fatty tissues to determine if they contain dioxin, and continues to insist that it will be 1987 before it can complete its epidemiological study.

"In the abominable history of war," said Dr. Ton That Tung in 1970, "with the sole exception of nuclear weapons, has such an inhuman fate ever before been reserved for the survivors?"[6]

A decade later a young mother whose daughter was born with sixteen birth defects testified before the U.S. Senate Committee on Veterans' Affairs about what has happened to many of the survivors of the Vietnam War. "Just as truly as the bullets and bombs killed on the battlefields in Vietnam," said Maureen Ryan, "maiming thousands of our men, Agent Orange has come home from those battlefields with our men. It has come home to maim and kill additional thousands of men who naively thought they made it home safely. It would have been tragic enough if it had ended there.

"But what the United States and what our Vietnam veterans did not know was that they carried home a tremendous legacy with them. They did not know that genetically on those battlefields were their children. So Agent Orange is now reaping an additional harvest of birth defects and cancers in our children and the men. We are losing our children through spontaneous abortions, through miscarriages, and perhaps most tragically in the surviving children, with the horrifying birth defects."

Angered by the VA's argument that it had not conducted an Agent Orange outreach program because it did not wish to confuse or frighten veterans and their wives, Ryan said, "It is not frightening when you are handed knowledge. It is much more frightening when you are kept in the dark. It is much more frightening to give birth to a child with birth defects. It is much more frightening to know your husband is dying of cancer."

Summing up her testimony, Ryan told Senator Alan Cranston: "The echo of pain that you are hearing in this room may come off as a tremendous amount of bitterness. I don't know whether bitterness is the right word so much as it is the level of frustration that has been reached. I think these people have lived private hells, and I don't think we would be sitting here today if we didn't believe in this country. What we are saying, though, is that the government is the people and the government has to stand behind us."[7]

At the age of five Lori Strait entered kindergarten. At seven she finished first grade, joined a square-dancing club, and played softball in a league for handicapped and retarded children. But Lori still wears a brace on her right leg, has only limited use of her right hand, and requires speech and occupational therapy. After the attention of nearly forty-five therapists and doctors, several stays in the hospital, and many thousands of dollars in medical expenses, Lori remains a handicapped child.

In spite of the pleasure they feel watching their daughter progress, the Straits are highly critical of their government's handling of the Agent Orange tragedy. Why, they ask, is the government unwilling to do the kind of grass-roots research Dr. Tung and his colleagues are conducting in Vietnam? Rather than spending hundreds of thousands of dollars designing studies that may eventually demonstrate that veterans are ill, why doesn't the United States send a team of medical doctors, dioxin experts, scientists, and dermatologists to examine firsthand the devastating effects of dioxin on human health? (Working out of mobile clinics the team could examine veterans and then make recommendations to the VA regarding a veteran's claim for service-connected disability.) Why doesn't the Department of Health and Human Services hire competent geneticists to examine the chromosomes and germ cells of every veteran who fathers a child with polygenetic birth defects? Perhaps most perplexing to the Straits is this: if Dow Chemical knew in 1965 that 2,4,5-T was contaminated with dioxin, and the U.S. knew in 1962 that dioxin is toxic, then why were extensive scientific studies not conducted on the possible mutagenic, carcinogenic, and teratogenic effects of Agent Orange *before* it was used in Vietnam?

According to Thomas Whiteside, none of the manufacturers of 2,4,5-T did any formal testing on the chemical's possible teratogenicity until after President Nixon's science adviser, Dr. Lee DuBridge, proposed in 1969 that limited restrictions be placed on the use of the herbicide in the U.S. and Vietnam. Dr. DuBridge's statement was prompted by the results of a study conducted by Bionetics Laboratories of Bethesda, Maryland, which concluded that even in the lowest dose given, 2,4,5-T caused cleft palates, missing and deformed eyes, cystic kidneys, and enlarged livers in the offspring of laboratory animals. The study was also important because, writes Whiteside, "the rat, as a test animal, tends to be relatively resistant to teratogenic effects of chemicals."[8]

Although the study was conducted in 1965, its findings were not released until a member of Nader's Raiders discovered a preliminary report submitted to the Food and Drug Administration by Bionetics Laboratories. The report's conclusions were passed on to Matthew Meselson, Arthur Galston, and other scientists, who then demanded to know more about the study, including why the Bionetics Laboratories did not release its findings sooner. The manufacturers of 2,4,5-T had failed to test its teratogenic properties because neither the Department of Agriculture nor the Food and Drug Administration required such tests.

"When I went to Vietnam," says Jerry Strait, "I took my chances. I was a soldier and I knew what to expect. There was always the possibility that I would be killed or wounded, but I didn't think my children would ever be a casualty of the war. And maybe it's too late for me, the damage has been done and whatever happens just happens. But I still wonder about our future generations. What about all the kids who didn't have anything to say about all this? The chemical companies insist that it's all a 'legal issue.' But I think that putting something into the air and water that will maim future generations isn't a matter of law. It's a moral issue. Am I bitter about Vietnam? No, but I am bitter about the spraying and about what happened to Lori. To tell you the truth, I would go back if they asked me. I think most of my friends feel that way. But we want some answers about this thing, and we keep asking how the government can get any answers if it doesn't ask questions."

On August 31, 1982, officials of the Veterans Administration told the VA's Advisory Committee on Health-Related Effects of Herbicides that the epidemiological study has been delayed because the VA "still must determine whether it can adequately identify soldiers who came into contact with the herbicide." Unless this can be done, said the officials, the study will not be conducted. In addition, said Dr. Barclay Shepard, chairman of the advisory body, "a pilot program must be conducted to show the study is feasible." All this, said Dr. Shepard, will take another six or seven years. The VA does plan to investigate whether veterans are fathering a "disproportionately high number of babies born with birth defects," and this study is scheduled to be completed, provided there are no bureaucratic snags, by 1984.[9]

5

DYING DOWN UNDER

Sweeping his empty beer stein aside, Jim Wares places his left hand on the table, fingers outstretched and pressed tightly together. His right hand forms an ax, which he raises in an eyebrow salute then slams down on the supine fingers and thumb of his left hand.

"If you took a guillotine and just dropped it straight across, including the top of the thumb, *that* is his hand. There's a little bud there, and a bud there," pointing to the first and fourth knuckle, "and a hole here where the finger should be, and then one here. And you could honestly put a spirit level across there and it's so even that it's as though an ax had fallen and chopped them right off. But in spite of it all, it's mild compared to a lot of things that other veterans' children suffer from."

Wares signals the bartender, who—moonwhite, emaciated and bored—delivers another round to our table, then settles down in front of the television. On *Wide World of Sports* a boxer, inspired by a delirious crowd, is battering his opponent unconscious. Three men at the bar give a desultory cheer as the referee steps between the two contestants and stops the fight. "I thought he was going to kill the poor bastard," Wares announces, breaking the bitter silence that has followed his description of his son's birth defect. The interview, stalled as others have behind a wall of anger, continues.

By 1962, Wares explains, the Australian government had committed thirty military instructors to Vietnam, a number that was increased to approximately one hundred by 1965. But by then the South Vietnamese government appeared to be floundering. The war against "communist insurgents" was going poorly, and a plea went out to the United States and Australia for more help. Convinced that the insurgency was part of a "thrust by Communist China between the Indian and Pacific oceans," a move that would mean a direct threat to his country, the Australian prime minister, Sir Robert Menzies, agreed to send a full infantry battalion to Vietnam. As the Australian government's involvement in the war increased, its troops were given an area of operations that included Phuoc Tuy Province, southeast of Saigon, with its center of operations based at Nui Dat. The area was considered vital to the South Vietnamese government because it was situated between Saigon and the important port of Vung Tau, and one of the Australians' primary tasks was to keep Route 15 open between Saigon and Vung Tau. To accomplish this they would fight many bitter engagements with both VC and NVA units. That much of the local populace was sympathetic to the VC was well known, and to reduce the chance of ambush, the Australians eventually began using herbicides in Phuoc Tuy Province. By the war's end approximately 50,000 Australians had served in Vietnam, with many of the men serving two tours.

One of Wares's most vivid memories of Vietnam is the mosquitoes—attacking like schools of piranhas, tattooing his skin with welts, which when scratched turned into festering sores. The mosquitoes also carried malaria, so when a C123 flew over the base camp trailing white fog from its wings, the men almost felt like cheering.

"What I saw them spraying was a mosquito killer, and that's all we knew it to be at that time. What we didn't know was that it was malathion. The C123s came over once a fortnight, or once a week or month, but it was very regular. And we were *very* happy with it because it killed the bugs. It smelled for a while, but it did the job, and that's all we cared about at that time, mate."

Wares also observed backpack spraying and spraying from trucks, but he had been told nothing about herbicides and had no reason to question the purpose of the spraying. Until his son was born with missing fingers and only a partial thumb on one hand and he began hearing stories of other Australian veterans whose children were born with deformed feet, cleft palates, missing limbs, holes in their hearts, partial brains, and skin rashes, Wares gave the spraying little thought.

Thirteen years after he returned from Nui Dat, Wares and I are seated in the lounge of a Ramada Inn in New York City. He has arrived from London to see Bob Gibson, an Australian Vietnam veteran who has been touring the United States for eight weeks, talking with American veterans and leaders of the veterans' movement, and gathering information he hopes will be useful to Australian veterans suffering from the effects of exposure to toxic chemicals.

In 1967 Gibson was an infantryman in Phuoc Tuy Province. Returning from three days in the bush he was handed a gas mask and ordered to begin spraying herbicides on the barbed wire surrounding his base camp. Gibson reluctantly complied, wondering why, since he had no training for this kind of work, he had been chosen for such miserable duty. Wearing a gas mask in Vietnam was like burying one's face in hot wet sand, and Gibson and others assigned to the detail quickly discarded their protective gear. Their clothes stuck to their skin, sweat drained into their eyes, and the spray was often blown directly back into their faces. Within ten days the mucous membranes in Gibson's nose had deteriorated so much that he suffered from frequent nosebleeds. His skin was covered with a painful rash, and his stomach was constantly upset. But he was nineteen and "very patriotic" at the time, and he believed that if the herbicides reduced the enemy's cover, then he could easily suffer a bit of discomfort.

Gibson's commanders "did tell us what we were spraying, and as infantry soldiers we thought it was a good thing. It done the job. We could see what it was doing, and it was making it easier for us. But they didn't tell us what the outcome would be, the health problems it could cause. We were told that they were going to defoliate, and we thought this was the best thing that they'd ever come up with. And we used to laugh about it; you know, we thought it would be a good idea if they defoliated the whole of South Vietnam. It would be kind of like fightin' in the desert.

"They did issue us gas masks that first day, but we couldn't breathe in them because of the humidity. And I was an infantry soldier just come back from three days of ambushes, and we were just picked out at random to use the stuff. We know now that it was nothing more than experimental. We've got documents on the scientist who was controlling the spraying. He was sent there by the Australian Department of Defense to experiment with various chemicals, 2,4,5-T, 2,4-D, and others. But the fellows who were picking us out at the time to do this work were infantry sergeants, and they knew as much about chemicals as I did, and that was damn nothing. So we told the sergeant after that first day that we couldn't breathe using this stuff, and he said, 'I'll check on it tonight for you,' and the next day he said, 'Don't worry, leave the gas masks and everything off.' So we used to get in back there and spray this stuff through the barbed wire, and it would come back on us. And your nose would start to bleed, your lips would all get blisters on them, your mucous membranes would break down, and he, the scientist in charge, has documented it all."

Like their American counterparts in Vietnam, Australian soldiers had been told very little, if anything, about the health effects of long-term exposure to herbicides. According to an Australian army handout, "Instructions for Spraying Herbicides," the spray was not "toxic to humans when dispersed as a spray on vegetation," but "casualties can be caused by spillage of the chemical concentrates on the skin and clothes by the spray. Therefore protective clothing and equipment is worn, and simple safety precautions are to be followed." Side effects from weedicides and soil sterilants are:

a. Blistering of the skin.
b. Toenails dropping off.
c. Systemic poisoning with fatal results from continued absorp-

tion, inhalation or swallowing of the spray or any of the concentrates.

d. Breakdown of mucous membrane, e.g., nosebleeds, red eyes, mouth ulceration.

But Graham Bell, Queensland president of the Vietnam Veterans Action Association, recalls that members of his unit were told that they had absolutely nothing to worry about. "In my unit we were told the chemicals were harmless to humans and animals, that they did no permanent damage to the environment, and that the major disadvantage was that when regrowth occurred (a few weeks after spraying) it would be much more vigorous—just like giving the vegetation a burst of fertilizer. Troops of another unit, 5 R.A.R, were drenched with chemicals sprayed by American aircraft; they were told, 'It won't even hurt dumb animals.' "[1]

Had Australian military personnel in charge of defoliation efforts consulted the U.S. Army on the effects of herbicides on human health, they would have read that Agent Orange was "relatively nontoxic to man and animals No injuries have been reported to personnel exposed to aircraft spray. Personnel subject to splashes from handling the agent need not be alarmed, but should shower and change clothes at a convenient opportunity."

According to the American manual Agent Blue was also "relatively" harmless. "Normal sanitary conditions should be followed when handling Blue. Although it contains a form of arsenic, Blue is relatively nontoxic. It should not be taken internally, however. Any material that gets on the hands, face, or other parts of the body should be washed off at the first opportunity. Clothes that become wet with a solution of Blue should be washed afterwards . . ."

Neither the American nor the Australian military explain how grunts in the field might be able to shower or change their clothes immediately after exposure to toxic chemicals, or avoid eating food or drinking water contaminated with arsenic* or dioxin.

---

*By the war's end, Operation Ranch Hand had sprayed 1,933,699 pounds of arsenic on the Vietnamese countryside.

Shortly after he was assigned to spray herbicides, Gibson, his face covered with a burning rash, entered Nui Dat hospital complaining of severe gastroenteritis (an inflammation of the stomach and intestines) and suffering from high temperatures. The doctors who examined him were bewildered, concluding, just as American doctors examining personnel with similar symptoms in other regions of Vietnam did, that their patient was suffering from overexposure to the heat. Entering the hospital for a second time, Gibson was transferred to Vung Tau, where he was examined by nine doctors, all of whom seemed mystified by his symptoms.

"I was really concerned because I just couldn't walk. The whole of my body, all over my groin and everywhere, was covered with a rash. But it was weeping and everything was just sort of falling off. And I said to these guys, 'What the bloody hell have I got?' And they said, 'Don't worry, don't worry, we think we know what it is. We think we can . . .' But I says, 'Yeah, you think you can *what?*' And they said, 'Oh, just take it easy, mate, we can fix you up.' But hell, when you've got nine doctors looking at you and they don't know, and when they come back with some younger doctors and start pointin' and lookin', it makes you a little bit worried. And still to this day the VA isn't able to tell me what it was, or is."

Draining his glass, Wares grimaces and with mincing sarcasm announces, "Why, it was the *heat*, mate, don't you know that? The heat of course. We accepted that explanation at the time because that was all they ever told us, all we ever heard. It's the tropics, boys, that's what it is. And that, we now know, is just so much *bullshit*. Because people here in Queensland live in the tropics, and do they all run around with bloody skin diseases? We accepted the explanation at the time that our rashes were due to the heat, but we don't believe a bloody word of it anymore. And I can tell you this. Never, never did they tell us anything about herbicide spraying, or about putting on any extra clothing or taking precautions against the spray. In fact at the time I wouldn't have known what the word 'defoliant' meant, and that's a fact, mate. I just wouldn't have known. Bob Gibson of course knew something more because he actually sprayed, but the average serviceman, the average Australian, wouldn't have had a clue."

Gibson nods his head in sad agreement. Since his return from Phuoc Tuy Province he has suffered from skin rashes, insomnia, violent rages, and other problems symptomatic of dioxin exposure. His ability to work impaired by physical and emotional conditions for which he could find no cure, Gibson applied to the Australian Repatriation Commission for disability payments. But the commission, using language that might easily have been excerpted from an American VA form letter, rejected his request. About Gibson the commission's psychiatrist wrote: "In this particular case, the patient is a thirty-two-year-old man who has a mild anxiety state. He sets himself up as a martyr and has suffered basically at his own hand by not allowing the memories of Vietnam and their associated emotions to fade with time. His present condition is due to his basic inherited personality pattern and his wish for martyrdom."

During the twelve months he spent in Vietnam, Gibson had gone on numerous ambushes and had fought in a fierce two-day battle with North Vietnamese regulars in which the Australians were outnumbered and nearly destroyed. His unit's motor positions wiped out, ammunition running low, and the NVA preparing for a final assault, Gibson had given up all hope of surviving the battle when American helicopter gunships arrived. Before the "Puffs"* appeared, says Gibson, he had concluded that "we were all dead men." In its initial rejection of his request for disability, the commission informed Gibson that he had spent very little time in combat; therefore, wrote the commission's psychiatrist, "Vietnam could not really have been as traumatic as he now tells." But later the commission reversed itself, acknowledging that Gibson was indeed a combat veteran while continuing to argue that his experiences in Vietnam were not responsible for his "anxiety condition."

---

*Puff the Magic Dragon: C-47 cargo plane equipped with three electric-powered Gatling machine guns.

In retrospect Gibson says that he and the nineteen-year-olds with whom he served may have placed too much trust in people who either did not know or did not care what the effects of toxic chemicals might be on Australian soldiers. "As infantry soldiers we thought we knew what the hell we were doing, but really we were so naive. We never thought that our government or our own military commanders would allow the use of anything that might have adverse effects on us as troops. And we used to walk through plantations of rotten banana trees that were just burstin' at the bottom, you know, rottin', stinkin', with these tiny dwarf bananas on them. So we'd just walk through and pick them. They were sweet as hell, and we used to eat them all the time. No one ever told us not to. And the water, we used to get it out of streams and drink it. And one time I can really recall quite well. We went through this thick foliage, and it had all this sticky shiny stuff on it, and it stunk, I mean it really stunk. And we were going through this stuff and there was no two ways about it, it had been defoliated. And yet no one ever gave it one second thought that we were there, touching the stuff, getting it on our arms and face. Not one thought."

Gibson's observations are substantiated by Australian authors John Dux and P. J. Young, who through careful examination of U.S. General Accounting Office reports, including "grid coordinates and details of all missions flown by the C123s from 1965 to 1968," found that Phuoc Tuy Province had been heavily sprayed with Agent Orange. Matching the GAO reports with Australian Defense Department maps, the authors concluded: "One can prove conclusively that Australian troops operated in defoliated areas, sometimes within a day of missions."[2] Dux and Young also point out that although the U.S. Ranch Hand operations may have been responsible for the destruction of 12 to 21 percent of the total land in South Vietnam (an area approximately the size of Massachusetts), C123 spraying was only one source of the toxic herbicides to which Australian and American veterans were exposed. Helicopter pilots, for example, needed only the approval of their unit commander before leaving on a defoliation mission, and it is quite possible that some areas of the province—particularly around base camps—were unofficially sprayed on numerous occasions. Spraying from trucks, riverboats, and by backpack also required only the approval of the unit commander.

Another possible source of contamination was from tanks that were used to spray both pesticides and herbicides directly upon or near base camps. Australian pilots have stated that following herbicide missions, empty spray tanks were refilled with pesticides that were then sprayed directly upon the base camp. Commenting on the possibility that residues from herbicides might have been dispersed in this way, one pilot said: "An interesting thing is that after the spraying missions, which occurred about every month with these aircraft, the rubber trees with which the Task Force area was covered shed their leaves rather alarmingly. After spraying for anti-malarial purposes there would be a sudden increase in skin infections for no particular attributable cause, apart from the fact that it followed the spraying."[3]

When one considers the amount of semi-authorized, unauthorized, and clandestine spraying in Vietnam, as well as wind drift and the fact that an estimated 14 percent of the Agent Orange sent to Vietnam is unaccounted for, it is apparent that the full extent of the defoliation campaign may never be known. What is clear is that Vietnam veterans whose units are not listed by the Department of Defense or General Accounting Office as having been in spray zones could very well have been exposed to toxic chemicals either in and around their base camps or on ambushes and search-and-destroy missions in the surrounding jungle.

When his son Cameron was born with a "noncorrectable" birth defect, Jim Wares wanted to know why. But doctors were unable to give him a satisfactory explanation, and he decided not to dwell on the boy's misfortune. After all, Wares told himself, he had survived Vietnam, was married to a fine woman, had a good job, and the boy, except for missing fingers, was beautifully formed, an optimistic and intelligent child whom Wares says is fond of making up stories and playing practical jokes with his hand. One evening, for example, Wares and his wife left their son with a babysitter who, summoned to the bathroom by the boy's cries, discovered him standing near the toilet bowl. Feigning distress and holding out the hand with the missing fingers, the boy announced that he had accidentally "flushed the fingers away." The babysitter, says Wares, didn't know whether to laugh or cry.

Wares had heard stories about Agent Orange and wondered if it might have something to do with Cameron's deformity, but the government's official position was that Orange had not been used at Nui Dat. Besides, argued government officials, scientists had found "no link" between exposure to herbicides and human health problems. But the Australian news media were becoming increasingly interested in the veterans' problems, and after reading an interview with a veteran whose eyesight was failing and who was suffering from constant trembling, diarrhea, fatigue, and vomiting, Wares decided to begin his own research into the matter. Calling people whose names had appeared in news articles, Wares was amazed to discover that each person he contacted knew other veterans who were sick, whose wives had suffered miscarriages, or whose children were deformed. Wares soon realized that something was seriously, perhaps disastrously, wrong with his fellow Vietnam veterans.

Wares began listing on filing cards the symptoms of veterans with whom he had spoken or corresponded by mail. Sorting through a stack of fifty cards one afternoon, he discovered that nearly one in four of the men he had contacted had fathered a deformed child. Four of the cards actually listed children born with deformed hands, and three out of the four were born with four fingers and half the thumb missing from one hand. On other cards Wares had listed cases of deformed legs, clubfeet, deafness, and missing ears. With each passing day Wares found himself increasingly involved in trying to sort out the truth about his own and his fellow veterans' exposure to toxic chemicals. With each rebuff from the government his anger—and the veterans' movement in Australia—grew. The country's enormous size and the scarcity of money sometimes made logistics rather difficult; but like their counterparts in the States, Australian Vietnam veterans drew support from the realization that they had at least three things in common: they had served in an area of Southeast Asia that had been heavily sprayed with defoliants; many of them were sick, dying, or had fathered children with birth defects; government officials, while expressing concern, were doing little to resolve the issue in a fair and compassionate manner.

"When we first got involved with the movement in Australia," Wares explains, "I went to the Royal Alexandria Hospital for Children in Sydney, saw the chief pediatrician, and asked some questions. I said, 'My son has been born with no fingers on one hand,' and I asked if he had any statistics on that kind of deformity. Now, in Australia most of the hospitals don't keep that kind of statistics. There's no national statistics on birth deformities. Some hospitals keep them, some don't; it's very ad hoc. So I told this guy that my son was born with no fingers, 'but his arm is perfectly normal, the palm of his hand is normal, his arm isn't withered, it's not short, there's just no fingers. It's only affected one limb, which in itself I understand is rather unusual.' And I said, 'What are the chances of this happening?' And he said, 'Well, I would say that using statistics, one in fifty thousand is way over the odds.'

"So I told him, 'What would you say if I told you that I know another two kids with exactly this same deformity? Exactly the same.' And he said, 'My God, that's incredible.' And I said, 'Well, if I told you that both their fathers were Vietnam veterans, and there were only forty-five thousand men from this country who went to Vietnam, and of the three children I know with this deformity all of their fathers are veterans, how would that affect you?' He was absolutely staggered. To such an extent that he said, 'What we will do is we'll test all of the veterans' children who are deformed free of charge at this hospital.' And that was in the Sydney press, and in the Australian national press. But one week later that decision was reversed. Politics. The hospital board decided that it wouldn't be done!"

Wares, Holt McMinn, and John Harper eventually formed the Vietnam Veterans Action Association. McMinn had served in Vietnam with an elite commando unit, the Special Air Service Regiment; but after several months in the bush he began coughing blood, his hands were covered with rashes, and, diagnosing his condition as bronchial asthma, Army doctors sent him back to Australia. McMinn attempted to return to Vietnam in 1968, but after examining his health records the Army refused to grant his request. His health continued to deteriorate and he was forced to enter a repatriation hospital where, after three months of tests, doctors told him they could find no reason for his hemorrhaging. His problem, they said, was obviously psychological. Discharged from the military and given a 20 percent disability pension, McMinn was accused by an examining doctor of being a "malingerer" who was trying to "rip off the government."

Although Wares and Harper had each fathered a deformed child—Harper's daughter was born with two clubfeet and had already undergone five corrective operations when the two veterans met—they were not suffering from the kind of catastrophic health problems that seemed to be endemic among other Vietnam veterans. "I wasn't angry for myself," says Wares, "because even though I had suffered from a rash in Vietnam and had experienced this strange tingling sensation in my limbs since my return home, I was fairly healthy compared to Bob Gibson, Holt McMinn, and too many others I could name. But I wanted to know whether my son could ever have children. I really didn't think the government owed me a damned thing, but for christsake they do owe it to these kids to try and find out what caused their deformity, and whether or not they can ever have normal children. Because that is the bit that I just can't handle, I mean the kids and their kids, the generations that are not yet born that might end up with two noses or one ear missing or no arms, no bones, no brains—that is the bit that is just so hard to take."

Wares knew that establishing a correlation between his exposure to toxic chemicals and Cameron's birth defects would not be an easy task. By 1969 public opinion in Australia had already turned sour on the war, and a decade later most people simply did not want to be reminded of Vietnam. To those who would rather practice selective amnesia than disentomb a bitterness that had once swept the nation like a virus, Wares, Gibson, McMinn, and other veterans' advocates were considered "gadflies," distraught over the fact that they had not been given a hero's welcome when they returned home and intent on making someone suffer for their neglect. The premier of Queensland, Joh Bjelke-Petersen, incensed by the activities of the Vietnam Veterans Action Association, suggested that the veterans' physical and emotional problems were the result of their having been exposed to a particularly virulent strain of venereal disease. Damaged livers, cancer, and deformed children were apparently just a few of the wages of sin. "And do you know what the man does for a living?" Gibson laughs. "He grows peanuts, and he's got his own crop-spraying company. That's right. His own spraying company."

"They call us communists, radical environmentalists, hippies, you name it," says Wares, who immigrated to Australia as a boy and is fiercely patriotic, "but that is just so much bullshit. I'll admit that I was a bit surprised at the animosity toward me and my mates when we returned home, but I didn't go to Vietnam to save Australia from the screaming communist hordes. I went because my country wanted me to go, and because at the time I just never, never believed that my own country would lie to me."

Concerned over the growing number of complaints about the domestic use of 2,4,5-T and 2,4-D, the Australian government commissioned its National Health and Medical Research Council to review the current scientific literature on these herbicides. NHMRC's researchers found no link between herbicide use and an increase in the number of birth defects and spontaneous abortions; lauding the council's work, the Australian government cheerfully concluded that it had found a scientific cornerstone for its refusal to take the Agent Orange issue seriously. Some scientists, however, were not willing to accept the council's report with such alacrity, arguing, as did Dr. Donald MacPhee, a geneticist at Melbourne's La Trobe University, that the council "might just as honestly have said that neither is there any scientific basis to disprove a link."[4] The council's conclusions were also criticized by Dr. Barbara Field, a pediatrician with an extensive background in the study of birth defects, and Dr. Charles Kerr of the School of Public Health and Tropical Medicine. In the course of their research, Drs. Field and Kerr discovered a "linear correlation" between the use of 2,4,5-T and the frequency of birth defects.

But perhaps the most serious criticism of NHMRC's review came from Vietnam veterans, who pointed out that the study had been based on the domestic use of 2,4,5-T in bush control, thus failing to take into account the fact that the T used in Vietnam was 500 times more potent than that used for domestic purposes. Samples of 2,4,5-T used in Vietnam contained up to 50 parts per million TCDD-dioxin, while that used in Australia was limited by law to .1 part per million. Veterans' advocates also argued that the government's "cornerstone" was rather shaky because undiluted herbicides were used in Vietnam and the same areas were sprayed again and again—making it quite possible that dioxin, which can remain in the soil for up to thirty years, would accumulate and enter the food chain.

While chairman of the New South Wales branch of Vietnam Veterans Action Association, Wares became increasingly aware of what he calls the "uncanny similarities" between the Australian and American governments' approaches to the toxic chemical issue. After much lobbying by Vietnam veterans and veterans' advocates, officials of both nations had agreed that something had to be done to "test the validity" of veterans' complaints. The "acid test," officials decided, would take the form of an epidemiological study, which, though it might take as long as a decade to complete, would answer "some if not all of the many perplexing questions surrounding this complicated issue." Ordered by the U.S. Congress to commence such a study, the Veterans Administration, after a game of bureaucratic cat-and-mouse, invested $125,000 in a study design that took eighteen months to complete and was rejected by reviewers from the Office of Technology Assessment and scientists at the Center for Disease Control. In

Australia, a proposed study of 41,000 Vietnam veterans, 100,000 of their children, and a 20,000-person control group had cost the government $1.2 million and gone absolutely nowhere after twelve months.

"They tried to buy us off with this study just before the last elections," says Wares, shaking his head in disgust. "They actually tried to give us two million dollars—that's what the entire study was supposed to cost—to shut us up. But for christsake, mate, that wouldn't even buy the bloody paper clips and everybody knows it. And the study was supposed to have been completed by two years, but the feasibility study hasn't even been finished, and it's taken *three* years."

At one point Australian veterans received a questionnaire in the mail that was a carbon copy of one mailed to U.S. veterans in 1978. One question asked whether the recipient had been exposed to chemicals in trenches and foxholes. The form, according to Wares, was similarly ludicrous throughout.

Meanwhile, the Australian Department of Veterans' Affairs assured Vietnam veterans that it was keeping a close watch on developments at the Veterans Administration in Washington, a watch that included a visit by the Australian minister for veterans' affairs, Senator Anthony Messner, to the VA in the United States. Once back in Australia, Senator Messner announced that he had been privy to information that might resolve much of the controversy surrounding the Agent Orange issue. He had learned, for example, that Australian veterans might be suffering from the same malady that, according to the VA, was affecting the health and behavior of many American veterans. The trauma of war, Messner claimed, not exposure to toxic herbicides, was responsible for the veterans' problems.

Australian veterans advocates knew just how traumatic Vietnam had been for many of the young men who who spent 365 days living in fear, seeing their friends die sudden, often brutal deaths, and discovering that the people whom they had been sent to "save" might work at the base camp during the day and plant booby traps in the jungle at night. More than a decade after their return from Asia, veterans were still suffering from flashbacks, night terrors, cold sweats, depressions, rages, and guilt. But night terrors are not synonymous with soft tissue sarcomas, flashbacks do not produce deformed children, and liver disease could hardly be considered a symptom of "war neurosis." Messner's attempts to sweep the toxic chemical issue under the rug with a broom he had acquired in Washington angered Australian veterans and convinced Jim Wares that the Australian and U.S. governments might be deliberately withholding information on the health effects of herbicides used in Vietnam.

"I never knew how naive I was," Wares sighs, calling for another round and refusing my offer to pay, "until I got involved in this. I just never really knew. There are things that have happened that until this day I just can hardly believe. I mean, you hear about the CIA and ASIO [the Australian counterpart to the CIA] and you hear how the CIA can destroy people, but in Australia it's a different world, and I never really considered any of it real; it was all TV stuff to me. But I believe now it's all real. *Every bit of it is real.* Do you know, for example, what happened to the scientist that Bob mentioned earlier, the one who was assigned by the government to test herbicides in Vietnam. His name was George Lugg, and he was an honorary major during the war. Part of his job was to advise the U.S. Army on the use of herbicides and pesticides in Vietnam, and he was a brilliant scientist, absolutely brilliant. We got ahold of some of his papers and reports and, of course, a copy had always gone right to the chemical warfare people at Fort Detrick. Brilliant fellow, and when he came back from Vietnam they said he had a 'personality disorder,' that's what they called it anyway. And do you know what they did to him, and we've only just discovered this. He ended up in a convalescent home, an old man's home, and he's fifty-seven. Fifty-seven years old! None of us knew anything about Lugg until the association got going; then we discovered that George Lugg existed and who he was and what he did, and that he was in an old man's home in Victoria. So we tried to set up a meeting with him and a journalist, but a 'salmonella' outbreak occurred that weekend at the home and no one could see George Lugg."*

Wares lights a cigarette and watches the smoke curl lazily around his fingers. "I'm not really a melodramatic person. I don't see ghosts everywhere, and I'm not paranoid at all, but there's pieces to this puzzle that are missing and I wonder if we'll ever find them all and put the whole thing together before we all die. Sometimes I really doubt it."

Bob Gibson and his wife have been advised by a physician that because of Gibson's exposure to toxic chemicals they should "under no circumstances" consider having children. Thirteen years after his army discharge, Gibson still suffers from skin rashes, insomnia, and stomach problems. But in spite of his many maladies, Gibson feels that he is more fortunate than many veterans. One of the most mysterious aspects of toxic chemical poisoning is that different species of animals are affected to a greater or lesser degree by substances like dioxin; it might very well be the case that human beings exposed to the same quantity of dioxin will react in dissimilar ways. For some the exposure may manifest itself in skin rashes, chronic allergies, migraine headaches, and personality changes, while others die in a matter of months or years from cancer, liver disease, kidney failure, and what has been called "wasting disease."† Still others—like Jim Wares, whose tentmate in Vietnam suffers from chronic allergies and has won the first round with a bout of lymphoma—appear to have escaped

---

*According to Australian authors John Dux and P. J. Young, George Lugg suffered "what was described as a 'breakdown' " in 1973. But a friend of Lugg's, Mr. Geoffrey Foot, says that following the breakdown Lugg "became very irrational in his behavior and the government fobbed that off as psychiatric disorder, but it was certainly more than just a mental breakdown; it was a distinct physical breakdown in his appearance and everything." Although Lugg was obviously exposed to herbicides over a period of time, no one is absolutely certain whether his physical and emotional collapse was caused by this exposure. "In his day he was a very brilliant man," says his sister, Mrs. D. A. Hardy, "but at fifty he lost it all."

†Some scientists believe that dioxin attacks the enzyme system, lowering the body's ability to fight infection and making the exposed individual more susceptible to disease. Experimental rhesus monkeys given minute quantities of dioxin develop rashes, lose weight, become listless and literally waste away in a matter of days or weeks, depending on the amount of dioxin they ingest.

the more devastating effects of exposure to toxic chemicals. In short, dioxin has crept through the ranks of Australian and American Vietnam veterans, maiming some, destroying others, and leaving the survivors bewildered, angry, afraid. Bob Gibson and Jim Wares are survivors, but they know too many veterans who, while still in their prime of life, have succumbed to the cumulative effects of toxic poisoning.

They knew Collin Simpson, a thirty-five-year-old Vietnam veteran who had been fighting to stay alive for a number of years. Dying of lymphoma, Simpson was absolutely certain that his illness could be traced to his exposure to toxic chemicals, including Agent Orange, during his ten-month tour of duty in Vietnam. He died just a few days before he was to become the subject of the first major Agent Orange case in Australia.

After he returned from Vietnam, Simpson lived in a suburb of Sydney where the trees had been bulldozed and, just as sketched on an architect's drawing board, houses had been built in symmetrical patterns. The neighborhood was friendly enough. On weekends neighbors would get together for a barbecue, a game of cards, and a bit of gossip while the children swam, raced their bikes, or bickered over a game of sandlot soccer. But inside some of the homes were men who "bashed" their wives during fits of uncontrollable rages, men whose bodies were covered in patches of chloracne, men who were suffering from rheumatic pains, fevers, and constant headaches. One veteran had suffered two suspected heart attacks and partial paralysis, at the age of twenty-three.

The children in the neighborhood also had problems. In one of the homes lived a five-year-old boy who could recite only one nursery rhyme; in another, a girl who was hyperactive and had to take medication to correct a chemical imbalance in her brain; in still another, a baby had died of cancer at the age of twelve months; and in the Simpsons' home, the father was dying and his son had asthma, a partially collapsed lung, and a permanent rash on his chest and back.

The men on Monrobe Street knew that things were not right,

and they scoffed at the minister of veterans' affairs when he claimed that they were suffering from "war neurosis." Had they been asked to fight again, most of them would have readily returned to the jungles of South Vietnam, even though they could recall walking through defoliated areas and, years later, wondered whether the water they drank or the food they had eaten in Vietnam might be responsible for their present maladies.

Collin Simpson died before his claims that he had been poisoned by toxic herbicides could be proven or disproven. But Simpson's wife and veterans' activists requested and received further hearings before the Repatriation Tribunal, a judicial review board with powers to grant dispensation, arguing that Simpson died of "war-related causes" and that his wife and children were entitled to a full war pension. One year after her husband's death, the tribunal ruled that the claim was valid and granted Mrs. Simpson her pension. In a ruling that Vietnam veterans have called a "worldwide breakthrough," the tribunal conceded that Simpson's death might well have been caused by his exposure to toxic chemicals. While unwilling to concede that Simpson's cancer was definitely caused by his exposure to toxic chemicals, the tribunal emphasized that it had been unable to "disprove the causal relationship." "This onus," declared the tribunal, "is not satisfied beyond a reasonable doubt that there were insufficient grounds for granting the claim. . . . It is a real possibility that the applicant's malignant lymphoma resulted from his exposure to phenoxyacetic acid herbicides during his period of special service in South Vietnam."

"I celebrated that night, the night when this decision came out," says Wares. "I tell you, I had a party that night. What a breakthrough. What they said was that it was *possible*, and highly likely, that his exposure to chemicals caused his cancer. What they didn't say was that his exposure *definitely* caused the cancer. But what is important is that they mentioned 'toxic chemicals.' Because in Australia we have written off the Agent Orange issue because we don't want to give the government the chance to eliminate any of the substances to which we were exposed and therefore close the issue. So we're including in our arguments Agent Blue, White, Pink, and Green. What we would like to know is what happens when you get all of these chemicals together. When you use them indiscriminately like they did in Vietnam, then what the hell can that do to a human being? We know that all of them except Blue contained some form of dioxin, and that Collin Simpson is dead and a lot of others are dying, not to mention the veterans who are screwed up, really in bad shape, and the kids who are still being born with serious problems."

Although the tribunal's decision has been hailed as a major precedent by American and Australian Vietnam veterans, Wares and Gibson realize that it is only one step down the long road toward winning compensation for those who are so seriously ill that they cannot work, and for the survivors of those who have died. Responding to the tribunal's decision, Senator Messner remarked that it should be regarded only as a single case. He had "always encouraged veterans to take their claims before the Repatriation Commission and would continue to do so." But veterans' advocates, having spent $250,000 on legal fees for the Simpson case, argue that this approach could take years and require millions of dollars, and that what is needed is a judicial inquiry into the government's handling of the toxic chemical issue, an inquiry that Senator Messner has steadfastly opposed.

"I've said it before and I'll say it again, mate," Wares announces. "You could fill up this bloody room with gold bars and it wouldn't compensate for Cameron's birth defect. Nothing will ever compensate for what's happened to the guys who went to Vietnam, and to their families. Nothing. We don't want money. That's just a bunch of bullshit. No one really cares about the fucking money. What we want people to know is just what has gone on, the bullshit we've put up with, the cover-ups, the . . ."
—Wares's voice fades and slides, then regains composure, clarity—"Someday people will look at this thing, the whole thing, and they'll be amazed, they'll just be amazed and, I would think, damn frightened when they realize what's happened to us could very well happen to them. I hope to Christ it never does, mate. I just really hope it never, never happens to anyone else."

6

STONEWALL

The VA's record on Agent Orange is so bad that it almost
defies belief. Nobody, you will feel, would be that insensi-
tive. And so, precisely to the degree I tell you the truth,
to that degree I fear I will seem irrational, unresponsible.

—Robert O. Muller, executive director,
Vietnam Veterans of America,
testifying before the
Subcommittee on Medical
Facilities and Benefits

With an annual budget of approximately $24 billion, a staff of
nearly a quarter million, and an empire that includes 172 regional
hospitals and 58 regional and local offices, the Veterans Administration is the U.S. government's second largest bureaucracy. But
in spite of the enormous sums of money it spends to maintain its
programs and hospitals, pay its bureaucrats, and at least appear to
take seriously the mandate given it by Congress to work on behalf
of America's veterans, the VA's record on the Agent Orange issue
is abysmal.

Just two years after the last helicopter lifted off the roof of the
U.S. embassy in Saigon, the VA began receiving calls and letters
from Vietnam veterans who believed they had been exposed to
Agent Orange. The veterans complained of chronic skin rashes,
fatigue, cancer, respiratory problems, impaired hearing or vision,

depression, and loss of libido. Their wives, veterans told the VA, were giving birth to stillborn and deformed children and had suffered numerous miscarriages.

In 1977, Maude DeVictor was working in the Benefits Division of the VA's regional office in Chicago when she received a call from the wife of a Vietnam veteran named Charles Owen. Her husband was dying, Mrs. Owen said, and he believed his terminal cancer was the result of exposure to Agent Orange. DeVictor had never heard of Agent Orange, but when she received another call from Mrs. Owen telling her that Charles had died and that the VA had refused her claim for survivor's benefits, she decided to learn something about this obscure-sounding chemical.

She began by asking the widows of Vietnam veterans whether their husbands had been exposed to Agent Orange. She asked each veteran who visited or called her office a series of questions, including: "Were any of your children born with birth defects? How many miscarriages has your wife had? Do you suffer from skin rashes?" Astonished, many veterans replied: "How did you know?" When her supervisor demanded she stop gathering statistics and get back to business as usual, DeVictor refused. Instead, she contacted Bill Kurtis, a local television news correspondent whose skepticism gave way when he examined DeVictor's findings. In March 1978, WBBM, a CBS affiliate in Chicago, aired an hour-long documentary entitled *Agent Orange, the Deadly Fog.* In the following weeks DeVictor received hundreds of calls from veterans who were sick or dying from symptoms remarkably similar to those of laboratory animals exposed to TCDD-dioxin.

By 1978, articles about Agent Orange were appearing in local and national publications, and officials at the VA decided it was time to begin mapping a strategy for dealing with the veterans' complaints. First, the VA held a series of meetings from which veterans, independent scientists, and members of the public were excluded. Meeting behind closed doors with representatives of the chemical industry, the VA established its "no health effects" position on Agent Orange, thus commencing what the National Veterans Law Center (NVLC) calls "a two-year history of closed and secretive decision making."[1]

Approximately one year after its first closed Agent Orange meeting, the Veterans Administration, faced with a lawsuit for violating the open-meeting provision of the Federal Advisory Act, agreed to invite scientists who were not employed by the chemical industry. The VA also established an Advisory Committee on the Health-Related Effects of Herbicides, but according to the NVLC, "the pattern of unlawful action had begun."[2] Although the advisory committee was a good idea in principle, it was clear from the beginning that the VA intended to ask for its advice only after crucial decisions had been made, placing the committee in the position of a surgeon who is called in for consultation a few hours *after* an operation has been performed. "As a practical matter," reports the law center, "the advisory committee has been ineffective as a device to obtain scientific advice on Agent Orange matters. This is a result which is the agency's by design, not the fault of committee members."[3]

Following the formation of the advisory committee in December 1978, the NVLC wrote the VA on behalf of the National Association of Concerned Veterans, suggesting that the agency conduct a comprehensive outreach program to locate veterans who might be experiencing "unusual" health problems and to encourage those veterans to visit regional VA hospitals for a complete medical examination. The NVLC also suggested that the VA conduct an epidemiological study "to determine whether an increased incidence of health problems was occurring among Vietnam veterans." The letter questioned the VA's policy of denying all Agent Orange disability claims when the agency had already stated that "it did not have adequate information on exposure or causation to decide intelligently the merits of these claims."

On May 30, 1979, Max Cleland, director of the VA at the time, responded by rejecting all of the center's suggestions. His argument against establishing an outreach program was curious. Although he knew that veterans were anxious and confused about contradictory reports on the toxicity of herbicides, Cleland felt that an outreach program would only cause veterans "needless anxiety." According to the VA, men who had survived ambushes in the A Shau Valley, fought door to door in Hué, and humped through the swamps in the Mekong Delta simply could not handle the anxiety of an outreach program.

Cleland also instructed the VA to deny all claims for service-connected disability due to Agent Orange exposure, arguing that it might take "another decade" for scientists to make a rational judgment on whether dioxin adversely affected human health. Cleland's statements that the VA knew little or nothing about the health effects of dioxin, however, appear to be contradicted by a memo circulated to all 172 VA hospitals and 58 regional offices on May 18, 1978. According to this memo, the VA felt it knew a great deal about the effects of dioxin on human beings. For example, the VA knew that herbicides used in Vietnam "have a low level of toxicity, both individually and when mixed. Furthermore they appear to be rapidly absorbed and completely excreted in both the human and the animal. Humans exposed repeatedly . . . may experience temporary and fully reversible neurological symptoms; however, the only chronic condition *definitely* [emphasis added] associated with such exposure is chloracne."

Advising VA health personnel to approach Agent Orange complaints with extreme caution, the memo explains: "If the veteran has no objective symptoms or signs, simple reassurance should be offered. The veteran should be told that a record of the medical examination will be kept for future reference, but that if the veteran does not now have symptoms and did not previously experience any, the likelihood of herbicide poisoning is virtually zero." It does not explain why veterans would visit VA outpatient clinics to complain about symptoms they either did not have or had not "previously experienced."* But it does warn VA staff not to make any entries in a patient's file that might indicate a relation-

---

*For a copy of this memo, see Appendix, pp. 191–194.

ship between an illness and defoliant exposure "unless unequivocal confirmation of such a connection has been established."

While publicly stating that it could not make a decision in favor of the veterans' claims for disability, the VA had obviously come to the private conclusion that laboratory research showing dioxin to be carcinogenic, teratogenic, and fetotoxic could be dismissed by a bureaucratic edict. This particular memo is also important because it formulated just one of the many Catch-22s that would frustrate the efforts of veterans to secure disability payments. An entry into the patient's file could not be made without "unequivocal confirmation" that the veteran's illness was related to herbicide exposure. But according to a General Accounting Office report, "VA regional offices have been instructed to send copies of completed ratings of herbicide-related claims to headquarters for review. In addition, regional offices have been instructed to request information from a veteran's service record to verify herbicide exposure. However, service records normally do not contain specific information on chemical exposure. As a result, responses to such requests are neither verified nor denied by military service record personnel."[4]

In order to substantiate their claims for disability, veterans were asked by the VA to produce information that did not exist.* It is difficult to imagine that the VA was unaware that the Department of Defense, whose records would presumably "verify" the veterans' exposure to herbicides, had already stated that: "(1) no such personnel records were maintained, (2) it would be difficult to estimate meaningful exposure data because the potential for exposure varied widely among personnel, and (3) only a few military personnel would have been exposed directly to spraying."[5]

While VA health personnel were informed that the human body could "rapidly absorb" and "completely excrete" the herbicides, Max Cleland encouraged veterans to visit outpatient clinics

---

*In 1980 the VA rescinded the requirement that veterans prove exposure when asking for information, assistance, or treatment for what they believed to be Agent Orange–related illnesses.

for a "clinical evaluation." These evaluations, said Cleland, would provide the basis for discovering any "unusual" health problems among Vietnam veterans. What Cleland did not say, of course, was that no matter how "unusual," the illnesses would be treated by VA health personnel as having little or nothing to do with the massive defoliation of South Vietnam.

In his attempts to justify the VA's policy on Agent Orange, Cleland often referred to his agency's "Agent Orange Program Guide," a seven-paragraph, one-page "no health effects" document that set down the official line for denying all disability claims. The "guide's" brevity, however, was not the only reason why veterans and their supporters rejected it as a scam sheet and hype. Demonstrating once again its predilection for cloak-and-dagger politics, the VA had drafted the document "in secret and without the participation of other government officials knowledgeable about the scientific evidence."[6]

Before long the VA faced yet another lawsuit, this time on behalf of veterans who might have been, or would be, affected by the program guide—perhaps several hundred thousand. The VA then astonished legal observers by declaring that veterans had "no standing" to "challenge the agency's refusal to conduct rulemaking."[7] Lawyers representing the veterans noted that the VA made "the rather incredible argument that Vietnam veterans have not been sufficiently injured by the rule to challenge the fact that public rulemaking was not conducted before the rule was adopted and used . . . The agency takes the extraordinary position that it has the discretion, unlike any other federal agency, to decide whether it would comply with its own regulations at 38 C.F.R. S1.12 which require the agency to conduct rulemaking . . . Confronting this lawless position compels the obvious remark that such a view leads to a government of men, not law."[8]

To a nation that has accepted, albeit with anger and frustration, the idea that bureaucracies are cumbersome and unreliable, the VA's resolute stalling might not seem so extraordinary. Moreover, if one accepts the idea that bureaucracies are inherently incompetent, the fact that the VA took "only" twelve months to open its meetings to the public might be interpreted as a kind of miracle. But with its response to the Environmental Protection Agency's ban on domestic use of 2,4,5-T, the VA demonstrated that even top-heavy bureaucracies can move swiftly when they wish to. Taking only seven days to review the EPA's decade of research, the VA announced that the studies on which the EPA's ban was based did not "offer definitive evidence for an adverse effect of herbicides on human health." But when asked through a Freedom of Information Act request to provide scientific evidence supporting the VA critique, officials said that no documents were available.

During the year following the EPA's order, neither the VA's Agent Orange Steering Committee nor its Agent Orange Advisory Committee discussed the matter further. When the VA held two "educational conferences" on Agent Orange for its hospital staff, representatives from the EPA were not invited. Requested by Congressmen David E. Bonior (D-Mich.) and Thomas A. Daschle (D-S.D.) to consider the importance of five newly discovered human epidemiology studies on workers and others exposed to dioxin, studies the EPA had spent a great deal of time and money to evaluate, the VA again responded with astonishing speed that the studies were not persuasive enough to encourage the VA to any further action.

While the VA argued that the suspension order was "premature" and continued to promulgate its policy of "no health effects" from Agent Orange, Cleland's public statements were based in part on a 1974 study of herbicide use in Vietnam by the National Academy of Sciences. But in his zealous use of the NAS report Cleland seemed unaware that the academy's president, Dr. Philip Handler, did not share his absolute certainty that Agent Orange was harmless. Testifying before the Subcommittee on Medical Facilities and Benefits of the Committee on Veterans' Affairs, Dr. Handler said: "At the time the NAS report was issued, I foresaw the serious implications of dioxin on human health. In a letter to Secretary of State Henry Kissinger, I noted: ' . . . The hazard could well be serious and indeed is so regarded by knowledgeable individuals in this country as well as in Southeast Asia . . .' Many of these issues are more sharply focused today."[9]

Dr. Handler also told the committee that the "perhaps limited data collected by the NAS committee failed to indicate direct damage by herbicides to human health." However, there were consistent, although "mostly secondhand," reports from certain areas of acute and occasionally fatal respiratory distress, particularly in children. There were also reports of "severe irritation to the eyes and skin, as well as digestive disturbances. However, no independent medical studies of exposed populations were available from the time of spraying, to confirm or deny these reports."[10]

One rather serious methodological limitation of the NAS study was that in 1974 the war in Vietnam was still raging, and considerable portions of the country were in the hands of the Viet Cong and North Vietnamese. Visiting scientists could not have expected to find archives filled with scientific information on the effects of massive defoliation on Vietnamese peasants and U.S. military personnel. Vietnamese doctors, farmers, and mothers had been complaining about the suffering caused by the defoliation campaign for many years, but their complaints had been dismissed by American officials as enemy propaganda. Defoliation, according to Pentagon and government spokesmen, was taking place only in areas "remote" from population centers, and neither American soldiers nor Vietnamese peasants were being exposed to the deadly rain of herbicides.

However, in *Chemical and Biological Warfare*, Seymour M. Hersh writes: "A 1967 Japanese study of U.S. anti-crop defoliation methods, prepared by Yoichi Fukushima, head of the Agronomy section of the Japan Science Council, claimed that U.S. anti-crop attacks have ruined more than 3.8 million acres of arable land in South Vietnam and resulted in the deaths of nearly 1,000 peasants and more than 13,000 livestock. Fukushima said one village was attacked more than thirty times by C123 crop dusters spraying agents more caustic than the arsenic-laden cacodylic acid."[11]

It is not clear whether a Japanese study of U.S. anti-crop and defoliation methods would qualify as "independent" verification of what Dr. Handler had called "secondhand" reports; however, Dr. Handler did inform Congress that the NAS Committee "did not study or review the effects of herbicides on U.S. military personnel who served in South Vietnam, nor had any reason to do so been called to our attention."

In the process of reading and rereading transcripts of testimony by Veterans Administration and Department of Defense officials before congressional committees and subcommittees, one begins to feel the presence of a bureaucratic Dr. Jekyll and Mr. Hyde. At the hearings Dr. Jekyll is the epitome of bureaucratic finesse, his statements sensible, reassuring, supportive of veterans, and often promising. On May 6, 1981, for example, Dr. William J. Jacoby, Jr., deputy chief medical director, Department of Medicine and Surgery, Veterans Administration, told a congressional hearing: "Mr. Chairman, I wish to state at the very outset that from the time this issue first began to emerge, the VA has taken a leading role in the government's efforts to keep abreast of the problem. It is largely because of this visible, and therefore perhaps vulnerable, position that the VA has at times come under heavy criticism. I would submit, however, that despite perceptions to the contrary, this agency has remained faithful to its primary mission as the true advocate of the veteran. Within the body of law that governs its operations, the VA has made every effort and has embarked on a series of bold initiatives in an attempt to respond to the many and varied concerns of our Vietnam veteran beneficiaries as they related to the issue of Agent Orange.

"Further, we are firmly committed to the policy that all veterans reporting for examination and participation in our Agent Orange Registry will be treated with the dignity and respect to which they are entitled. Every effort is made to ensure that from the time the veteran first enters a VA facility, to the conclusion of the physical examination, the experience is one which responds to medical or other needs in a compassionate manner."[12]

As ludicrous as Dr. Jacoby's testimony must sound to many veterans, it is conceivable that the VA's Washington headquarters issued orders to treat Vietnam veterans with "dignity" and "compassion," and that regional staff were simply choosing to disobey. Might it have been possible that Dr. Jekyll just did not know what Mr. Hyde was doing outside congressional hearing rooms and the VA's bureaucratic fortress?

But this theory is easily disproven by the administrator's many policy statements—which, if followed by regional hospitals, would contravene any public declaration of his agency's good intentions. Why would the regional staff bother to find out anything about the effects of Agent Orange on human health if Washington's policy was to dismiss such complaints as unfounded? And how, after receiving the memo cited earlier, could anyone expect doctors and administrators to treat veterans with dignity and respect? One does not advise health personnel to consider their patients' complaints as groundless and then expect those same doctors, nurses, and physician's assistants to behave compassionately.

One of the most absurd arguments the VA uses to rationalize its behavior on the Agent Orange issue is that it has been unable to locate a "study population" that could provide "scientific verification" of veterans' claims. The fact that a "study population" has been filing for disability, demanding medical care, lobbying the government, testifying at hearings, forming organizations and coalitions, and all too frequently, dying from cancer, seems to have escaped the VA. Had the agency really been interested in locating a "study population," it might have held public hearings similar to those sponsored by the New York State Temporary Commission on Dioxin Exposure. At these hearings VA officials would hear grunts testify that they entered spray zones not six weeks *after* a defoliation mission, *but on the very day of the spraying;* that while guarding a base camp perimeter or on patrol they were soaked in herbicides jettisoned from a C123; and that since their return home they had been beset by a host of debilitating ailments. And the VA's "no health effects" nonsense would be challenged by the sight of men who, when asked to give their ages, appear ten, fifteen, even twenty years older. These prematurely aged men tell a story that the VA has not wanted to hear. For example, one former combat infantryman told New York's commission about assaulting a hill just seventy-two hours after it had been sprayed: "In October of 1968," he testified, "we saw helicopters spraying intermittently in the valley in front of us. There were hills among us. Three days later we assaulted the hill before an artillery barrage hit it, and they napalmed it also. We assaulted the hill, and that night we slept on the ground, ponchos just covering us. At the time we saw the spraying, we thought it was nerve gas. We had no idea it was Agent Orange. No one had told us. That same night we also had to fight on that hill.

"In December 1968 a hill, a ridge, was sprayed by helicopters. Again, we thought it was nerve gas. And Phantom jets strafed the hill with napalm, causing gas and a lot of smoke. I'm told now— I didn't understand it then—that this causes more dioxin to be present.

"I sweat all the time, my hands and feet. My joints are always sore. I have chronic diarrhea. In general, I consider myself a physical wreck. And I am thirty-three years old. I feel like I am sixty years old."[13]

Had they been willing to listen, VA officials would have heard a former aircraft crew chief announce: "I am compelled to testify because I probably won't be alive for the next meeting of the Commission.

"I was exposed approximately twenty to thirty times of flying through the mists . . . There was heavy defoliation in that area for a whole month. We were getting mists practically every day, coming into the compound. I had no health problems prior to my service time, and I was healthy up until six years after I left the army. In 1975 I suddenly became ill, and I went to see doctors. I had $12,000 in medical expenses. I spent all my savings . . .

"No diagnosis was ever reached. I was forced to go to the VA for help. I stayed in the VA hospital for two and a half months. The doctors told me it was my gall bladder and I should have an operation.

"I went through an exploratory laparotomy, in which they

removed my gall bladder, they removed part of my spleen, and they also removed my appendix.

"They had told me that if I underwent this operation, I would be okay. After the operation I was sicker than before, and the doctor, my surgeon, came and told me after the operation that my liver didn't look so good. He couldn't tell me at that time what it was.

"When a biopsy came back, it came back as nonspecific hepatitis. I asked the doctor what that meant. He told me, that means you have a liver disease, that nobody knows what it is.

"Between 1975 and the present time I have been over three and a half years in the VA hospital in Brooklyn. I get terrible pains in my right-hand side. I have lost over fifty pounds. I get nausea, vomiting; I can't keep anything down.

"In 1978 I also developed chronic idiocrasy and pancreatitis. I am getting worse and worse, and the VA cannot figure out what to do.

"Now they tell me I have priority treatment. Priority treatment doesn't mean anything to me because medical science doesn't even know how to deal with my illness, an illness that's never been seen before. But it's not so unusual to me because all the years that I spent in the hospital, there have been other Vietnam veterans who have liver diseases that are also undiagnosable. They are unable to come here today because they are too sick to even get out of bed.

"So I think that we need medical help, but I would also like to stress the fact that these poisons that were dealt out in Vietnam, they have created diseases that medical science cannot even deal with today. There is no treatment for me. There is medicine that can only relieve my pain and try to help my symptoms, but there is no treatment that is going to help me get well. I am going to continue to deteriorate until I die."[14]

And the Veterans Administration or congressional committees would have heard Vietnam veterans and their wives testify that their treatment at VA hospitals had been anything but dignified and compassionate. They would have heard that following cursory physicals, which veterans had been led to believe were "comprehensive Agent Orange examinations," they had waited weeks, even months, for the "results," only to be informed that the problem was "all in their head" and to be given a public relations packet that, said one veteran, "told you Agent Orange had saved your life so don't worry about it." VA officials would have heard a veteran testify that, unable to treat a fungus-like growth on his scrotum with over-the-counter remedies, he had visited the VA clinic, where a doctor ordered him to "drop his pants" and, without administering even a local anesthetic and using an unsterilized scalpel, proceeded to remove the fungus "as though he were scaling a fish." The VA hierarchy would have heard, as I did at New York state's public hearings on dioxin exposure, seemingly endless stories of abuse, neglect, incompetence, arrogance, faulty diagnosis, altered records, and ordinary stupidity.

But perhaps the most disturbing thing these officials would have heard was that as the number of Vietnam veterans applying for disability increased, regional VA hospitals frequently resorted to a strategy perfected by totalitarian governments to silence dissidents. The dissident, in this case, is a veteran asking to be examined for bladder or liver cancer, who instead is given a psychiatric examination. Dissent is the desire to be seen as a rational human being with a genuine, urgent medical problem, rather than as a traumatized guerrilla fighter whose problem is postwar confusion. Had the VA been willing to listen, its medical staff would have heard veterans expressing their outrage at being treated as children, neurotics, and con artists.

"Why," demanded a veteran at the New York State dioxin hearings, "is every Vietnam veteran given a psychological examination first? Or, if you are admitted to the hospital, it is always under a psychiatric guise. Why can no proper diagnosis be made? Men have a history of a multitude of psychological, organic, and/or neurological problems that are not being assessed or documented properly at the Veterans Administration. They are denying men their rights. They are committing a crime. They are violating the Federal Code of Regulations, Title 8, as it is. And doctors are violating their code of ethics."[15]

On February 21, 1980, Max Cleland, testifying before the Committee on Veterans' Affairs, U.S. Senate, answered the question about the VA's penchant for seeing Vietnam veterans' problems as "psychological." After telling the committee that Vietnam veterans had a lower unemployment rate than the U.S. population as a whole, were going to school, buying homes, and, thanks to the concern and generosity of the Veterans Administration, generally adjusting rather nicely to civilian life, Cleland said: "Vietnam era veterans are utilizing VA outpatient health care facilities at about the same rate as veterans of other wars but have a lower rate of hospitalization due to their younger age when compared to veterans of other wars. As may be expected with younger veterans, those Vietnam era veterans treated have relatively fewer physical medical problems than do older veterans and, conversely, as a result for those treated, their care is more apt to be for psychiatric disorders. Of those VEVs [Vietnam era veterans] discharged from VA hospitals during FY 1979, 46 percent had received care for psychiatric disorders, including alcohol and drug abuse."[16]

There can be little doubt that being sent to war as a hero only to be greeted upon one's return home as a pariah has angered, frustrated, and confused many veterans. Nor would anyone deny that the horrors of guerrilla warfare have taken their toll on veterans of America's longest and most unpopular war. But in its attempt to invalidate the veterans' claims for service-connected disability, the VA has resorted all too frequently to labeling the symptoms of dioxin exposure as just one more example of "post-Vietnam syndrome." A veteran in his early thirties who is told that his many ailments are incurable and who is then turned down for disability payments is very likely to experience depression, sleep disturbances, and other symptoms commonly associated with his tour of duty in Vietnam. By arguing that the sudden weight loss, chronic skin rashes, migraine headaches, and gastrointestinal pains that thousands of Vietnam veterans have complained of are symptomatic of a collective neurosis, the VA is attempting to place veterans who were exposed to Agent Orange in a no-win situation. Ironically, the VA would have veterans believe that whatever ails them can be traced directly to their experience in Asia, just as long as that experience does not include exposure to toxic herbicides.

It would be unfair, of course, to deny that there are dedicated doctors, nurses, administrators, and bureaucrats within the VA; but the agency's failure to conduct an outreach program or to provide genetic counseling and family support services, and its refusal to begin an epidemiological study until ordered by Congress to do so (Public Law 96-151), have tarnished the VA's reputation and posed serious questions about the protection Americans can expect from government agencies. Speaking of the VA's denial of all disability claims based on Agent Orange, Senator Alan Cranston, chairman of the Senate Veterans' Affairs Committee and floor manager of the bill signed into law by President Carter mandating the VA to conduct an epidemiological study, said: "The denial of almost all Agent Orange claims by the VA is viewed by some Vietnam veterans as suggestive that a deliberate cover-up or irresponsible action by the federal government is being carried out in much the same way as information about the adverse health effects from radiation was withheld from nuclear weapons test participants in the 1950s and 1960s."[17]

Yet even after Congress ordered the VA to begin an epidemiological study of Vietnam veterans, the agency continued to exclude veterans and independent scientists from participating in the planning of the study. Before the actual study could begin, the VA needed to develop a design or protocol that would assure the study's scientific objectivity and accuracy. (Although it did not have an epidemiologist on its staff, the VA planned to "contract out" only for the study design and to use its own personnel to conduct the study.) To secure a study design the VA developed a "request for proposals," which it intended to send out to scientists who might be interested in participating. But at this stage the National Veterans Law Center confronted the VA once again, arguing that its "request for proposals" lacked scientific validity. "Examples of defects in the solicitation are legion," said NVLC attorneys. "The proposal omitted important . . . data that would be necessary to develop a scientifically valid epidemiological study design, such as the facilities of the agency, the personnel to be used, the type of study populations available for the study, the nature of access to the study population, or the funds available to gain access to the study population. The absence of this essential data is not typical of other government research proposals. Indeed, scientists who reviewed this proposal for the law center concluded that only a scientist with inside information about the study design could likely submit an acceptable proposed design."[18]

Moreover, the "request for proposals" also stated that "anyone associated with a prior position regarding the effects of phenoxy herbicides and/or their constituents on human health" would be disqualified from bidding for the study design. This, said the VA, would assure that the study would be free of bias. By excluding anyone who may have published a paper or written an article on phenoxy herbicides, the VA was denying virtually all of the leading scientists in the field of dioxin research the chance to bid for the study. And while the exclusionary clause would keep highly qualified scientists from bidding for the study design, it did not prevent industry scientists or consultants from making a bid for the study. Consistent with its obstructionist position, the VA had devised just one more Catch-22 that hindered progress.

When the VA finally did award the contract for the epidemiological master plan, it was to a ULCA epidemiologist who would be quoted by the *New York Times* as telling a California assembly committee: " 'Agent Orange was used primarily in areas where few or no troops were located,' and therefore, 'the likelihood of substantial exposure to ground troops in Vietnam' was not great.

"Dr. Spivey also told the panel that 'there is to date little evidence' of any 'specific human health effects' as a result of the powerful herbicide. 'The fear which is generated by current publicity is very likely to be the most serious consequence of the use of Agent Orange,' he said."[19]

Two years after Congress ordered the VA to begin an epidemiological study of Vietnam veterans, Dr. Spivey submitted his protocol to the American scientific community and Congress's Office of Technology Assessment. But the protocol was rejected by scientists and members of the OTA. After reviewing the protocol, John Sommers, deputy director of the American Legion's National Veterans' Affairs and Rehabilitation Commission, said, "The design is incomplete and unacceptable as presently written. The authors are so obsessed with secrecy that information pertaining to diseases or symptoms of interest to the study and details relating to veterans they consider to be in high or low exposure groups have been withheld."[20]* Sommers also told a Senate Veterans' Affairs Committee that even the protocol's authors admitted that their work was incomplete because, said Sommers, "the investigators were denied access to certain classified military records because *the VA failed to obtain a security clearance for the contractor or his assistants.*"[21]

Vernon Houk of the Center for Disease Control was also critical of the protocol. In fact, said Houk, the proposal "had such insufficient information that we did not indeed even classify this as a protocol."[22] Following the scientific review and comments from OTA officials, the protocol was returned to UCLA for modifications. After twenty-four months, the epidemiological study was still mired in the planning stages.

The revised protocol was returned to the National Academy of Sciences for review, but even if the NAS had found the design acceptable it would have been years before the VA reached any conclusions on the health effects of Agent Orange. Although the agency said it was planning several new studies, including one of identical twins, one of whom served in Vietnam, officials continued to insist that the epidemiological study could not be

---

*For the American Legion's August 24-26, 1982, resolution no. 410 (Iowa), "The American Legion Policy on Agent Orange," see Appendix, p. 197–199.

finished until 1987. And while VA officials were searching for ways to improve the agency's credibility among veterans, Illinois State Senator Karl Berning told a VA panel that he sensed "a lack of commitment, a lack of concern, a lack of interest on the part of the national government" regarding this issue.[23] While conceding that studies may be necessary, Berning told the panel: "However, I remind you that while you and I are talking, men and women, our fellow citizens, are suffering and dying now—and, from what we have had in the way of testimony, with little or no help from their government."[24]

On March 3, 1982, four years after the VA first responded to Agent Orange claims, I asked Victor Yannacone, lawyer for the 2.5 million Vietnam veterans who are suing companies that manufacture Agent Orange, whether he had seen any change in the VA's attitude in recent months. Yannacone had been cheerfully, almost endearingly bellicose during our interview, answering my questions with the candor and compassion that have won him the trust and respect of Vietnam veterans. But when I asked about the VA he paused, rose slowly from his chair, and, facing my tape recorder as though it were a jury, shouted: "Yes, the attitude has hardened. The attitude has become patently vindictive, the attitude has become *militantly* anti-Vietnam veteran. The management has become, if anything, more inept. And the trail of broken bodies and dying veterans is getting longer."

On October 14, 1982, Robert P. Nimmo, who just a few days before had announced his resignation as VA director, informed reporters that the VA had decided to turn over its much-delayed and controversial study of the health effects of Agent Orange to the Center for Disease Control in Atlanta. While denying that the VA had intentionally stalled the study, Nimmo conceded that a "broad consensus" had developed to support the "belief that it would be in the best interests of veterans to have a non-VA scientific body conduct the Agent Orange epidemiology study."[25] Two weeks later the General Accounting Office released a report that had taken its auditors two and a half years to complete. The report states that the VA did not actively attempt to locate and screen veterans suffering from symptoms potentially related to Agent Orange. It also chastises the VA for its inconsistent procedures at the agency's 172 hospitals. In its rebuttal the VA argued that the GAO's evidence was dated and that treatment at VA hospitals has improved considerably since the GAO's auditor did his research.

7

WHEN YOU CAN'T SUE THE GOVERNMENT THAT KILLS YOU

Victor Yannacone has been called flamboyant, arrogant, a genius, and, I'm sure, many less complimentary things by those whose vested interests he challenges in the name of what he calls the "public good." Certainly he is not overly modest, calling the Agent Orange class action suit "the most important product liability case in the history of the United States." Nor is he always gracious or polite, thundering like an evangelist, occasionally answering questions with the clipped irritability of a man who has little time for fools, because he knows only too well that they can be depended on to lose; and Yannacone doesn't intend to lose when he goes to court on behalf of 2.5 million Vietnam veterans and their families.

He can be charming. He will bring you coffee, buy you lunch and spend the morning, perhaps even part of the afternoon, helping you sort things out, defining legal terms, correcting misconceptions, and speaking always with the confidence of a man who, through his successful campaign to remove DDT from the market, has shown that the chemical industry and its multi-million-dollar Washington lobby is not invincible. Yannacone loves a good joke, a humorous story, or a satirical account of court proceedings, but he is not a cynic, and beneath the bravado it is easy to see the intense compassion he feels for the "kids" who served in Vietnam and returned home with what Yannacone calls "an aging disease."

Victor Yannacone possesses another important attribute. To men who have been lied to, misled, maligned, treated as pariahs, psychopaths, malingerers, hypochondriacs, and disposable war matériel, he just may be the one man in America whom Vietnam veterans feel they can trust.

I am waiting for him to finish a rather long story about how he once defended a man who wanted to keep pigs in his backyard on Long Island. Somehow Yannacone managed to prove that the pigs' ancestors had provided a valuable service to the community and, he laughs, to convince the judge that the pigs therefore had every right to be where they were. At a nearby desk Carol Yannacone sorts through mail, examines and files autopsy reports on Vietnam veterans and their children. She explains that "many times they don't really know why the children are born dead or don't live very long after birth. Everything seems to be perfectly normal, but the child dies. So the doctor just files an autopsy report and we get them from lawyers who are working on the class action suit. It is a sad job, sometimes too sad."

In nearby rooms typewriters clack, computers hum, and Vietnam veterans phone from all over the country seeking advice, asking for help, offering assistance. People enter the office, ask questions, leave notes, and exchange bits of information or gossip with Carol and Victor.

Although he was aware as early as 1969 that defoliants may have resulted in permanent damage to Vietnam mangrove forests, Victor Yannacone's involvement in the Agent Orange controversy did not really begin until August 1978, when he accepted a luncheon invitation from a group of Long Island attorneys who wished to discuss the Paul Reutershan case. Reutershan, the lawyers told Yannacone, was a young Vietnam veteran who never drank or smoked; he considered himself a "health nut" but was dying of cancer. As a helicopter pilot in Vietnam he had flown through herbicidal mists on numerous occasions, and he believed that his exposure was responsible for his terminal cancer. He had filed a $10 million damage claim against Dow Chemical and two other Agent Orange manufacturers.

Yannacone left the luncheon saddened by what he had heard, but unconvinced that a large number of Vietnam veterans might be suffering from symptoms similar to those that had destroyed Paul Reutershan's health; however, during the next few months he continued his own research into veterans' claims that they had been poisoned by Agent Orange. By December 1978 he had learned about Maude DeVictor's documentation of at least one hundred cases of possible dioxin poisoning; and following Reutershan's death at age twenty-eight on December 14, 1978, Yannacone began receiving numerous calls from Frank McCarthy, a Vietnam veteran, Paul's close personal friend and a co-founder of Agent Orange Victims International. Convinced that many of his fellow veterans were suffering from herbicide exposure, McCarthy insisted that Yannacone take legal action against companies that manufactured herbicides for use in Vietnam. On January 8, 1979, having concluded that at least 400 veterans might have been poisoned by herbicides—but due, in large part, to McCarthy's persistence—Yannacone filed a class action suit against Dow et al. on behalf of "all those so unfortunate as to have been and now to be situated at risk, not only during this generation but during generations to come." The risk was exposure to dioxin, and the lawsuit demanded:

An immediate ban on all advertising, promotion, distribution, marketing and sale of the contaminated herbicides;

A declaration that the corporate defendants are trustees of the public health, safety and welfare, with a fiduciary responsibility to the public.

Disclosure of everything the companies know about the dangers of the contaminated herbicides.

Establishment by the companies of a tax-exempt reserve fund sufficient to cover damages from use of the herbicides (reimburse the VA and Social Security Administration for benefits, compensate victims and their families and protect consumers from any attempt to pass along cost of damages resulting from use of utility or railroad rights-of-way).[1]

According to the *Chicago Tribune* (February 1979), the estimated reserve fund would require more than $4 billion.

Soon after Yannacone refiled Reutershan's initial lawsuit as a class action, Yannacone's office was deluged with calls from Vietnam veterans and veterans' widows seeking advice and asking to join the lawsuit. By May 1979 it appeared that at least 4,000 claims would be included in the suit, possibly more. According to Yannacone, the question of how the litigation was to be managed became equally as important as the immediate problem of defeating the chemical companies' various motions to dismiss the complaint. Yannacone was also receiving calls and letters from attorneys throughout the country who wanted to work on the case, and he knew that he had to devise a workable scheme for organizing a task force that would be separated by great geographical distances and, unless the attorneys involved made a very concerted effort to avoid it, the traditional competitiveness of their profession.

"Normally," explains Yannacone, "in a personal injury case of this magnitude there would be a certain amount of, oh, I wouldn't say ambulance chasing, that's not the appropriate expression, but let's just say jockeying for leadership roles. And because of the size of the litigation that we were envisioning early on—four thousand cases is what we were thinking of—we decided to try something new in the history of personal injury litigation. We would make an agreement with each attorney to divide the case into two parts. liability and damages. We here in New York would handle liability and what we call 'Cause in Fact' or *Generic Causation.* In other words, how toxic is dioxin? And just what can it do? Not what *did* it do to a particular veteran, but what *could* it do. Then each individual attorney around the country would handle his own client as a personal injury case as far as proximate cause and damages were concerned, proximate cause meaning: 'Did this particular veteran manifest the kind of symptoms that would be attributed to dioxin-contaminated herbicides used in Vietnam? And if so, how much damage is he suffering?' We agreed also to divide whatever fees were awarded by the courts equally, and we agreed from the very beginning—and this is also unique—that we would subject our fee ratings to the court for supervision. We then agreed that we would limit our fees, which are contingent of course only on winning, to no more than one-third of recovery, even though some states still allow 50 percent. We also adopted a rule requiring every attorney to file an affidavit saying they didn't chase the case, they didn't offer anybody money to get the case, and they violated no disciplinary rules or ethical considerations in acquiring the case. And we have those filed from all of our attorneys. The fact that we've filed our agreements and made our financial arrangements known from the beginning is unique in personal injury litigation."

Meanwhile, the five chemical companies named in the suit filed various motions to dismiss, arguing, among other things, that "its very length was an affront to the Federal Rules of Civil Procedure." The chemical companies also held that no federal interests were involved and the veterans' complaints should therefore be heard in state rather than federal courts. If the case were heard in state courts, Yannacone countered, "a nightmare of court administration would begin that would make the present disastrous state of affairs in the asbestos cases look like good management."

Had the chemical companies been granted their wish and the case heard in state courts, each veteran would have been required to file and serve a document alleging that he had been an American serviceman and that while in the U.S. military had spent time in Southeast Asia. He would also have had to document that while there he had been exposed to phenoxy herbicides such as 2,4,5-T which were "manufactured, formulated, advertised, marketed, promoted, and sold" by subsidiary corporations of the chemical company defendants, even though these companies knew that the herbicides were contaminated with "toxic synthetic organic chemicals." Each dying or disabled veteran would then have to file a claim arguing that his illness was directly related to his exposure to herbicides. If he believed that his child or children's birth defects were due to this exposure, he would also have to file this claim separately. The veteran's wife or widow, or both parents of a child suffering from developmental defects, would have been required to file a claim. And each plaintiff would have claimed money damages ranging from $10 million to $100 million, depending on the veteran's age or loss to his family, loss of services, and developmental damage claims. These claims would be filed and served in the home jurisdictions of each veteran, a process, says Yannacone, that could easily take more than the lifetime of all the plaintiffs involved.[2]

On November 22, 1979, District Judge George C. Pratt, to whom the Multidistrict Litigation Panel had assigned the cases at Dow's request, refused to accept the chemical companies' motions to dismiss the complaint and grant "summary judgment in favor of the defendant war contractors." Pratt also accepted jurisdiction as a federal question, holding that "some federal common law rule would be applied uniformly to the claims of all the veterans regardless of the state in which the action may have originated."[3] The chemical companies (war contractors) did not like this ruling and appealed, arguing that because the U.S. was not a party, the case lacked substantial federal interest. On November 24, 1980, two Second Court of Appeals judges accepted this logic, reversing Judge Pratt and stating that there really was no "clearly identifiably federal or national interest in the outcome of the veterans' claims sufficient to concern the federal courts as 'federal questions.'" But Chief Justice Feinberg dissented, setting the stage for a "certiorari petition to the U.S. Supreme Court, which caused that Court to invite the Solicitor General of the U.S. to brief the question of national interest."

On June 18, 1981, the U.S. Supreme Court met in conference to examine petitions from Yannacone, and counterpetitions from the war contractor defendants, regarding the question of federal interest in the Agent Orange lawsuit. After perusing the arguments before them, the Chief Justices decided to seek the opinion of the executive arm of the federal government on "the substantiality of federal interest." To secure this opinion the court asked the attorney general to inquire into the matter. After questioning officials at the Department of Defense and Veterans Administration, who told him they could see no reason why there would be federal interest in the case, the solicitor general returned to the Supreme Court and, according to Yannacone's associate, Keith Kavenagh, announced: "Oh my, how could you ever have thought there was any federal interest in this case? Good heavens, how misled could you be? At that point, of course, the Supreme Court denied our petition, which put us in the stance we are in now, which is diversity jurisdiction as one private party against another. But the Court, contrary to a number of misleading news articles, did not dismiss the case. All they did was deny our petition because they didn't really want to be bothered reviewing it. And by denying the petition they simply said they would allow the Court of Appeals decision to stand."

Faced with a lawsuit on behalf of thousands of angry Vietnam veterans and their families, the war contractors resorted to what has become a classic American corporate reaction to being sued: you simply sue some "third party," someone related tangentially but significantly to the case, to whom you can shift the blame. So Dow decided to sue the Department of Defense because, said Dow, it had sold its product to the DOD in good faith and from then on it was really the government's responsibility to use it properly. If anyone was injured by herbicides in Vietnam, and according to Dow this remains to be proven, it was the government's fault, not theirs. Second, as a government war contractor the company was only following orders; and government contractors who follow orders cannot be sued, even if the resulting action happens to injure, maim, or kill friendly troops.

Claiming that the doctrine of sovereign immunity protected it against such lawsuits, the U.S. government moved to dismiss Dow's third-party suit. But for Dow the government's reluctance to be sued was only a temporary setback. Even if the courts ruled negatively on Dow's attempts to sue the government, the company's lawyers could still argue that because it had been employed by the government as a "war contractor," Dow Chemical could not be sued. To advance this argument the corporate defendants filed a motion to dismiss the veterans' complaints based on the claim of *derivative sovereign immunity,* an ancient doctrine that

Yannacone says has "fallen into disfavor in this country because the people with a capital P are the sovereign. In England the sovereign was the king and of course the king could not be sued. The government of the U.S. as a general rule can not be sued either. And there is a rule of law that during combat, mistakes, no matter how dramatic they may be, are not actionable. A classical example is the 'Charge of the Light Brigade.' Somebody made a big mistake. But the survivors and the widows couldn't sue. Because it is the duty of the soldier to go 'Onward into the valley of death, down into the volleying and thundering' and all the rest of that. So in Vietnam no matter how wrong the command decisions might have been the soldiers can't complain.

"But what we're saying in the Agent Orange lawsuit is that our soldiers ran the risk of being killed, both through the action of the enemy and the ineptitude of their leadership, but they did not accept the risks of being poisoned by their own war materials. The chemical companies say that whatever happened is not actionable in the courts of this country because it occurred during wartime and 'we the war contractors were only following orders and are just the same as fellow soldiers. And just as you can't sue your fellow soldier for dropping a live round, or a short round, on you, you can't sue the company that manufactured the defective round.'

"Well, we say that is utter nonsense. The government contracted to get war materials, but under no circumstances did the government contract to have its own men poisoned or killed.*

---

*At the first "Defoliation Conference" sponsored by the Department of Defense and attended by several chemical companies (including Dow and Monsanto), General Fred J. Delmore, commanding general, U.S. Army, Edgewood Arsenal, told the companies' representatives that the DOD wanted to make sure that whatever it used for defoliants would be "perfectly innocuous to man and animals and at the same time will do the job." Albert Hayward, chief of the program coordination office at Fort Detrick, told the conference that "it goes without saying that the materials must be applicable by ground and air spray, that they must be logistically feasible, and that they must be nontoxic to humans and livestock in the area affected." In a 1964 press release, Dow asserted that its 2,4,5-T was absolutely nontoxic to humans or animals, but by 1965 the company confirmed that it contained TCDD. Dow also admitted that it had not informed the USDA or the DOD that it had discovered 2,4,5-T to be contaminated with TCDD.[4]

Therefore, the material that the contractors delivered was *not* what the government expected, and that means that the contractors were in fact liable. But they say, 'No, whatever occurred did so during wartime, and we were only following orders. We're war contractors and you can't sue us.' That's *their* definition of *derivative sovereign immunity,* but it's really no more than the good Nazi defense that was used at Nuremberg back in 1946, a defense that is a little discredited by the fact that some of the people who used it were hung. Of course, not everyone was hung, and both Krupp and I. G. Farben are back in business." On December 29, 1980, Judge Pratt denied the chemical companies' motion to dismiss the class action suit on the basis of derivative sovereign immunity.

In opposing the first of many motions to dismiss their complaint, Vietnam veterans and their families made it clear to the court that they did not want to become recipients of public assistance. They also expressed their belief that American taxpayers should not have to bear the burden of medical care and treatment for veterans and their children. They wanted, said the plaintiffs, "to compel the corporate defendants to make restitution to the American people by reimbursing those federal and state agencies that have provided benefits, medical care and treatment . . . for conditions attributable to the toxic effects of contaminated phenoxy herbicides . . ."[5] They also wanted a resolution to the scientific controversy over the toxic effects of phenoxy herbicides contaminated with toxic synthetic organic chemicals "such as polychlorinated dibenzo-p-dioxins (PCDDs) and the polychlorinated dibenzo furans (PCDFs) fomented by the promotional efforts of the corporate defendants . . ."[6] They challenged the claims of those who were still making phenoxy herbicides that their products were safe, and sought punitive damages in an amount that would "convince corporate management they serve as trustees of the public health, safety and welfare to an extent commensurate with the economic power and technological resources of the corporations they manage."[7]

The corporations, says Yannacone, owe the veterans a "non-delegable fiduciary duty of care," a concept which, to proponents of laissez-faire, must sound like unadulterated socialism. But Yannacone argues that he and the consortium have taken this approach because they have no desire to bankrupt the chemical companies. Nor are they advocating nationalizing any of the Fortune 500. They are asking that corporations assume responsibility for their products from "cradle to grave" and that the task of monitoring the effect of a product on the environment and the health of the American people not be the sole responsibility of inefficient and frequently ineffective bureaucracies like the Environmental Protection Agency and the Food and Drug Administration.

"You see," Yannacone explains, "the chemical companies manufacture a product, and if it doesn't kill you within forty-eight hours of use, they assume that their responsibility toward the consumer is over. But we know that in the Agent Orange suit there may well be over forty thousand victims,* and if each one asked for and was granted the appropriate amount of damages it would be possible to bankrupt all the companies we are suing. The whole thrust of this lawsuit is to impose on the chemical industry and its leaders a *non-delegable fiduciary obligation* as trustees of the public health, safety, and welfare to notify the public when there is any indication that there might be something wrong with the material being sold. We feel that Dow, Hercules, Monsanto, Diamond Shamrock, or Uniroyal are so large and their advertising promotion and public relations budgets so much greater than the federal regulatory budgets that this is hardly an unreasonable thing to ask. And I'm more than willing to pay the extra penny for the product to see the Dow diamond or some other symbol that I recognize, knowing that that company will do what it can to make sure that the product is safe, and more

---

*Although the class action suit has been filed on behalf of all veterans who served in Vietnam, the number of veterans who were listed as sick or dying at the time of the interview was approximately 40,000. More veterans will undoubtedly be added to this list in the future.

efficient, because the company's image is one of long-term service to the public. And I would like to impose this obligation on these companies just as a matter of law. So in the Agent Orange class action suit we're saying that if anyone has been injured, then the companies are responsible for the people whose health was damaged by their product."

The class action is not only unique but ironic in many ways: 2.5 million Vietnam veterans suing chemical companies that were, theoretically, manufacturing a product that would save American lives in Vietnam; the chief attorney for the veterans confiding that he gets his most incriminating information on the effects of dioxin from scientists who work for one of the plaintiff war contractors; and the chemical companies arguing they were just "following orders" when they made Agent Orange, some of which was 15 to 15,000 times more contaminated with dioxin than the 2,4,5-T sold for domestic use.

Perhaps the most fascinating thing about Victor Yannacone is that while scientists may spend another decade quibbling over the effects of dioxin on human beings, and refusing, for one reason or another, to come to a conclusion that would affect governmental regulatory decisions, he has no doubts that dioxin is a killer. So little doubt, in fact, that he has put his legal reputation on the line and, because many of his veteran clients are impoverished, has worked for years with little remuneration to prove this point.

"There's enough evidence to convict dioxin by even criminal standards today," he says forcefully, half standing, pointing at me as though I am the jury that will decide the most important product liability case in the history of the United States. "If you had an alleged criminal with the kind of evidence against him that we have against dioxin, he'd be convicted no matter who was sitting on the Supreme Court or how the evidence was obtained. But just what do we know about Agent Orange? We know that during the Vietnam era 8 million young men were in military service. And the average age was about eighteen and a half years old, and those kids were duly certified by at least one and in some cases three agencies of the federal government as the healthiest people in America. The people who weren't healthy stayed home. So we're saying that if you count the cancers, birth defects, suicides, and serious illnesses among the 2.5 million that went to Vietnam and compare those statistics to the approximately 6 million who did not go—all of them chosen by the same rigorous standards—you will find that the group that went to Vietnam is much, much sicker than the group that didn't. The kids in Vietnam were exposed to something that seems to have accelerated their aging processes. They are suffering from the diseases of old age, and they are only in their thirties.

"So we've established clearly that the Vietnam veterans are sick, and we've identified a known toxicant to which they were exposed that is capable of causing the illnesses or the aging that we see in the combat veterans. The burden now shifts to Dow, Monsanto, and the other manufacturers of toxic materials to show that it wasn't their fault, that the products they made didn't poison our army. We've done our job. Let's see what they've got."

Unfortunately, seeing what they've got may take a lot longer than Yannacone or anyone involved in the case, with the possible exception of the war contractor defendants, had anticipated. By filing various motions to dismiss the Agent Orange suit, the defendants actually delayed replying to the suit for one year, and through appeals and other legal maneuvering more than three years will have passed before the "war contractor" defense is actually heard in court. Still, Yannacone has no doubt that he will win "on the merits of the case." The government contractor immunity defense will be tried first, and if the "jury doesn't buy it, then we go to a trial on the issue of fault. That is: did the chemical companies make the product? Was it contaminated with dioxin? If it was contaminated with dioxin, did they know the dioxin was toxic, and did they have a duty to warn the Defense Department and the president during the war, and the veterans and the Veterans Administration after the war? If the answer to all those questions is yes, then the next question will be 'What is it that dioxin can do?' That's the long trial; that will take some time. The others are relatively short. If we win and establish the

toxicity of dioxin, then the cases go back to their individual jurisdictions where the individual veterans face their home juries and
prove two things: first, that they were in Vietnam, and second,
that they are sick."

After years of waiting, Vietnam veterans suffering from the
effects of dioxin poisoning will still not be home free—even if
Yannacone wins his case against the war contractor defendants.
Because there is one more roadblock, one more "legal means" by
which the chemical companies can attempt to prevent veterans
from winning compensation for their injuries. The roadblock,
says Keith Kavenagh, is the statute of limitations; and he believes
it is quite possible that the war contractors will make use of this
tactic to thwart, perhaps for the final time, veterans' efforts to
secure compensation for their injuries. In some states the statute
of limitations is determined by the "time of injury." This means
that a Vietnam veteran exposed to dioxin in 1967 but suffering no
ill effects until five or ten years later would be *time-barred* by that
state's three-year statute of limitations. In other states the statute
of limitations begins only *after* discovery of one's illness. Regardless of how much time has elapsed since the original exposure, a
veteran can file a claim for compensation two or more years after
he becomes ill. Because toxic chemicals often do not cause illness
or death until years after the original exposure, veterans' advocates argue that a statute of limitations based upon "time of injury" is inherently unjust. Responding to the veterans'
complaints, at least one state legislature, New York, has revised
its statute of limitations law so that veterans will have two years
from the time the law was passed, or twenty-four months *after* the
discovery of their injury, to file a claim—depending on which
time span happens to be longer. Should Yannacone win the suit
against Dow and veterans then return to their local jurisdictions
in order that the amount of their compensation can be determined, the issue of statute of limitations will, says Kavenagh,
"loom large in the war contractors' defense."

Before Yannacone sent me upstairs to talk with Keith Kavenagh, I asked about the lawsuit he has pending against the Veter-

ans Administration. Yannacone explained that Dow had actually told him about the kind of treatment, or lack of treatment, veterans were receiving at VA clinics.

"After the war the VA's treatment of Vietnam veterans was so bad, Dow told us, that much of the illness and death and serious disability among Vietnam veterans might be due to the negligence, carelessness, and disregard of the Veterans Administration. We checked this out, and found it to be true, and that's why we're suing the VA. But it wasn't our intention to sue them. We pleaded with the VA in private meeting after private meeting to please look at our victims, look at our data. And we asked the famous Dr. Paul Haber, the VA's medical director, if he would consider our liver damage among Vietnam combat veterans. And he said, 'I don't see any cases of porphyria cutanea tarda.' Now porphyria cutanea tarda is a terminal state of liver derangement where you turn jaundiced yellow, your eyeballs turn yellow, and you're very, very sick. I said, 'Doctor, I'm not interested in porphyria cutanea tarda. I'm interested in urinary porphyria derangements which are premonitory of the final stage. Let's treat it before the guy dies!' And he accused me of trying to practice medicine without a license. And I told him, I said, 'I can't believe that a physician at the head of the VA could be so stupid as to ignore the current scientific literature which I lay on the table in front of you, if you don't have the wit and wisdom to read it in your own library.' I said, 'It's not my quote. It's from the literature. *Here it is.*' And their reaction, by the way, was not to have physicians at this meeting, but there was Paul Haber and seven lawyers! I wasn't suing the VA. That was February 1979, one month after we filed the lawsuit against Dow. But we were not suing the VA."

Yannacone persisted in his efforts to avoid a lawsuit and to persuade the VA to recognize that Vietnam veterans needed help. He talked to Max Cleland in Los Angeles, and agreed on an arrangement to meet again with Haber and other "experts" to work out a cooperative program of dermatological investigation. The plan was to use the expertise of World War II dermatologists who knew "what jungle rot really was," as well as industrial dermatologists from Dow and the workmen's compensation board who could recognize chloracne. Clinics would then be established in all of the major veterans hospitals throughout the country on a "road-show basis," and Yannacone would produce fifty to one hundred of his clients at each of the clinics to determine whether they had "chloracne or just spots." All this was agreed, says Yannacone, in the presence of cameramen from one of the major networks. But "in front of ABC-TV in the Patriot's Hall in L.A., Max Cleland reneged on that agreement and said there was *no* evidence and they would not cooperate with the plaintiffs on the Agent Orange suit. They were not going to do anything to help a lawsuit, Cleland said, that they believed to be nothing more than a publicity stunt. Well, Dow sure as hell doesn't think it's a publicity stunt."

Since he initiated the lawsuit against the VA, Yannacone says he has been placed under surveillance by the Justice Department, has received threats in writing, and has been threatened with an investigation to determine how he acquires his information on the medical effects of Agent Orange.

"They think I've got a mole in the VA. They demand to know who my sources are. But they know they have more information than I do. They have withheld. They are lying. *They are killing veterans!*"

Yannacone realizes that he has been shouting. He sighs, shuffles a stack of papers on his desk and, it appears, waits for the jury to return with its verdict. I talk with Mrs. Yannacone for a few moments and then, accepting Yannacone's offer of another cup of coffee, wander upstairs to find his law partner. Shortly after two, Carol Yannacone invites me to lunch, but before I leave his office Kavenagh and I talk briefly about Ireland. I explain that I once lived on an island off the coast of Connemara, and he tells me that he and his family toured the country in a rented car just the year before. Driving through County Wicklow they decided to take a road that led up a mountain. But after considerable winding the road simply narrowed and then disappeared altogether. They stopped and an elderly farmer emerged from a clump of trees and Kavenagh's wife asked if he knew where the road "really went." Without a moment's hesitation, says Kavenagh, the old man winked and replied, "To eternity, ma'am, to eternity."

A light snow is falling. Mrs. Yannacone is driving and Victor is pointing out the sights of the town. For a moment I have the urge to tell them Kavenagh's story, but I assume they have already heard it, probably more than once. Then it occurs to me that the most remarkable thing about the Yannacones may not be that they have dedicated their lives to helping Vietnam veterans and their families, or that they spend every day working within the milieu of a monumental tragedy.

The surprising thing about the Yannacones, Keith Kavenagh, and others who work at the law office in Patchogue is that they can still laugh, tell a joke, and on occasion take an hour off to go to Fadeley's Deli Pub, where they serve German beer, Guinness stout, and corned beef sandwiches with exotic names. We eat our lunch in one corner of the deli while Yannacone leafs through stacks of legal papers, handing Carol a number of medical reports, and smiling, it seems to me, in anticipation of victory against Dow et al.

8

CASUALTY
REPORT

Until a former Green Beret walked into his office complaining of symptoms that physicians call "exotic," Dr. Ronald A. Codario had never heard of Agent Orange. "I don't know how common my experience was," says Codario, "but I went all through medical school and my training in internal medicine without ever hearing the word dioxin." The veteran told Codario that since his return from Vietnam he had spent many hours each week practicing martial arts, becoming highly skilled in using vigorous physical exercises and meditation to control his emotions. But recently, he said, he had been losing the dexterity and speed that had taken him many long years of discipline and practice to develop. His muscular power seemed to decrease almost daily, and he suffered from headaches and numbness and was easily fatigued. But most bewildering, the self-discipline that had enabled him to survive Vietnam and the years following his discharge from the Special Forces seemed to be slipping away; he was afraid he was losing control. Although his training in martial arts helped to lessen his fear and enabled him at times to regain his poise, he was disturbed because there seemed to be absolutely no reason for what was happening.

Dr. Codario listened patiently for nearly three hours but, he confesses, not without a considerable amount of skepticism. As a doctor he had been trained to perceive that certain causes produce readily identifiable effects, and nothing the veteran was telling him fit into this conceptual scheme. Still, he had an intuitive feeling that the man was more than a hypochondriac who, having run out of friends who would listen to his laments, had searched through the phone book until he found an M.D.

During the course of a routine physical examination, Codario discovered that his patient's liver was slightly enlarged and his blood pressure was high. He admitted him to the hospital, where further tests showed signs of liver inflammation, and a liver spleen scan suggested sclerosis. A liver biopsy found fibrosis of the liver and fatty degeneration. These are the findings, says Codario, that one might expect in the tissue of someone who had been a heavy drinker, but also what one could expect to find in someone exposed to a toxic material. When asked if he used alcohol excessively, the veteran said that the use of alcohol and drugs was incompatible with martial arts training, and an examination of the biopsy failed to show the alcoholic hyalins that are usual in cases of alcoholic liver disease.

"So I simply told him," Codario explains, "that he had been exposed to some type of toxic substance, but what it was I just didn't know; and the most important thing was to make sure he didn't expose himself to any further toxic substances. At that time he didn't know anything about Agent Orange, and neither did I."

During the next few months the veteran's condition continued to deteriorate and, still unable to satisfactorily diagnose the source of his patient's problems, Codario resorted to the explanation that, he now realizes, has been used all too often by VA and private physicians to dismiss the complaints of Vietnam veterans.

"At the time I was just unable to come up with answers, so, like most doctors who can't make sense out of what a patient is saying, I suppose I resorted to thinking that maybe his physical symptoms were getting worse because of the stress he was under, maybe as the result of his combat experiences in Vietnam. There were times when I did wonder if some of his problems weren't psychological." But Codario's initial gut reaction resisted this as being too easy, a facile, unsatisfactory solution. On one visit the veteran asked if Codario had ever considered the possibility that Agent Orange might be responsible for his problems.

"I said, 'What's Agent Orange?' " recalls Codario. "I thought it was something out of a McDonald's hamburger ad or something. So he said, 'It was a defoliant that was sprayed in Vietnam while I was there.' I said that I thought it might be possible that a herbicide could cause liver damage, but that I really couldn't say for sure. But I told him that it wouldn't be unreasonable, considering the state he was in, for him to consider pursuing a claim for disability."

Codario was unaware at the time that the Veterans Administration had been routinely denying disability to Vietnam veterans, even those who were nearly totally disabled from the effects of their exposure to toxic herbicides. He sent his patient to his own lawyer for legal advice, and after listening to the veteran's story, Codario's lawyer suggested he see another attorney who was working with Victor Yannacone on the class action suit against wartime manufacturers of Agent Orange. The attorney, Hy Mayerson, was so impressed by the fact that an M.D. would show so much interest in a Vietnam veteran that on the following day he forwarded more than a thousand pages of information on Agent Orange and the effects of dioxin on animals and humans to Codario's office. Included in the material were approximately one hundred articles from toxicology journals dating back more than a decade, as well as data about where herbicides had been sprayed, what the effects of dioxin had been on animals and humans, and every accident in factories where herbicides were produced or dioxin was a contaminant of some chemical reaction.

Codario found the material fascinating. He read, for example, about a doctor in the Soviet Union who had examined four hundred workers in a herbicide factory over a ten-year period, describing symptoms that Codario would come across often during his examinations of Vietnam veterans: neurasthenia, headaches, loss of libido, personality changes, chloracne, and depression. A decade later researchers who had been studying fifty of the original four hundred workers found that 20 percent of them were suffering from porphyria cutanea tarda, an often-fatal stage of liver disease associated with exposure to TCDD-dioxin. Codario also read Lennart Hardell and M. Eriksson's studies on the relationship between soft tissue sarcomas, malignant lymphomas, and exposure to chlorophenols and phenoxy acids, and he continued seeing veterans who seemed to have stepped from the pages of the material he was reading. Codario had wanted to believe that the Vietnam War was over, that the wounds of that era were at least beginning to heal, but he would discover that for many veterans the struggle for survival that began in mangrove forests, rice paddies, and jungles has not ended. And Codario would begin a war of his own—to save the lives of veterans poisoned by toxic herbicides.

One of the more intriguing things Codario came across during his research was that workers exposed to dioxin during industrial accidents often have in their urine elevated levels of a substance called "intermediate porphyrins." Porphyrins, he knew, are substances that act as building blocks for hemoglobin—it takes four porphyrin molecules with an iron molecule in the center to make hemoglobin—and hemoglobin is similar structurally to chlorophyll, the material that enables plants to carry out photosynthesis. Because they are extremely sensitive to light, conditions for testing for porphyrins must be carefully controlled if the test is not to be invalidated by a change in their chemical structure.

Codario concluded that he needed expert advice if he was to find a way of analyzing the porphyrins in his patient's urine, so he contacted Drs. Schwartz and Watson's laboratory at Abbott Northwestern Hospital in Minneapolis, where a clinic had been established some years before to treat cases of porphyria. In the early 1970s researchers at the hospital had developed a "miracle drug" for treating patients with elevated porphyrins, and Codario was interested in the possibility of using this drug to help some of the veterans he had been seeing. After a brief correspondence, the clinic's director, Dr. Petryka, agreed to organize the analysis of the veterans' urine.

Codario collected urine specimens in special dark containers kept in an ice bath, and sent the containers to Philadelphia's St. Joseph's Hospital, where a registered nurse had volunteered to help out with the project. Upon receiving the containers, the nurse measured the exact amount in each container, then poured out 100 ccs for packing convenience, and, mixing it with a preserving chemical, shipped it via Federal Express to Minneapolis, where Dr. Petryka would then use thin-layer chromatography to analyze the specimens for elevated levels of porphyrins. Over the next few months, Codario examined 270 Vietnam veterans, performing urinalysis on 120 of them and discovering that the same unmistakable pattern appeared again and again.

"In fact," he says, "*68 percent* of the people we've examined have an elevated level of one particular type of porphyrin in their urine, a type we call copro. In addition to the elevated level of coproporphyrins, *90 percent* of the veterans I've examined have what we call a positive Ehrlich reaction. Now the Ehrlich reaction was a test that was done several years ago as a test for porphyrin problems. It is a reaction that takes place when a measured amount of urine is added to an acidified benzaldehyde solution. Before the advent of thin-layer chromatography and all the sophisticated methods of picking up the various types of porphyrins, it was a good screening test for picking up a particular type of porphyrin called porphobilinogen, which is an intermediate type of porphyrin. Dr. Petryka was the first person to actually describe a positive Ehrlich reaction in certain alcoholics because of the appearance of certain pyrroles in their urine.

"But the important thing here is that in the world's literature one can find only about ten different compounds that will cause a positive Ehrlich reaction, and to our surprise we're finding that 90 percent of the Vietnam veterans we see have this positive Ehrlich reaction. So naturally Dr. Petryka was intrigued by this and he went about searching the urine samples to see if they contained any one of these ten chemicals. And he discovered that the veterans' urine contains none of them. So we concluded that the compound that is causing the positive Ehrlich reaction must be a new compound, and I jokingly told Dr. Petryka that he should name it after himself, calling it the Petryka compound. But he went and named it after me, so now it's called the 'Codario-Ehrlich positive metabolism.' But we do know the molecular weight—it is 220—of this compound, and Dr. Petryka is in the process of defining its chemical structure. And when he finds the chemical structure it may be very interesting because it could very well be a way of determining whether or not a person has been exposed to herbicides. Obviously, with the coproporphyrin elevation and the curious positive Ehrlich reaction, we now have a biochemical way of saying yes, these people are different. And there are abnormalities in these patients that we are not finding in those who didn't serve in Vietnam."

In addition to his willingness to work for very little financial gain (Codario sees all Vietnam veterans initially for free and often spends his weekends flying free of charge to the home state of any veteran who has called for help), Dr. Codario has another remarkable quality. During our interview the phone would ring, as one might expect in a busy doctor's office, and he would listen patiently, replying to the caller's questions or complaints with genuine concern. Then almost before he had replaced the receiver, he would continue exactly where he had left off, even if this meant in the middle of a complicated compound sentence.

"The other thing that is of interest is that Dr. Strik of the Netherlands, who is one of the world's authorities on porphyrin problems resulting from exposure to chemicals, and has published several papers on what happens to people whose porphyrin levels are elevated due to their exposure to herbicides, has clearly stated that porphyria progresses in a stepwise fashion from asystematic coproporphyria auria to the much more devastating uroporphyria auria. And that disease is called porphyria cutanea tarda, which is a condition characterized by episodes of severe crampy abdominal pain, high fevers, schizophrenia, and often death. So it seems that the coproporphyria auria that we are seeing now merely represent the tip of the iceberg, or the beginning of the abnormality that if left unchecked may progress to porphyria cutanea tarda and death."

Codario feels that he may have discovered a way to check the progressively destructive effects of herbicide poisoning; however, he fears that he may only be able to arrest, rather than cure, the problem. "I'm hoping that once we have established a significant statistical correlation, which we seem to be moving toward right now, that we can get approval to treat some of these porphyrin problems with the drug that they have developed in Minnesota called Hematin. But that may be an oversimplification because Hematin was designed to treat patients with acute severe porphyria—for example, patients suffering from porphyria cutanea tarda. The results have been nothing short of miraculous and are well-publicized in the journals of internal medicine. But in those cases the porphyrins they were producing in their urines were thirty to forty times higher than those we are seeing in our veterans. And we have to keep in mind that Hematin has never been used to treat chemically induced porphyrin problems, so we're really treading in new territory and can't be certain that it will work this way. But based on the mechanism of its action, it is certainly possible that it will be beneficial here. The thing we don't know is, even if we are able to reverse the production of excess porphyrins, will we stop it forever just by giving the patient Hematin? And even if we return the porphyrin count to normal, will their symptoms go away? In examining the veterans and listening to their stories, I suspect that even if Hematin works it will only be temporarily effective and that after a period of time the individual will probably relapse. And I also suspect that all of the symptoms about which Vietnam veterans are complaining are not due solely to porphyrin problems but rather are a direct toxic effect of the herbicide in general and dioxin in particular."

Another thing Codario would like to determine is how many of the veterans' problems are due to the storage of TCDD in their fatty tissues because he believes it may be possible to flush these residues from the human body. But his efforts to test this theory have been hampered by the fact that the VA has done only a very limited fat biopsy study on Vietnam veterans, and when I spoke with him, he had already been waiting for nearly six months for the return of five biopsies.

"I sent the five fat biopsies to Dr. Thomas Tiernan at the Brehm Laboratory at Wright State University because Dr. Tiernan had done research on dioxin for the government and he is considered an 'independent' researcher. He was involved in studying dioxin levels on the ship *Vulcanus,* * and seems to be an expert in the field."

Although dioxin can be stored in the human body for many years, standard laboratory tests commonly used by the VA in its "Agent Orange examinations" fail to detect traces of dioxin in the blood, urine, or spinal fluid. "They take your blood and urine," one veteran told me, "and when they don't find dioxin in it— which they knew goddamn well they wouldn't in the first place —they conclude that you're clean, you weren't exposed to Orange in Nam. Just more fun and games, because they know that TCDD is stored in the fatty tissues of the body. Their own research has shown that."

The research the veteran refers to is a "blind" study conducted by Dr. Michael Gross of the University of Nebraska, on contract to the Veterans Administration. In this study, 30 grams of fat were removed from twenty Vietnam veterans who believed they had been exposed to Agent Orange. An additional 30 grams were removed from ten veterans who presumably had no contact with Agent Orange and from three U.S. Air Force officers who had done dioxin research. The samples were forwarded to Dr. Gross's

---

*In 1970 when the order to stop using Agent Orange in South Vietnam was issued, the U.S. military was left with thousands of fifty-five-gallon drums containing this herbicide. Some of these barrels were stored on Johnston Island in the Pacific, while others went to the Naval Construction Battalion Center at Gulfport, Mississippi. But the drums started to rust and their contents began leaking, making it imperative that something more "final" be done about the surplus stocks of herbicide Orange. In February 1972, the Mississippi Air and Pollution Control Commission ordered that the Agent Orange stored at Gulfport be removed immediately. Faced with this, the Air Force tried returning the remaining stocks of Agent Orange to its manufacturers, who refused to accept the offer. Air Force officials also suggested that the surplus herbicide be disposed of "by the prudent disposition of herbicide Orange for use on privately owned or governmentally owned lands." This plan also failed and, seven years after the barrels were removed from Vietnam, the EPA finally granted the Air Force a permit to incinerate the remaining stocks of Agent Orange on the German-built ship *Vulcanus* in the South Pacific. By the time the permit was granted, more than 5,000 drums containing over a quarter million gallons of Agent Orange had rotted through.

laboratory, where they were analyzed for residues of TCDD-dioxin. Two of the three men who had been described as heavily exposed had TCDD in their fatty tissues of approximately 25 to 100 parts per trillion, while three of the five who were classified as receiving "light exposures" had concentrations of from 5 to 7 parts per trillion. *Ten out of the twenty Vietnam veterans had TCDD in their fatty tissues.* Two of the control samples contained low levels of TCDD and the tissue taken from the Air Force officers had levels of TCDD in the abdominal adipose ranging from 5 to 6 parts per trillion.[1]

Called as an expert witness at the Environmental Protection Agency's 2,4,5-T suspension hearings, Dr. Gross said: "It appears that Vietnam veterans heavily exposed to herbicide Orange will carry low levels of TCDD in their body fat. This conclusion is supported by the observation that two of the three most heavily exposed men have the highest levels detected in this blind study. It is extremely unlikely that this finding is a matter of chance or has occurred because of herbicide or other TCDD-related exposure in the United States. Furthermore, 50 percent of the veterans of Vietnam tested in this study exhibited low levels of TCDD in their abdominal fat whereas only 20 percent of the controls were found to be positive.

"Additional support for this conclusion comes from the replicate analysis of the adipose samples from the 'heavily exposed' veterans, and from the validation analyses performed by Mr. Harless. We recognize the need for additional validation studies, and these are planned.

"We propose that the results are relevant to the cancellation hearings. They constitute support for the concept that exposure to TCDD can lead to long-term storage in human fat tissues."[2]

Dr. Gross's discoveries seem to have been received by the VA with the same amount of enthusiasm that the Atomic Energy Commission displayed when informed by John Gofman and other researchers that long-term exposure to low-level radiation could be dangerous, even deadly. In the two years following Dr. Gross's testimony at the EPA hearings, the Veterans Administration conducted no further tests to determine the extent to which Vietnam veterans may have TCDD in their fatty tissues. However, the VA recently announced that it does intend to conduct further studies on the adipose tissue of veterans.

Should he discover that the fatty tissues of veterans he has examined contain residues of TCDD, Codario will attempt to flush dioxin from their bodies with a drug used to treat victims of kepone poisoning. Kepone is an insecticide which, like dioxin, collects in the fatty tissues of the human body, producing numbness of the hands, headaches, personality changes, and other dioxin-like symptoms. Another similarity between kepone and dioxin is that it is eliminated in the bile fluid, passed into the intestine, and then reabsorbed in the body in what physicians call an enterohepatic cycle. At the University of Virginia, a researcher administering cholestyramine (a bile-salt binder commonly used to treat patients with elevated levels of cholesterol and, in some cases, jaundice) to workers who had high levels of kepone in their bodies discovered that within two months all of the workers showed dramatic improvements, and within one year seven of the twenty-two workers were totally kepone free. The results were published in *The New England Journal of Medicine* (1978, vol. 298) by Dr. Philip S. Guzelian et al., and Codario believes that Guzelian's findings may be vital to physicians working with Vietnam veterans or victims of domestic herbicide spraying.

"So if dioxin behaves similarly to kepone, and we have evidence that it does," says Codario, "it would certainly be tempting to postulate that it could be eliminated from the body by the aid of cholestyramine. And so, once I get the fat biopsies back, I can start giving my patients this drug and doing follow-up examinations to measure for dioxin in their bowel movements. In that manner I can determine if TCDD is actually being washed from their bodies."

Ronald A. Codario seems to find nothing unusual about the fact that he is doing work that should have been done years ago by the Veterans Administration, or that, without a grant from any of the national health institutes or foundations, he has discovered a medical basis for proving that Vietnam veterans were exposed to Agent Orange and that their exposure is now crippling and killing them. As a specialist in internal medicine he could demand fifty dollars an hour for his advice, yet he donates twenty to thirty hours each week to the people whom many Americans still prefer to use as scapegoats for the Vietnam War.

Will the Veterans Administration listen to his theories, accept his statistics, and take action on behalf of Vietnam veterans? Codario thinks they will. He believes that the men and women who run the VA are honest people who are stifled by the inherent inefficiency of big government; moreover, he intensely dislikes what he calls "Monday morning quarterbacking," and says that trying to place blame for what has happened to Vietnam veterans will only prolong their agony.

"Look," he says, shuffling a stack of papers on his desk, "it's just too easy if you ask me to say, 'Hey, Dow did this, and the VA did that.' Sure, maybe there was conflict of interest back then, and we all know that somebody makes, or rather made, a lot of money from selling herbicides. But it's just too easy, if you ask me, to look back fourteen years and place the blame. That just isn't the thrust of my work. I'm just trying to show that these fellas have a problem, and I want to get them some help. And in getting help for them I want to say, 'Hey, listen, these things have caused the problems.' Let's just make sure it doesn't happen again because certainly the people that can help the veterans much quicker than I can are the federal government and the chemical companies. I think that where we have to exercise our diligence and care now is trying to make sure that mass herbicide spraying and pollution of the environment doesn't continue to happen in the future."

Codario and I shake hands and he walks me to the waiting room, where his receptionist and an elderly black woman are watching television. I ask directions to the subway, explaining that on my way to his office I had gotten off at the wrong stop. Codario, the elderly woman, and the receptionist appear shocked that I would have taken the subway, and insist on calling a cab. During the drive to the train station, the cab driver chats pleasantly, weaving skillfully in and out of the rush-hour traffic and laughing happily at his own jokes. But I am mesmerized by the clicking meter and unable to put out of my mind what Codario said as I was about to leave. The Green Beret, he told me, has continued to deteriorate. His liver and spleen are swollen, his arms and legs are often numb, and he has lost much of his coordination. Rising from a chair or sofa, he often falls down, walks into walls, stumbles about the room. He has episodes in which he goes blind for fifteen minutes, and has lost consciousness while driving, ramming into the car in front of him. Sometimes he "goes off" for a couple of days, flying into terrible rages, banging his hands through walls. X-rays have failed to determine why his urine is darkened and his head throbs and he has blood in his bowel movements.

As I pay the driver and prepare to enter the station, I remember something else Codario told me about the first Vietnam veteran to enter his office complaining of "bizzare" and "exotic" symptoms. The man's wife, said Codario, had given birth to a horribly deformed baby girl who died in the veteran's arms.

9

HUMANS, RATS, AND LESSER BEINGS

On one wall of the receptionist's office at the Oregon Regional Primate Research Center in Portland a large female monkey and her baby snuggle beneath the caption LOVE US OR LOSE US. On the opposite wall a sullen great ape informs visitors that AROUND HERE WE CAN USE ALL THE SMILES WE CAN GET. After checking the appointment roster and handing me a name tag (NO ACCESS TO ANIMAL ROOMS), the receptionist suggests I wait in the center's cafeteria. Fifteen minutes later Dr. Wilbur McNulty, whose research into the effects of TCDD-dioxin on rhesus monkeys has often been quoted by opponents of domestic herbicide use, appears. Thin and polite, he answers my questions with the cautious reserve of a scientist who has been drawn, somewhat against his will, into the controversy over dioxin.

The Oregon Regional Primate Research Center, McNulty explains, is one of seven primate centers established in the early sixties as scientific institutes under the assumption "that because primates are our nearest biological relatives they might in many cases be good or even superior models for handling diseases." Because the supply of rhesus monkeys appeared to be inexhaustible, they were considered ideal for laboratory experiments, but in recent years an international controversy has developed over the capture and sale of this species of primate. After several decades the rhesus population has been so depleted that at least one Asian nation has placed a ban on their export.

"But we don't have to worry too much about all that," McNulty explains with a touch of pride. "In fact, we now have over 2,500 primates living on the grounds of our center. And they live outdoors all the time all year round, and they seem to do quite well in this climate. We're pretty self-sufficient, at least where the rhesus is concerned, and no longer depend on capture from the wild."

When he first began feeding a select group of rhesus monkeys minute quantities of TCDD-dioxin, McNulty was actually doing research into polychlorinated biphenyls (PCBs), which he describes as his first love. "Back some years ago, the thought was around that the toxicity of PCBs might not in fact be due to the PCBs themselves, but rather to a contaminant that was contained in the PCBs, something called polychlorinated dibenzofurans. But there really wasn't any information available at that time on the relative potency of PCBs and/or the dibenzofurans. So, obviously, in order to investigate whether the toxicity of commercial PCBs might be due to the contaminants, I had to know just what the potency of the contaminant might be. But the contaminants were not available; however, since the polychlorinated dibenzofurans are a very close relative of dioxin, which was indeed available, I started testing with a dioxin compound called TCDD. I wanted to see just what its relative potency might be, and as you can well guess, it was enormously more potent than PCBs, although qualitatively the diseases they cause are the same. On a per-weight basis dioxin is much, much stronger."

In the beginning McNulty placed what he thought were small quantities of dioxin in the food of his rhesus monkeys. "As fools rush in," he admits, "the doses, in retrospect, were astronomical. They were in the parts per billion instead of parts per trillion range, which is more relevant when it comes to food. I think the first level I used was 20 parts per billion in the diet, and that killed a young male rhesus monkey in twelve days. This was an estimated total intake of well under 10 micrograms (TCDD) per kilogram (body weight). A level of 2 parts per billion was lethal in seventy-six days. I discovered that monkeys are several times more sensitive to TCDD than mice, rats, rabbits, and dogs."

Dioxin turned out to be so toxic to his experimental animals that McNulty decided to suspend all research with TCDD until the primate center could construct a special building with carefully controlled access, assigning the care of his monkeys to only one or two well-trained people in an effort to minimize the risk of contaminating other areas of the center.

"Dioxin," says McNulty, "is the most toxic small man-made molecule we know of. It is less toxic on a per-gram basis than some biological toxins like botulin, but that's a very huge molecule. So molecule for molecule dioxin is probably the leader of the pack."*

After consuming food containing minute amounts of TCDD, McNulty's primates became very quiet, began losing weight, lost their appetite, grew progressively thinner and weaker, and then "just laid down and died." Sometimes they would have episodes of retching or vomiting, but, says McNulty, "these were at the higher doses. At much, much lower doses a certain fraction of the animals remain well for one to three or four months, and then will suffer from an ailment characterized by failure of the elements of the bone marrow. They will have low white counts, very low platelet counts, so that they suffer from hemorrhages and infections and are essentially carried away by bone marrow failure."†

Unlike Vietnam veterans who have complained of fluctuations in weight patterns, gains as well as losses, the monkeys did not regain the weight they lost. "They just go down," says McNulty, "although I did have one animal who lost a lot of weight over a period of about three and a half months, without showing any of the other characteristic signs of toxic poisoning. And then she began to regain her weight and is still alive today, and appears to

---

*According to Harvard researcher Matthew Meselson, dioxin is also much more poisonous than the most toxic military nerve gases, which also consist of small molecules.

†"What appears to be happening," says Matthew Meselson, "is that cell division stops. Spermatogenesis stops, the replacement of red blood cells stops, the regeneration of the epithelial lining of the gut stops. After a few days or weeks without cell division the animals simply fall apart."[1]

be quite well. But usually if they are sufficiently poisoned that they lose a significant amount of weight, they don't recover from it. It simply goes on and they become worse and then they die."

Although TCDD, when given to rats and mice in minute doses, causes congenital abnormalities, including fetal deaths, cleft palate, and kidney abnormalities, McNulty's research failed to indicate that TCDD acts as a teratogen in rhesus monkeys. McNulty did find, however, that TCDD is *fetotoxic* in rhesus monkeys. "The experiment," says McNulty, "was designed to explore whether short-term exposure to dioxin, either in a single or a few closely spaced doses during that period in early pregnancy when the organs are forming, would result in malformations. At the highest dose it was very toxic to the mother, and since I wasn't really interested in that, I did very little at that particular level. At the intermediate level there was a fairly high level of abortion, or loss of the fetus. But those which did not abort gave birth to normal offspring. We were unable to find any malformations. Also, at the level that TCDD caused a fair number of abortions there were some late toxicities and deaths among the mothers. But the number of animals was relatively small, and unlike experiments with rats and mice, you can't use the number you would like for statistical significance. Still, with the relatively small number of animals I used it seems extraordinarily likely that TCDD is toxic to the fetus, but I did not conclude that it causes malformations in the offspring of rhesus monkeys."

Fetotoxic effects, which means the ability of TCDD to destroy developing fetuses, have been observed in three different mouse strains, two rat strains, and one species of monkey. In a study by Dow Chemical, rats fed one nanogram (billionth of a gram) of TCDD per kilogram body weight per day exhibited increased stillbirth and shortened life spans for surviving pups. Skeletal birth defects have also been observed in four different mouse strains as well as other types of defects in rats when pregnant females are exposed to TCDD.[2]

Dr. McNulty has not researched the possible mutagenic effects of TCDD on male monkeys because, he says, "there isn't any reason to think it would be a good experiment. As you recall, I said there is *no evidence* that TCDD is a mutagen, and any reproductive failures in terms of abortions or malformations that are going to be transmitted through the father almost necessarily have to be due to the mutagenicity of *his* germ cells. So it's not the kind of experiment that's likely to get results. Now, I'm sure Vietnam veterans would raise the question: 'How do you know if you haven't done it?' Well, with mature monkeys now running around a thousand dollars each, it becomes a matter of choosing experiments that one has some reason to assume will give one conclusive results. It's always difficult to prove that something doesn't exist. In other words, how many males would I have to expose and then breed with females before I could say with confidence that TCDD *does not* cause reproductive failures through the male? One sure wouldn't be enough. Would ten be enough? Not likely. Would a hundred be enough? Well, maybe, but still a little bit doubtful. And that's just an impossibly expensive experiment if you don't have any good reason ahead of time to think that it's going to pay off."

But not all scientists would agree with McNulty's conclusions regarding the mutagenicity of TCDD. In their paper "The Mutagenacity of Dioxin and Its Effects on Reproduction among Exposed War Veterans," Vietnamese doctors Ton That Tung, Ton Duc Lang, and Do Duc Van suggest that scientists should at least consider the possibility that TCDD might act as a human mutagen. Comparing birth defects among children born to North Vietnamese soldiers who had served in the South to those among children of soldiers who had remained in the North, and noting that "none of the wives of exposed or non-exposed veterans received any exposure themselves," the doctors wrote:

> The congenital malformations are of many types, with an increased frequency of anencephaly in the children of former soldiers . . . In spite of the limitations of the available data, it is striking to compare the absence of anencephaly among the births in the unexposed civilian population to the seven cases among births to

former soldiers. The excessive incidence of congenital malformations in the children of soldiers exposed to dioxin were discovered by interviewing each couple. In relation to national and international norms, the incidence of neural tube malformations is particularly elevated.

Likewise, the rate of abortion, premature births, and sterility is significantly higher in the group of exposed veterans from the South. Moreover, the number of molar pregnancies* in Hanoi seems abnormally high; the Institute for Mothers and Children (The National Ob-Gyn Institute) has just reported the hospitalization of nineteen cases of molar pregnancies or chorioepitheliomas, of which nine were diagnosed in women married to former soldiers from the South.

A plausible explanation for the association established between exposure to dioxin and excessive congenital malformation in first-generation offspring is that exposure may affect the father's genetic material. This association calls for a vigorous epidemiological study taking into account the various factors which could interfere with reproduction. It also indicates that a cytologic and biological study of sperm of both man and animal exposed to dioxin should be carried out."[3]

A scientific paper by David Kriebel, published by the Center for the Biology of Natural Systems, Washington University, also gives a number of reasons for considering the possibility that TCDD might act as a human mutagen.

RATS ARE NOT PEOPLE: WHAT DOES ALL THIS MEAN FOR US?

Two points must be made about the significance of the experimental animal data to human health. First, bacteria, rats and people have very few things in common. But one of those few is a genetic code made of deoxyribonucleic acid (DNA). If TCDD can damage DNA in salmonella, and lacking evidence to the contrary, we

---

*A molar pregnancy is one characterized by the presence of a uterine mole, a fleshy mass formed in the uterus by the degeneration or abortive development of an ovum.

must assume it can damage it in humans as well. Second, chemicals *known* to harm humans (benzene, vinyl chloride, cigarette smoke, to name a few) via mutational damage almost invariably do it to other organisms as well. With only one exception (arsenic) all the known human carcinogens cause cancer in laboratory animals as well.

TCDD—A HUMAN MUTAGEN

Scattered evidence supports what experimental studies suggest— that TCDD is probably a human mutagen. There is often conflicting data, and room for different interpretations; however, there is much more evidence now than there was two years ago, and this trend will probably continue. Chromosome damage has been reported in Hungarian workers exposed to TCDD in a chemical plant, and in Vietnamese civilians sprayed with the herbicide Agent Orange, which contained TCDD in small amounts (parts per million).

BIRTH DEFECTS FROM AGENT ORANGE?

Could the exposure of veterans to Agent Orange in Vietnam over ten years ago cause birth defects in their children born today? There is no direct proof, but a mechanism capable of causing this effect certainly exists. If TCDD is a human mutagen, and if it causes mutations in male germ cells, then children born of men exposed at any time in their life could develop abnormally. At least three other environmental pollutants have been shown to cause birth defects or other reproductive problems; most likely via mutations in male germ cells.[4]

Neither Dr. Tung and his associates nor Kriebel argue that there is indisputable proof that TCDD is a human mutagen, but both papers suggest that the possible mutagenicity of TCDD should be examined further. Dr. Steven D. Stellman, assistant vice president for epidemiology, American Cancer Society, has also suggested that scientists continue research into the mutagenicity of TCDD. Testifying before the Subcommittee on Medical

Facilities and Benefits of the Veterans' Affairs Committee, Stellman said that it is conceivable, though not provable at this time, that Vietnam veterans exposed to Agent Orange may have increased the odds that their children would be born with defects. Stellman and his wife had been coding and analyzing some of the thousands of questionnaires sent out to Vietnam veterans by Citizen Soldier, a veterans' organization headquartered in New York. Although they found some of the exposure histories to be "unreliable," Stellman felt that "the next best thing to an exposure history *may* be an exposure marker.* Since we asked about skin effects in four different ways, we compared the association of one particular health outcome—namely, the presence of any birth defect in a child born after the father's return from Vietnam—with the presence or absence of this exposure marker. Odds ratios ranged from 1.3 to 1.8 . . . Continuing this line of inquiry, we also found a quantitative association between the number of gastrointestinal complaints reported, and the likelihood of fathering a child with a birth defect. Taken literally, this *could* mean that men having the stated skin conditions were 30 to 80 percent more likely to father children with birth defects. However, without more objective clinical evaluation of the men and their children, I would caution a more conservative interpretation, and simply state that the results are highly suggestive of a possible effect, and that they should be confirmed by new studies in which the subjects are selected on a random basis rather than on their own initiative."[5]

"The problem," Dr. McNulty explains, "is that there are enormous differences in the reactions of species to TCDD. The hamster, for example, will take a dose 5,000 times as large as a guinea pig, and the hamster excretes TCDD quite rapidly. Other animals will store TCDD in their fat tissues, but the problem with doing a half-life study of this stored dioxin is that you've got to give *just enough* TCDD that you won't kill or seriously damage the animal.

*The most readily observable symptom or marker of dioxin exposure is chloracne.

And there are various estimates of what it costs to measure the dioxin in one piece of tissue, and most of them run to the order of two to five thousand dollars per sample. So we're talking dollars again like we were with the monkeys. When people ask why these things haven't been done, why they haven't been measured, the answer, at least one of the basic answers, is *money.*"

Dr. McNulty apologizes for a persistent cough, pauses while I examine my notes, and appears not to notice as a woman enters the office rather brusquely, lays a manila folder on his desk, and leaves. But when I ask whether the primate center has done any research into the carcinogenicity of TCDD in rhesus monkeys, he replies with the convivial irritation one might expect from a congressman asked once too often about his voting record.

"No, neither I nor anyone else has, or probably ever will, for several reasons. In general the latency period for induction of cancer into an animal is correlated with the life span of the animal. So one can get skin cancers in mice by painting them with polyaromatic hydrocarbons for just a matter of weeks or months, but then a mouse only lives for about a year and a half. Some years ago a researcher here was trying to reproduce these sorts of things in monkeys by painting them with polyaromatic hydrocarbons and exposing them to ultraviolet light. And he finally pretty much gave up. But several years later the animals were still around and did begin to show up with skin cancers. So it just isn't practical, at least in the research environment today, to conduct an experiment that would go on for twenty or even forty years, particularly when there is no evidence that TCDD is carcinogenic in animals or humans."

Observing my surprise, McNulty points to a large file drawer and declares: "It's all there, and it's all, or at least 90 percent of it, negative."

But McNulty's insistence that TCDD has not proven to be carcinogenic in laboratory animals or humans only demonstrates, once again, that scientists disagree on just how much and exactly what kind of damage TCDD does to living organisms. For example, Dr. Samuel S. Epstein, a human and experimental pathologist and toxicologist who has devoted the past thirty years to the study of the hazardous effects of chemicals and chemical pollutants believes that "TCDD is the most potent known carcinogen." An expert on the delayed and chronic toxic effects—most notably cancer, reproductive and genetic—of chemicals and chemical pollutants, including pesticides and herbicides, Epstein testified before the House Subcommittee on Medical Facilities and Benefits of the Committee on Veterans' Affairs that

> In tests with small groups of rats over a dose range from 1 ppt (0.0003 ug/kg) to 1000 ppb (500 ug/kg), all animals receiving doses in excess of 500 ppt died within 95 weeks. TCDD induced a wide range of malignant tumors in doses as low as 5 ppt (Van Miller et al., 1977). These include squamous carcinomas of the lung, cholangiosarcoma of the liver, and malignant histiocytomas at 1 and 5 ppb levels, and carcinomas of the ear duct, kidney and skin, malignant histiocytomas and testicular tumors at the 5 ppt dose. In more large-scale carcinogenicity tests by Dow Chemical, which are generally confirmatory of the Van Miller studies, TCDD was administered orally to rats at levels of 0.001, 0.01 and 0.1 ug/kg (Kociba et al., 1978). Carcinomas of the liver, lung, palate and tongue were induced at the highest dose levels, neoplastic liver nodules at the intermediate dose level, and toxic liver effects at the lowest dose level tested.[6]

Contradicting the VA's contention that there is no evidence that TCDD is harmful to humans, Dr. Epstein told the subcommittee about a study of forestry, paper pulp, and sawmill workers in northern Sweden who were exposed primarily to 2,4,5-T and 2,4-D. The study concluded that the risk for soft tissue sarcomas in the Swedish workers was five times greater than in those not exposed to these herbicides.[7] A "statistically significant excess of stomach cancer" was also found in Swedish railroad workers exposed to phenoxyacetic acids and amitrole over a ten-year period,[8] and a study conducted in southern Sweden found "statistically significant excess risks for soft-tissue sarcomas."[9] In the follow-up of the 1953 Ludwigshafen (West Germany) accident in a TCP plant, a seven-fold excess in stomach cancer over expected rates was noted.[10]

Among Vietnam veterans, Epstein testified, "the incidence of testicular cancer appears high, even allowing for selection bias. In one group of about 5,000 plaintiffs, approximately 200 testicular cancers, mainly seminomas, have been recognized. There are also suggestions of an increased incidence of lymphomas and leukemias." When Dr. Epstein described the "symptomatology" of TCDD in human beings, which he said is "well recognized in the clinical and toxicological literature," he might very well have been a Vietnam veteran talking about some of the problems he had experienced since returning from Asia. TCDD, said Epstein, "is a potent multi-system toxic agent producing a panoply of a wide range of acute and delayed effects, many of which can progress to the chronic. Recognized clinical symptoms include asthenia, muscular weakness, pains in limbs and joints, insomnia, photosensitivity, nausea, vomiting and diarrhea. Recognized signs include abnormalities in liver function, porphyria, peripheral neuropathy, elevated blood triglycerides and cholesterol, and psychological and personality changes . . . This disease complex is generally consistent with that recognized in preliminary surveys of Vietnam veterans, although no large-scale analysis has yet been published."*

What Epstein did not tell the subcommittee is that thousands of Vietnam veterans have been complaining of these *very* symptoms for a number of years, only to be given a Rorschach or Minnesota Multiple Personality Inventory (MMPI) test by VA hospital staff and sent home—or, all too often, to the psychiatric ward with a prescription for uppers or downers. Unfortunately Valium and Thorazine have not proven very effective in arresting liver cancer, and Gelusil (an antacid) seems not to have acted as an antidote to the destructive effects of TCDD on the stomachs, colons, livers, and even prostate glands of many young veterans.

---

*See Appendix, pp. 195–196, Letter to the Editor of the *Journal of the American Medical Association*.

Although many studies have shown that TCDD is carcinogenic in laboratory animals and there is now suggestive evidence that "exposure to phenoxy acids and chlorophenols might constitute a risk factor in the development of soft-tissue sarcomas,"[11] the VA has failed to conduct a national outreach program that might determine just how many Vietnam veterans are ill, have died, or may be dying from various types of cancer. With over a quarter million employees and a yearly budget of approximately $24 billion, the VA's failure to do cohort studies, says Victor Yannacone, is based not on scientific caution but on a singular lack of compassion.

"I can go to my terminal in my little country law office in Patchogue," says Yannacone, "and I can sit there and I can ask my relatively inexpensive computer to tell me the names and addresses of every veteran with testicular cancer. That is not terribly hard. I can tell the computer to tell me who had testicular cancer and the birth defects, and who was a Marine, and who served in a particular place during the month of January or February of 1968 . . . It takes two minutes and forty-five seconds to get the answer.

"Why hasn't the government done this kind of study? Because, quite simply, they don't really think the veterans are that important; the Vietnam veteran is an expendable commodity to the U.S. government."

Yannacone, whose first brief against the manufacturers of Agent Orange was 184 pages long and contained "every piece of scientific data that was then known about dioxin or phenoxy herbicides," believes that many veterans have already died from the "wasting effects" observed in rhesus monkeys by Dr. Wilbur McNulty and researcher Dr. James Allen. "People under the age of thirty-five don't waste away and die with an autopsy report that says the veteran looked considerably older than his stated age of thirty-two years. He looks like a ninety-six-year-old mummy fresh out of the tomb. There isn't a single piece of measurable fat on his skeleton. Now, that is ten years after his tour in Vietnam. What does that mean? It means somehow the amount that was loaded in his fat was mobilized and eventually killed him, and it killed him as if he had an acute dose years before. It just took ten years instead of ten days."

Since 1949 there have been a number of accidents involving the release of dioxin at industrial plants throughout the world, the best known of which occured at the ICMESA plant in Seveso, Italy, on July 10, 1976. The ICMESA plant was producing 2,4,5-trichlorophenol, and the accident took place in a chemical reactor. The explosion blew a safety disk out of the reactor, sending the bubbling brew up a venting pipe into the atmosphere, where it formed first a plume, then a cloud that eventually settled over a 700-acre area where 5,000 people lived and worked. Soon animals began to sicken and die, and those who were exposed to the dioxin-laden cloud suffered symptoms similar to those Vietnamese peasants had complained of following a defoliation raid: bouts of diarrhea, excruciating headaches, stomach cramps, dizziness, and sleeplessness.

During his tenure as VA chief, Max Cleland would on occasion draw Seveso from his grab bag of justifications for the VA's recalcitrance on disability payments to Vietnam veterans who had been exposed to Agent Orange. Seveso, according to Cleland, only demonstrated that human beings can be exposed to dioxin without suffering demonstrably calamitous effects. This argument is fallacious for at least two reasons: First, because Vietnam veterans, unlike victims of industrial accidents, were exposed to toxic herbicides over a twelve-month period and their exposure involved what scientists call "multiple routes"—which means that they drank water and ate food contaminated with dioxin, inhaled smoke from brush that had been sprayed with herbicides containing dioxin, swam in water polluted with dioxin, waded through brush coated with toxic sprays, and wore clothing for days, even weeks, which in some cases had been liberally doused with herbicides. Second, the accident at Seveso did have some very serious health effects on the residents of that community. In *The Pendulum and the Toxic Cloud: The Course of Dioxin Contamination*, Thomas Whiteside, who visited Seveso soon after the accident and again two years later, describes the aftermath of the explosion at the ICMESA plant.

> Bird life appeared to have been devastated; fields, gardens, and orchards were littered with the carcasses of swallows, martins, warblers, and goldfinches, and also with those of thousands of rats, mice, and moles. Both brown field rabbits and white rabbits that residents of the area had been raising for food had been dying by the hundreds, and chickens by the thousands. Cats that survived were meowing piteously; dogs, which are known to be comparatively resistant to dioxin poisoning, looked sickly, and their behavior was reported to be nervous and aggressive.
>
> ... Inside Zone A [the zone closest to the reactor], the scene was desolate indeed, inhabited only by occasional hooded figures encased in impermeable white decontamination suits and boots and wearing face masks; scientists monitoring soil samples and veterinarians collecting dead animals in plastic bags. From time to time, shots could be heard as dying animals were put out of their misery and those still capable of moving were killed to prevent them from traveling out of the contaminated zone. Toxicological analysis demonstrated beyond doubt that most of the animals found dead had died from dioxin poisoning, and post-mortem examination showed extensive liver damage.[12]

Returning to Seveso two years later, Whiteside interviewed four doctors at Desio Hospital about their impressions of the effects of dioxin on the population. After explaining to Whiteside that they had requested qualified epidemiologists be sent to the area but "nobody has been sent so far," the doctors said that, because of the lack of information on abortion rates prior to the accident, it was difficult to determine just how many spontaneous abortions had occurred since the accident. "Many spontaneous abortions had undoubtedly not been recorded as such, or perhaps even noticed by mothers if they occurred early in pregnancy," the physicians said. They also told Whiteside about a small herd of cows fed grass grown in fields near the ICMESA factory. Thirteen of the cows had experienced spontaneous abortions, and out of three calves that were born only one survived more than a short time after birth. Because of the considerable amount of organic damage that had been observed in animals (dioxin had been discovered even in the livers of animals that had been considered healthy), the doctors felt it would make sense to assume that human beings would also have been affected by TCDD. In a study group of residents living outside Zone A, as well as some living in the upper half of Zone A, 35 percent of those examined had enlarged livers, said the doctors.[13]

In an attempt to verify or supplement the information he had learned from the Desio group, Whiteside checked with scientific sources in Milan, only to be told that symptoms of dioxin exposure that had been observed in and around Seveso included "diminished white-blood-cell counts, neurological disorders of various kinds, such as blurred vision and loss of conduction time in peripheral nerve tissue . . . disturbances of the endocrine system, and the normal functioning of the enzymatic system. Between 1976 and 1977 the incidence of infectious disease among the affected population tripled, and this striking increase has been interpreted by some specialists as an indication of the capacity of dioxin contamination adversely to affect the functioning of the immune systems of people living in the Seveso area."[14]

The birth rate in the area had also dropped sharply, and although Whiteside writes that some physicians thought this might have been due to the increased practice of birth control by women who were afraid of bearing defective children, a study by Dr. James Allen at the University of Wisconsin has demonstrated that TCDD causes female rhesus monkeys to abort their fetuses or, in spite of repeated mating, not to conceive at all. Out of eight rhesus monkeys fed TCDD at levels of 50 parts per trillion for seven months and then mated, four suffered spontaneous abortions, two did not conceive "although they were mated on repeated occasions" and only two were able to carry their infants to term. All eight of the control group of pregnant rhesus monkeys carried their babies to term.[15]

Whiteside also talked with people who lived near, but not

within, the most contaminated zone and found that they were suffering from a variety of physical and emotional problems commonly associated with dioxin exposure.

> Signora Brambilla said that a number of the people in the apartment house had developed blurred vision, which made it difficult for them to watch television. "So many people seem to have disturbances here on the block," she said. "It's not normal at all. They get dizzy spells and headaches, and there is still a lot of diarrhea. The doctors say the people's platelet counts are very low. They have skin problems, and when they go to the sea and it's windy the itching is terrible—*un tormento!*" She said she was convinced that there were a number of people on the block who really weren't well, adding, "But they won't say anything about it to the health authorities because they're ashamed to say that they ate fruit from the trees after the accident."[16]

Even if an epidemiological study were conducted in Zone A, it would not be conclusive in accessing the damage to residents of the surrounding area because no one has determined the exact extent to which dioxin was dispersed. What is certain is that the dioxin released in the accident did not fall in neat patterns upon the residents of a prescribed area, who could then be subjected to various tests to determine the deleterious effects of dioxin on human beings. "Traces of dioxin," wrote Whiteside, "have been found in mud as far south as Milan, thirteen miles away. Also, significant dioxin levels—whether spread directly by the toxic cloud or indirectly by the Seveso inhabitants themselves—kept turning up outside Zones A and B for months after the evacuation of the residents. And the incidence of chloracne among children of the inhabitants continued to increase."[17]

To argue that the incomplete, confusing, and contradictory epidemiological information from the Seveso accident proves that dioxin has not yet been proven harmful to human beings is rather like concluding that the accident at Three Mile Island proves that nuclear power is safe. Dioxin does not enter the body like a bullet, smashing through vital organs, splintering bone, and leaving the wounded or dying person physically helpless. Sometimes its effects are felt immediately in the form of nausea, vomiting, diarrhea, dizziness, bleeding from body orifices, and in just a few days the individual *appears* to recover completely. This seems to have been the case for many Seveso residents, but without constant medical monitoring for elevated porphyrin levels, without liver or fat biopsies, and careful statistical comparisons of Seveso residents to Italians living in nonexposed communities, how can anyone be sure that five, ten, fifteen years from now those exposed to dioxin will not begin succumbing to a host of symptoms similar to those which have damaged the health and taken the lives of Vietnam veterans? A decade ago, when the majority of Americans had returned from Southeast Asia, the claim might easily have been made that troops exposed to phenoxy herbicides suffered no adverse effects, save an occasional upset stomach, skin rash, or headache. Today that claim has been proven tragically untrue.

On July 22, 1980, Robert O. Muller, executive director of Vietnam Veterans' of America, told the Veterans' Affairs Subcommittee on Medical Facilities and Benefits about a Vietnam veteran who had tried to convince the Veterans Administration that he had been exposed to Agent Orange. The veteran had rashes on his legs and other symptoms of dioxin exposure, including recurring migraine headaches, severe chest pains, and respiratory problems. But the only treatment he had received from the VA was three and a half weeks in the psychiatric ward, and prescriptions for Valium, lithium, and sleeping pills. Unable to cope with being told that his chronic medical problems were psychiatric in nature, or with the apparent indifference of the nation for which he had fought, the veteran sent his wife and children away for the weekend and, said Muller, "put the VA prescribed pills to their final use." Muller, whose spine was shattered by a bullet in Vietnam, concluded his testimony as follows: "Mr. Chairman, there is, and has been, human evidence on the health impact of exposure to 2,4,5-T. Now, finally, the public recognizes that the evidence exists.

"That recognition allows us to push past the meaningless threshold debates to the fundamental questions. It allows us to stop saying, vacuously, that we need more evidence; and to start asking the serious questions: precisely how much evidence, and precisely what type of evidence, do we need?

"The VA's answer to this question is becoming regrettably clear. They are waiting for something like absolute certainty. The VA's theory of some fundamental biological distinction between Vietnam veterans and the rest of the human race is, of course, laughable. But it is, unfortunately, only the final implication of the VA's underlying quest for absolute certainty. But what is this 'certainty'? What does it require? More importantly, is the VA's 'certainty' achievable at all?"[18]

Although he was speaking on behalf of his fellow Vietnam veterans, the answer to Muller's questions, provided answers are forthcoming, will have profound implications for people throughout the industrialized world. How many studies of the effects of dioxin on rats, mice, monkeys, and guinea pigs must be done before scientists are able, or willing, to extrapolate from the results of these experiments the effects that dioxin might have on human beings? If human beings are so biologically distinct from other animals, then why bother researching the effects of dioxin at all? Why not just concede that no matter how much "anecdotal evidence" indicates a connection between dioxin and the suffering and death of human beings, there will never be "conclusive" evidence—because human beings are not rhesus monkeys or rats or mice.*

According to the Environmental Defense Fund, "the American population as a whole is Dow's guinea pig and the environment

---

*It interesting that other substances, including the artificial sweeteners, cyclamates, have been banned under the Federal Food, Drug and Cosmetic Act on the basis of studies showing they were carcinogenic in animals. And although scientists know less about the effects of formaldehyde than the components of Agent Orange on human health, at least three federal agencies have proposed regulating formaldehyde, while the Consumer Product Safety Commission believes it should be banned in certain home products.

is Dow's laboratory . . ." But in spite of Eriksson and Hardell's studies of Swedish workers, warnings from the World Health Organization about the toxicity of dioxin, and outbreaks of chloracne among its own workers, Dow Chemical continues to manufacture and market a product that its own scientists have admitted contains an animal carcinogen, and residuals of which Dow's scientists have discovered in beef fat from cattle grazed on rangelands where 2,4,5-T was sprayed. Dow's argument for continuing the company's crusade to keep this particular herbicide on the market is based, according to company spokesmen, not so much on *profit* as on *principle*. "We think," said one Dow spokesperson, "that 2,4,5-T is a very important symbol. If we were to lose on this issue, it would mean that American public customs would be beaten back a couple of hundred years to an era of witch hunting. Only this time the witches would be chemicals, not people, and that's the importance of this issue."[19]

Today we are all living in a laboratory where the cancer victim must prove that his or her illness is the "direct result" of having been exposed to one of the many toxic chemicals that are spewn into our air and water, sprayed upon our food and forests, and that inundate many of the places where we work. In the name of science we seem to have banished common sense to the dustbin of "anecdotal evidence," allowing multinational chemical companies to tamper dangerously with the ecology of our planet and the health of future generations.

Vietnam veterans came home believing they could eventually forget the horrors of guerrilla warfare and live long and productive lives. Unfortunately, for thousands of veterans the past decade has been the latency period during which dioxin would begin to slowly and then more rapidly attack their enzyme systems, damage their livers, weaken their hearts, and induce various types of cancers that would eventually destroy their young bodies. Yet it would appear that, more than three decades after 2,4,5-T and 2,4-D were first developed and marketed for commercial use and twenty years after the first defoliation mission, no institutes will be established to house scientists who might wish to examine the effects of herbicides on human health. Nor have any chairs been endowed at universities for the study of TCDD-dioxin on human beings, and it appears that no agency comparable to NASA will be funded to pay the salaries of the world's best scientific minds while they seek to discover just what is responsible for the maiming and killing of thousands of veterans.

"One need only look toward the efforts of the National Cancer Institute, and its Asbestos Information Program, or the American Cancer Society and its information on smoking, or the diethylstilbestrol programs that exist nationwide," Dr. Jeanne Stellman, associate professor of public health at Columbia University, told the Veterans' Affairs Committee of the House of Representatives, "to see what can be done if the national will, energy, and commitment are present. Surely our veterans and their service organizations, the people who served our nation at the peril of their lives, they and their families deserve the finest in research, in outreach, in information, in medical care that our country can put forth. Only minimal effort has thus far been forthcoming."[20]

Outside it is raining, and the sky has turned the color of a well-ripened plum. Dr. McNulty appears tired, his cough has gotten worse, and the frequency with which he glances at his watch leads me to conclude the interview has gone on long enough. As we shake hands and prepare to leave his office I ask if he would be willing to say that 2,4,5-T should be taken off the market altogether.

"Well," he replies, "it's toxic enough that common sense would say the less the better. As far as exposure to dioxin can be avoided, it should be. And I'll broaden that to say to the class of compounds which all appear to act alike, and that includes the dioxins and the polychlorinated dibenzofurans which are present in pentachlorophenol.* It's a much bigger source of dioxin here in Oregon than 2,4,5-T. I'm willing to say what my data is to anybody at any time, provided it has passed the gauntlet and has been accepted—that

*Used extensively as a wood preservative.

is, published—by my peers. That's no problem. I'll do that for anybody. And if I thought there was a social danger from it, then I would feel a personal obligation to speak out. But I can't do that just because I know dioxin is toxic and I treat it with extreme caution around here. I can't leap to a conclusion that I feel is unwarranted on a scientific basis, that it all ought to be stopped. That's always subject to revision, the way science is. There may be something next year or next month that will change my mind completely on that."

10

THE VIETNAMIZATION OF AMERICA

During the height of the war in Vietnam, television crews, newspaper reporters, and freelance writers followed American and Vietnamese troops into jungles, through swamps, and up mountains. Between toothpaste and shampoo commercials, Americans could watch helicopters strafe "enemy strongholds," see young Marines returning from an ambush or firefight, and watch the wounded being evacuated or the enemy dead counted following a battle. News coverage of the Vietnam War was so extensive, in fact, that some cynics began referring to the war as a "media event."

But what Americans did not see during the late sixties or throughout the seventies was the war being waged on their own environment, sometimes right in their own backyards. There were no crews from CBS to witness the Forest Service's spraying of Bob McKusick's homestead near Globe, Arizona, in 1968; nor were reporters on hand to observe Boston Edison's spraying of herbicides near a heavily populated suburb south of Boston in August 1979. When the Long Island Rail Road, without notifying the residents along its rights-of-way, doused homeowners' gardens and children with toxic herbicides, it didn't even make the local news. Like the troops in Vietnam, those who lived near national forests, power-line and railroad rights-of-way, or privately owned tree farms had been told—if they were told anything—not to worry; herbicides were harmless.

From 1965 until 1970, when the spraying of Agent Orange was suspended in Vietnam, the U.S. military covered approximately 5 million acres of Vietnam with herbicides. During those same years, ranchers, farmers, and the Forest Service sprayed 4.1 million acres of the American countryside *annually* with 2,4,5-T. The Forest Service alone sprayed more than 430,000 acres of national forest every year with 2,4,5-T in an attempt to kill broad-leaved plants that might block sunlight from pine and other coniferous saplings. Ranchers used 2,4,5-T to destroy anything that might interfere with livestock grazing, while rice growers sprayed it on about 100,000 acres, primarily in Arkansas and Mississippi, to kill parasite weeds like arrowhead, gooseweed, and ducksalad. In 1970, the USDA announced a set of limited restrictions on the use of 2,4,5-T; however, although the ban affected only about 20 percent of all 2,4,5-T used in the United States, Dow Chemical went to court, obtaining an injunction to prevent the Environmental Protection Agency from further regulations until more testing was done.* Until 1979, when the EPA's temporary and limited suspension order (which excluded rangelands and rice plantations) was issued, 2,4,5-T had been the most widely used herbicide in the country.

When the National Forest Service first sprayed Bob McKusick's land, he had no idea that herbicides could be harmful: "The first time was in 1968. The kids were little, and we were out on the clay deposit in Kellner Canyon with two dogs, just standing there on my property. A helicopter came across—and we're in plain sight—and we tried to wave it off but the spray drifted down on top of us. I had no reason to believe it was harmful because the Forest Service said it was completely harmless to birds and animals and humans and it just worked on brush. But it caused a rash, and my dog, Coyote, got pneumonia and almost died. A few months later he did die. I notified the Forest Service that we'd been sprayed, but I didn't know the stuff was bad."[1]

*See Appendix for a history of 2,4,5-T, pp. 183–185.

One year later a forest ranger phoned McKusick, who at the time was a professional potter and was fortunate enough to have found a piece of land that included clay deposits, telling him to put pie tins at each corner of his clay deposits to mark the area so it would not be sprayed. But, says McKusick, "they sprayed my clay deposit too." All of the complaining neighbors were sprayed, including a woman named Billie Shoecraft, who compiled more than a hundred files on chemical poisons before she died of cancer. For three consecutive days the Forest Service sprayed, and, explains McKusick, "We all got bleeding ears; in fact we had bleeding from all body orifices. There's this disease called IHS—internal hemorrhaging syndrome. In Vietnam 1,300 war dogs got it and the government said it wasn't because they were spraying with Agent Orange. The dogs got a virus, they said, and had to be destroyed. Well, after the 1969 spraying, we had IHS and I can't tell you how many horses and cows had it."

Animals in the canyon began dying, giving birth to deformed offspring, lying paralyzed on the ground. Some even forgot how to breed. Before the spraying, McKusick recalls, there were no problems, no deformities or miscarriages. But in 1969, "60 to 70 percent of our goats were born deformed, and we've had heavy deformities ever since."

McKusick, who has had a series of heart attacks during the fourteen years since the spraying, adds, "I can't prove any of this was caused by the spray, but all I can say is that before the spray I was healthy as a horse. The doctor told me I would never have heart trouble. And our family did not have a history of illness . . ."

The McKusicks and other families living in the spray zone attempted to find help in their struggle to get the Forest Service to stop the spraying, but to no avail. "We went to everyone we could think of and nobody would help us. We went to Senator Barry Goldwater and he couldn't be bothered . . . We asked Governor Jack Williams for help and he laughed. Representative Sam Steiger was the only exception. He tried to help, but he simply didn't have the weight to stop it . . .

"When they first sprayed, the Forest Service said the stuff

would disappear in twenty-four hours. Then they changed their story and said it would be gone in three days, and then in thirty days . . . In [over fourteen] years, not one family here has dared to use their own well water."

The McKusicks sued Dow Chemical and, after nearly a decade of legal delays, agreed to settle out of court for an undisclosed sum. But money, says McKusick, can never compensate for so many years of insecurity and hardship. "It's very easy for somebody who has not had his family and himself sick for twelve years, his animals dying around him, and people laughing at him and criticizing him and never helping to say you should have gone and fought it for another three months and then when you won it and they appealed you could wait another ten or eleven years to get back in court and then they'd appeal it again and you could wait another ten or eleven years—just where in the hell does anybody think we're going to get the strength to do it?

"We settled because of what life we have left and I'll be honest with you, I don't know. My wife has had things removed from her; I've had growths removed from me; friends have had growths. I've had heart problems; three or four times I've collapsed. Of course, a lot of people have died.

"The only good thing we've got going for us is, I don't know if they'll spray it somewhere else, but I know they won't come back here."

Like Vietnam veterans Paul Reutershan, Charles Owen, and Ed Juteau, Billie Shoecraft died believing her cancer was the result of having been exposed to herbicides. Like other Americans who have sued Dow Chemical, the McKusicks grew tired of waiting for their day in court, settling as others have for an undisclosed sum of money from a company that insists there is still no evidence that 2,4,5-T harms humans. While publicly defending its product against "chemical witch hunters," Dow has quietly paid off those who seemed to have a solid case against 2,4,5-T, thus managing to avoid the possibility of an embarrassing day in court.

For the McKusicks the battle against toxic herbicides may be over, but for Americans living near power lines, railroad rights-of-way, national forests, or private timber companies, the continued spraying of herbicides is both disturbing and frightening. Their fears are often based on far more than what Dow has called "anecdotal evidence." For example, many residents of the Alsea region in Oregon, which includes the Siuslaw National Forest, are aware that dioxin was discovered in eight of thirty-two wild-life samples taken from the forest, in the breast milk of one out of six women living within the Siuslaw, and in "extremely high levels" in the garden soil of a young woman who had experienced four spontaneous abortions in three years while living adjacent to the National Forest. And they have read about seventeen tree planters working on Bureau of Land Management land that had been sprayed eleven months earlier with both 2,4-D and Silvex becoming ill with symptoms of herbicide poisoning, and an eight-year-old girl who contracted a rare blood disease, and whose tap water contained the same herbicides doctors discovered in her blood.[2] And of course they remember being told that when sprayed from helicopters herbicides are harmless to humans and animals because "they biodegrade so rapidly that by the time they hit the ground they are perfectly innocuous."

On April 11, 1978, a high school teacher by the name of Bonnie Hill, along with seven women residing in the Alsea region, sent a letter to the Environmental Protection Agency suggesting that until herbicides were proven safe, their use in the State of Oregon be stopped. The eight women had experienced a total of eleven miscarriages, all but one occurring during the spring (peak) spraying season, and nine of the miscarriages occurring in the first trimester of pregnancy. The one woman who experienced a miscarriage in the fall lived in an area that had been sprayed in the fall of that year. In their letter the women declared: "Even the latest Forest Service Environmental Impact Statement admits that 'All chemicals are capable of causing toxic effects upon the developing embryo . . . Chemicals can become available to the embryo in spite of the mother's excretion and metabolism capabilities.' " Copies of the letter were also mailed to Oregon legislators, agencies and companies using herbicides, the editorial pages of major Oregon newspapers, and other health and environmental agencies the women felt might be sympathetic.

The letter was the result of a grass-roots research effort by Mrs. Hill, which began when she read about the findings of Dr. James Allen at the University of Wisconsin and Dr. Wilbur McNulty at the Oregon Regional Primate Research Center. In their research with primates Allen and McNulty discovered that rhesus monkeys fed minute doses of TCDD frequently miscarried, often in the first trimester of pregnancy. Hill, whose home is completely surrounded by land managed by the BLM, had experienced a miscarriage in the spring of 1975, and when she discovered that Silvex and 2,4-D had been sprayed not far from her home just a month before she lost her baby, she decided it was time to find out if other women in the Alsea region had experienced similar problems.

"I just started asking around," Hill explains, "and every time I found out about a spontaneous abortion it had occurred in the spring. That's what was so unusual. Up until recently I didn't find out about any miscarriages that had happened at any other time of year."

We are standing beside a counter in the home-economics room of the high school where Hill teaches, and as we talk she mixes the ingredients for a dessert she plans to take to a retirement dinner that evening. Apologizing for having to make the dessert, Hill offers her young daughter a graham cracker, and continues. "I think I was fairly cautious about it in the beginning, but the evidence just seemed to build over a period of about a year and a half. Every once in a while I would find out about another miscarriage, and when I found out about the eleventh, I started asking some rather serious questions about the possibility of a correlation between springtime spraying and miscarriages in the vicinity surrounding or very near the spray zones."

Hill began calling agencies and private industries that owned land in the Alsea area to inquire about when and where they had applied herbicides. "I did tell them immediately about my concern. I didn't try to hide anything. I just explained that I had discovered that several miscarriages had occurred in the spring, and that I was trying to find out just where and when they might have sprayed. I wanted to go back for a number of years, and I do remember one man at a private company expressing great surprise that any kind of health problem might be associated with herbicides. But later he was very open about giving me information, something I didn't find everyone quite so willing to do. Another company gave me different kinds of information at different times, and in fact there were quite a few discrepancies in the information they gave me. But I think in general that the recordkeeping on the 'when' and 'where' of herbicide spraying has been nothing short of deplorable when you consider the possible health implications of these substances. Even Oregon State University, which has long been an outspoken proponent of herbicide spraying, has stated that the recordkeeping of the actual spraying is terrible.

"One of the problems is determining just who owns the land. If you look at a map of this area it's really a checkerboard pattern, with someone owning a few square acres here, and someone else owning a few square acres there, so if we saw somebody spraying with a helicopter out there right now"—pointing to one of the snowcapped mountains that appear to be just a short walk from Alsea's high school—"it would take us a long time to determine just who owned that land. Sometimes if someone is spraying even just across the hill from where you live, you still might not know just who owns that land.

"So there are really no natural barriers between the houses and the land being sprayed, and it's almost impossible to avoid drift from the spraying. In fact the Bureau of Land Management did a study in the Coos Bay area under very controlled circumstances, observing all the current required buffer zones along the streams, and they found that *70 percent of the time* the herbicide was entering the water. And the EPA has documented drift up to twenty-two miles. But most of the studies were done on flat land under pretty controlled circumstances of wind and weather, and herbicide users have based their conclusions on these studies. But when you consider the actual conditions on the coast of Oregon, where there are mountains and hills and air currents running in and out of those hills, it's just really unpredictable. And being twenty miles from the coast as the crow flies, our area has equally unpredictable precipitation patterns. They will be sure that we're going to have a nice day, and yet eight hours later it's raining. They're supposed to have a clear weather sign for twenty-four hours once they have decided to spray, but Oregon's weather is notorious for its unpredictability, especially in the spring, which of course is the peak season for herbicide spraying."

By establishing a "buffer zone" between areas to be sprayed and sources of water, the Forest Service and other proponents of herbicides have been able to rationalize the use of substances contaminated with dioxin. Theoretically this zone will keep herbicides and herbicide contaminants from entering the drinking water or food chain, but in reality the Oregon coastal area has been a herbicidal free-fire zone for a number of years. Theoretical buffer zones, explains Hill, do not prevent area residents from being exposed directly to herbicides. "Right after we sent our letter to the EPA an environmental group in Portland tried to get the buffer zones increased, but 75 percent of the State Board of Forestry is composed of timbermen, so needless to say the proposition failed. And just because the EPA temporarily suspended certain uses of Silvex and 2,4,5-T doesn't mean the spraying of herbicides hasn't continued. Just this year, for example, a woman was at her house one afternoon and there's a helicopter spraying across, just about a quarter of a mile from her house. And she had all of her windows open because it was a beautiful day, although quite windy, and all of a sudden she smells something and she knows it's a herbicide. So she gets on the phone and she tries to find out who it is that's spraying, but she can't find out. And she makes several telephone calls, and all of a sudden it's five o'clock and all of the offices are closed. She calls the Forest Service and they can't help her, even though all the helicopters use the same helipad, *all of them.*

"She calls the State Board of Forestry, which is supposed to have the permits for everybody, and they can't help her. She calls a few private companies, and she can't find out. Everybody's closed over the weekend, and finally it's Monday afternoon when she finds out the name of the company that has sprayed. Meanwhile, she has become very sick and her children are very sick. Her nose and throat were burning, her eyes were irritated, and her son was vomiting."

Four days later, on a Tuesday morning, the company responsible for the spraying sent someone to take blood and urine samples, which, when tested for residues of herbicides, turned out negative.

"But this is meaningless," says Hill, who has delegated the dessert-making to her teenage daughter and, having poured us each a second cup of coffee, is seated across from me at a table in the home-economics room. "There's a doctor in Coos Bay who has worked for some time with people who've been exposed to herbicides, and he points out that just because they don't find traces in your blood or urine doesn't mean it isn't someplace else in your body. For example, dioxin is stored in fat tissue. And even if the herbicide has passed through your body there's no proof that it hasn't done some damage in passage. An X-ray also passes through your body, but it can do some damage as it travels through. But of course this is all hearsay, you know. In a court of law it would be just that—hearsay."

One of the most fascinating and incriminating aspects of the history of herbicide use is that whether reports have come from Vietnamese peasants, Oregon housewives, Arizona potters, or mothers living near the Long Island Rail Road, complaints about the effects of 2,4,5-T on humans and animals have been remarkably similar.

In Minnesota, a homesteader who had searched for five years to find land that had not been sprayed with chemicals fired a shotgun at a Forest Service helicopter. But according to columnist Jack Anderson:

It returned the next day and thoroughly sprayed the forest adjoining the land. Subsequent testing of his water supply by Minnesota health authorities showed traces of herbicide containing dioxin.

Within a few days of the spraying, his family suffered headaches, nausea, dizziness and diarrhea . . .

Another horror story is told by Neddie Freedlund, a farm wife in Wisconsin. After a neighbor sprayed his land with 2,4,5-T, she reports her entire family was seized with intense bellyaches, fever and sleeplessness.

Her baby began screaming in agony and pulling out his hair until bald spots appeared. She subsequently has suffered three miscarriages although she had previously borne six healthy children.

Freedlund also claims that similar maladies affected her barnyard. There was a dramatic decline in the quantity and quality of the milk produced by two cows. Her pigs gave birth to piglets that were either abnormally large or small. Rabbits had premature and deformed offspring.[3]

In his paper "The Effects of Herbicides in South Vietnam," Dr. Gerald C. Hickey—who was affiliated with Cornell University's Southeast Asia Program when the paper was published by the National Academy of Sciences, National Research Council—describes the effects of defoliants on Vietnamese highlanders. The highlanders' descriptions of the effects of herbicides on their land, animals, and their own health are in many cases similar to those of Americans who have been exposed to herbicides.

There was a definite pattern in the perceptions regarding the effect of the herbicides on those residing in or near the sprayed zones. The most common symptoms reported were abdominal pains and diarrhea. Informants from Long Djon also reported that in addition to these symptoms, the villagers complained of experiencing a stinging sensation in their nasal passages just after the spray drifted into the settlement. Many developed coughs that lasted more than a month. At Dak Rosa, according to some residents, many villagers went into the swiddens following the spraying, and in addition to the common symptoms noted above, these people broke out with skin rashes that lasted many weeks. Dak Tang Plun residents also reported widespread skin rashes, cramps, diarrhea, and fevers. A Plei Ro-O informant reported these same symptoms, noting that some villagers coughed blood.

Polei Krong informants stated that the villagers suffered these same ailments, that the skin rashes looked "like they had been burned, with small blisters all over the red areas." Dak Siang informants noted that after some of the villagers drank from the stream which was in the sprayed area, they became ill with abdominal pains and diarrhea that lasted for days. They also reported that some villagers had eaten bamboo shoots from the sprayed area, after which they became dizzy "like you feel when you have drunk too much from the wine jar," and this was followed by vomiting. Polei Krong residents, according to one informant, fell ill with abdominal pains, diarrhea, vomiting, and fever within one day after the spraying . . .

A difficult area of inquiry concerned possible deaths due to the herbicides. Sickness and death are common occurrences in highland villages, and infant mortality is particularly high. Some of the informants expressed the opinion that there was an unusually high number of deaths, particularly among children, following the spraying. However, they were very cautious in concluding that the spraying affected childbirth.

Informants from Long Djon had reported a stinging in the nasal passages just after the spray drifted over the settlement, and this was followed by villagers being afflicted with coughs. They added that more children than adults were affected, and that "many children died." The victims developed skin rashes, and those with rashes that did not clear up died. One elderly lady noted that she knew of one stillborn case following the spraying, but she could not say whether it was due to the herbicide (she, like other informants, always pointed out that stillbirths were not unusual in their villages). At Dak Rosa informants attributed the outbreak of skin rashes to the fact that many villagers went into the swiddens following the spraying. They also noted that some women carried their small children on their backs in the fields, and they brushed against leaves containing the "medicine" that had been sprayed. Some of these children subsequently developed bad rashes all over their bodies. They looked, the informants said, "like insect bites," and all the victims died. One informant knew of three such deaths.

Another informant reported knowing of five stillbirths after the mothers, during pregnancy, had worked in the sprayed swiddens. The informants felt that there was an unusually high number of such deaths following the spraying.

Most of the informants interviewed reported widespread deaths among their domestic animals following the spraying. The Long Djon informants noted that since they were refugees they had few animals, but most of their chickens and pigs died shortly after the spraying, and the Dak Rosa villagers reported the same thing. Informants from Dak Tang Plun said that all of their chickens, most of their pigs, and some of their cattle died, and the young man from Plei Ro-O reported the same thing, specifying that this occurred within four or five days after the spraying. He also noted that villagers found a number of dead wild animals, particularly wild boar, in the nearby forests. Polei Krong informants also pointed out they found dead wild boar in the forest. They, too, saw all of their chickens, pigs, dogs, and small cattle die, although big cattle survived. Both the Polei Kleng and the Plci Jar Tum villagers said that their pigs, dogs, and chickens died, and the latter added that they also lost cattle. Plei Ngol Drong informants reported that all of their pigs, chickens, dogs, goats (they noted that goats are "very strong"), and cattle died . . .

Although some of these reports may sound highly exaggerated, Dr. Hickey and others have pointed out that before the U.S. sprayed their villages and farmlands, the highlanders of Vietnam had never been exposed to synthetic drugs or chemicals, and it is conceivable that their susceptibility to herbicides was much greater than that of people living in highly industrialized nations where even tests on young children have demonstrated that their bodies contain residues of synthetic substances. Some areas of Vietnam were also sprayed repeatedly with Agent Orange containing levels of TCDD hundreds of times higher than the dioxin content of 2,4,5-T now in use in the United States. Yet even after Dow had "refined" its production process to reduce the content of dioxin in 2,4,5-T, the effects of this herbicide on animals and humans have been extremely toxic, although without a national effort to determine just how many people have become ill, died, lost their farm animals, and left their land because of herbicide spraying, the full extent of the problem may never be known.

Consider, for example, the case of Eve and Vern DeRock, who were living on a farm in an Oregon valley sprayed by International Paper Company in March 1977. One week after the spraying, fifteen of the DeRock's experimental cows aborted their calves. But like so many people who believed that "killing off a few weeds" would never do anyone harm, the DeRocks dismissed the miscarriages as "bad luck" and tried to re-breed their heifers. Out of fifty-four, only six conceived and the DeRocks, totally unaware that TCDD could be stored in beef fat, wound up butchering a few cows for their own use and selling the rest. The following spring when the surviving cows gave birth, five of their offspring were born with gross deformities and died within four days. Soon the DeRocks began experiencing stomach pains, loss of strength, and "summer colds" that seemed to resist ordinary treatment. Following a fire in an area of their farm that had been treated with herbicides just a few weeks earlier, Vern collapsed. And after a series of tests, doctors performed exploratory surgery on Eve, only to discover chronic liver failure, sending her home with the expectation that she would die as soon as her liver stopped functioning.[4]

But through all this the DeRocks did not stop eating the beef and butter they had stored in their freezer. No one from the company that was spraying herbicides or a state or federal health agency appeared to explain to them how dioxin gets into the food chain and consequently into the human body. More than a year after their land had been sprayed and their lives disrupted, if not ruined, the DeRocks happened to see a documentary on Vietnam veterans that explained the health effects of Agent Orange. The documentary also described the research of Vietnamese doctors who have linked Agent Orange to liver cancer in their own country, and the very next day the DeRocks stopped eating the meat and butter they had stored. Their health began to improve, but they have not been compensated for their suffering and, they realize, the Vietnamization of Oregon continues. Even after the emotional and financial hardships the DeRocks have endured, they cannot be sure that the helicopters will not return—there is no law to prevent them from doing so.

Bonnie Hill has heard this story, and many others. But, she sighs, "after all that's gone on, it would still be virtually impossible to prove in a court of law that you had been exposed and then, even worse, that what happened afterwards was the result of that exposure. That's one thing that happened with the miscarriages. Dow just dredged up every possible factor that could influence a miscarriage or spontaneous abortion. Well, of course there are a lot of things that can cause miscarriages, but I really resent their insinuations—it's been a little more than that, actually—that this is a great area for growing marijuana, and it's because we don't want our marijuana plantations killed off that we're against spraying. Someone has also spread the rumor that our miscarriages are because we are 'remnants of the sixties flower children' who overindulge in drugs. I've lived here for eleven years, and I can assure you that opponents of herbicide spraying come from all walks of life. Some of them even work for the timber industry, and there are absolutely no marijuana plantations in the Alsea area. That's one ploy that just won't work—not here, anyway."

Dow has also challenged the EPA's decision to place a limited suspension order on domestic use of 2,4,5-T,* arguing that the Alsea study was not comprehensive enough to merit the EPA's conclusions.

"One of the problems we have had all along," Hill explains, "is that the media has always given people the impression that the EPA's study was based on only nine women living in the Alsea area, when in fact the EPA actually covered a 1,600-square-mile area, and of course years of research into the effects of 2,4,5-T influenced their decision as well. I don't mean to disparage the

---

*Although the EPA passed its suspension order on certain domestic uses of 2,4,5-T in February 1979, there is evidence that the use of this herbicide has actually increased each year since the suspension order was passed.

media altogether, because we received international coverage and it was rather surprising, even a bit overwhelming, because people came from New Zealand, England, Germany, and Australia to talk with us, and this of course increased people's awareness of this problem. Our main criticism of the EPA study is that they only examined hospital records, rather than talking with more of the people who lived in this area, because very few spontaneous abortions are treated in hospitals these days. They are almost all treated in doctor's offices, or people don't go to the doctor at all; it's just something that happens in their homes. Out of the first eleven spontaneous abortions that we found out about, only *two* had been treated in hospitals, and that's a fairly representational figure —all the rest being treated in doctor's offices—so if the EPA really wanted to get a true feeling of what was going on here they should have gone to doctors' offices, which is something we pressed for from the very beginning. So actually, in spite of our good feelings about the suspension order, we still feel that no one has really taken a thorough look at just what has been going on here."

Prior to the EPA's Emergency Suspension Order, 2,4,5-T was undergoing scrutiny through a process called RPAR, or "Rebuttable Presumption Against Registration." Having decided that on the basis of its evidence there were serious questions involved in the continued domestic use of 2,4,5-T, the EPA had announced that it was considering canceling registration for this product, but would give the manufacturer the opportunity to present arguments for keeping the herbicide on the market. The Emergency Suspension Order superseded RPAR and the two hearings were merged into one, which was to be divided into two sections—first, the risks involved in, and second, the benefits derived from using 2,4,5-T.

During the second section of the EPA's hearings, Dow Chemical was joined by fifty-four corporations and trade associations, including the National Cattlemen's Association, the National Forest Products Association, and the American Farm Bureau in opposing the EPA's possible cancellation of 2,4,5-T. The U.S.

Department of Agriculture also intervened with information that supported Dow's position. Intervening on behalf of affected citizens were the Environmental Defense Fund and the Northwest Coalition for Alternatives to Pesticides (NCAP), an organization with fifty member groups in five northwestern states. Following arguments in favor of and against the continued registration of 2,4,5-T, an administrative law judge was to make a recommendation to the EPA's administrator, whose decision would be subject to a lengthy appeals process. But in March 1981, before testimony had been completed, the EPA agreed with Dow's request to suspend the hearings and negotiate a settlement behind closed doors.

"Our reaction to the news was one of anger," wrote the NCAP staff in their quarterly magazine, *NCAP News*. "To so compromise a public process as to render it meaningless is an outrage to all citizens. Instead of an orderly public airing of the risks and benefits of 2,4,5-T and a decision by an administrative law judge, we have gotten the backroom deal. The closed-door negotiations have short-circuited the orderly hearing process, stifled the disclosure of essential information, and effectively excluded citizen representation."[5]

"I think they knew that no one really had any information on the benefits of T, either economic or otherwise," laughs Hill, "but no matter which way things go, Dow pretty much wins because the EPA will be closed down before long anyway. The Reagan administration didn't even appoint an administrator for the agency until four months after the president took office, and their funding has been cut by 40 percent this year; yet they were always *under* funded. And it's ironic that at a time when the EPA seems to be needed more than ever, some of the best people are leaving because they are unable to deal with the frustration of working for an administrator and an administration whose idea of regulating the environment is that you should pretty much let industry do whatever it wishes."

As I listen to Bonnie Hill it becomes increasingly clear that she has not come to these mountains to be a weekend woodswoman, stapling NO HUNTING OR TRESPASSING signs to the trees on her acreage so the rednecks won't ravage the wildlife. Nor has she chosen a life style that will enable her to return to her parents' suburban home and, while the bathtub fills with steaming water, rail against the parasitical and platitudinous quality of urban-suburban life. She does not like what some of the people who work for the BLM, Forest Service, or private timber companies are doing to the land, but she does not hate the men who are doing it. Having lived not just *on* but *in* the land for over a decade, she realizes that the ice-clear streams, the trees, centuries old and draped in layers of lichen, the elk and the deer and the trout can get along without human beings; but she cannot imagine her family getting along without the land. What seems to upset and bewilder her the most is why everyone doesn't love the forests as much as she and her neighbors do—a question that has perplexed Native Americans for more than two hundred years. The answer, as she has heard more than one professor of Ag-Economics say, "is of course complex."

Although even the most fervent opponents of 2,4,5-T would concede that Dow has managed to reduce the amount of TCDD in this herbicide, no one is quite certain just how much 2,4,5-T is currently being sprayed on rangelands and rice plantations, or even how much of this herbicide is actually manufactured each year. The amount produced is considered a trade secret, but even if one were able to determine the exact number of gallons produced, it would be difficult, if not impossible, to discover with any precision just where and in what quantities 2,4,5-T is being used. Neither the EPA nor the states in which herbicides are used have the financial resources or manpower to spot-check even a small percentage of the helicopters that douse our national forests, rangelands, and rice plantations with defoliants. Moreover, there is little if any environmental testing for residues of TCDD that might find their way into the water, soil, and food chain following the application of herbicides contaminated with dioxin.

Speaking of the difficulties involved in such testing, Dr. Arthur H. Westing, chairman of the Science Department at Hampshire

College and a man whom Dow considers one of the "fifty-nine top world experts on dioxin," explains that "In the whole world there are only about six or eight laboratories that have the capabilities of measuring dioxin at the levels of concern, and I think four of these labs are here in this country. There's one in Wisconsin, there's one at Harvard, Nebraska, Beltsville, and possibly Du Pont can do it; so there's four or five labs. There's one lab in Switzerland and one in Sweden, and those are the only labs in the whole world where you can do the kind of dioxin analysis that needs to be done in order to examine the levels of concern. But we're talking about a theoretical capability that, however, doesn't exist. For example, consider Canada, a developed country, a rich country with a large forestry industry that uses, or did use, a lot of 2,4,5-T, yet they could not test for dioxin. There was no laboratory in the country where they could see whether a problem was building up in the environment. On the other hand, it's not so difficult, although it is still difficult, to do the testing on the actual 2,4,5-T. Probably thirty or forty labs can do that around the country. You're talking about *parts of tenths of hundreds of parts per million* of a chemical, that is dioxin in this case, and so where the problem lies is that if Dow goes perking along and says, 'We're making the stuff and it's safe,' you have to take their word for it. But I shouldn't pick out Dow, I mean any company. You just have to take their word for it because you and I couldn't test for it. I was in Vermont and I discovered that neither the Vermont Department of Health nor the University of Vermont had the capability of checking whether or not the shipments of 2,4,5-T coming in were safe. No one in the entire state has this capability. Now you can tool up for that, but it hasn't been done.

"But to go back to the question of environmental testing, that now costs $750 to $1,000 a sample if you have it done by contract. For instance, you could ship it to the University of Nebraska and they'll do it for you, but obviously you can't do that very often. So the problem is not that you might not be able to reduce the content of dioxin in a herbicide so it might be a conceivably safe level, but that you must take the chemical companies' word that the shipments will come through safe. And secondly, you can't continually test to see whether there is a buildup in one place or another, because beyond the safe manufacture of chemicals there has to be some assurance that they will be safely used. In other words, even if the applicators are told that they shouldn't spray into a stream or reservoir, who's really going to find out whether they do it or not? Because who's out there in the woods watching them every day?

"And then, of course, what about accidents? In Missouri, for example, someone in totally good faith got rid of wastes that had dioxin in them, and then the people who were paid to get rid of the waste, rather than doing it in a proper way, simply dumped it along the wayside. Nobody can really test for it readily without a lot of money and expertise, so how do we really know whether or not Vermont Yankee [a nuclear power station], which is just up the road from here, releases an unsafe level of radiation one day? They aren't going to tell anybody about it. They do or they don't, but you don't know if they do or they don't. And it's the same with dioxin, and it's a nasty thing."

The Missouri incident to which Dr. Westing refers occurred in 1971 at three horse arenas in eastern Missouri that had been sprayed with waste oil containing approximately 328 parts per million dioxin. The oil came from a plant that produced 2,4,5–T for use in Agent Orange during the Vietnam War, and later made hexachlorophene. Shortly before the Northeastern Pharmaceutical and Chemical Company, which leased the plant, went out of business, it hired a waste hauler to remove 18,000 gallons of contaminated oil. The hauler, who later signed an affidavit declaring he was unaware that the oil contained dioxin, sprayed 5,000 gallons of his cargo on the three horse arenas to keep down dust.

According to Thomas Whiteside, of the eighty-five horses exercised in the arenas, fifty-eight became ill and forty-three died.[*] At least twenty-six pregnant mares aborted, and foals exposed in

---

[*]The total number of dead horses was approximately 62.

utero died at birth or soon after. Six of the foals were born with birth deformities. In addition to the horses, hundreds of rodents, birds, cats, and dogs died, ten people reported rashes, headaches, and diarrhea, and two children were hospitalized, one of them with an inflamed kidney and internal bleeding. Twelve years later the children are still ill and have been warned by doctors that they "face an increased risk of cancer and birth defects."[6]

In October 1982, the Environmental Protection Agency confirmed that significant levels of dioxin have been found in fourteen sites in Missouri, and that eleven more sites in that state may contain dangerous amounts of dioxin. The EPA also said that approximately *forty-eight pounds* of dioxin contained in the waste oil from Northeastern Pharmaceutical are missing. Investigators have found dioxin in fish caught up to eighty miles downstream from the plant, and dangerous levels of dioxin have been discovered in a residential area where soil removed from the three horse arenas was deposited in 1973.

Most disturbing about the Missouri incident is that the company responsible for disposing of the toxic waste did so without attempting to find out what effect the chemicals might have on the environment, a practice so widespread in the United States that at least one state, New York, has trained an armed task force to prevent the continued dumping of toxic wastes into its landfills, lakes, rivers, and forests. Shortly before the first members of the task force completed their training, dioxin had been discovered in striped bass caught in the Hudson River, and in forty-five fish samples taken from Lake Ontario.

Can the Environmental Protection Agency, inadequately funded and understaffed, really protect the American environment from the deluge of pesticides, herbicides, and other toxic substances that, their manufacturers argue, are necessary if we are to "maintain economic growth and a high standard of living"? There is reason to believe that it cannot. In 1972, with the passage of the Federal Environmental Pesticide Control Act (FEPCA), Congress provided the EPA with a legal basis by which it could "duly process all new pesticide registration applications and pesticide residue tolerance petitions," as well as review and, "only if compatible with human and environmental health," register some of the approximately 50,000 pesticides previously registered over the past thirty years. Congress set October 1976 as the deadline for the completion of this Herculean task.

Under FEPCA, the EPA was responsible for determining whether pesticides registered would "perform their intended function without unreasonable adverse effects" on human health and the environment.

> In addition to more conventional toxicity data, pesticide companies were required under FEPCA to show: 1) animal testing data, indicating whether their products could cause birth defects, tumors, and interference with reproductive capacity or other harmful chronic effects and 2) data on the effects of exposure to fish, mammals and birds. If the administrator of the EPA determines through a risk/benefit analysis of a certain pesticide that it causes "unreasonable adverse effects" he or she may "restrict, suspend, or cancel the use of the pesticide."[7]

Faced with a monumental task and a minimum of human power to accomplish it, the EPA began devising shortcuts for reviewing data, one of which was the organization of products of a similar chemical structure into "batches." Thus the EPA managed to cut down the number of products it reviewed from the 50,000 that are actually on the market to the 1,400 active ingredients in those products—a practice that failed to consider either the possible consequences of combining these ingredients in one product or the toxic properties of what scientists have called "inert" ingredients. Short of qualified staff that could evaluate complicated data on the effects of a particular substance on laboratory animals, the EPA's task force resorted to a cursory examination of data that had been submitted to the agency by manufacturers in support of reregistration of their products. Although manufacturers often failed to include any chronic toxicity testing in their "research conclusions," the EPA staff routinely decided the safety of a product on the basis of the manufacturer's "research." This "cooperation" continued in spite of the fact that "in virtually every instance, independent pathologists diagnosed many more cancerous and precancerous tumors in the test animals than did the original manufacturer's laboratory pathologists."[8]

The story of 2,4-D reregistration by the EPA in April 1976 is typical of the EPA's casual and cursory approach to the reregistration of pesticides.

On April 8, 1976, EPA mailed reregistration guidance packages to manufacturers of 670 products containing 2,4-D for which more than 45 residue tolerances have been granted on such foods as dairy milk, eggs, poultry, meat, corn, apples, vegetables, and citrus fruits. The guidance packages cited a two-year rat and dog feeding study performed by FDA in 1963 as "sufficient" to satisfy the "chronic" safety testing requirements for reregistration. Yet a summary report on the study in EPA's files stated that there was "increased tumor formation" in the rats . . . An independent pathologist, who reviewed the raw data on the study at the request of subcommittee staff, concluded that 2,4-D "is carcinogenic in rats."[9]

Despite its rather slipshod methods of determining whether a particular chemical should be reregistered, the EPA can not be held responsible for the *quality* of the data upon which it must base its decisions. Nor can one hold the EPA accountable for the fact that some of the data it has received is not only poor in quality but *fraudulent*. According to a federal grand jury's indictments against four former officials of Industrial Bio-Test Laboratories, once considered one of the most important industrial laboratories in America, the company fabricated results of two cancer studies on the herbicide Sencor and the insecticide Nemacur, submitting the results of "tests" to the EPA in support of registration of those products.

The indictment also accuses the officials of "concealing the fact that TCC (trichlorocarbanilide), an antibacterial agent used in deodorant soaps manufactured by Monsanto Corp., caused atrophy in the testes at the lowest dose tested in mice . . ."[10] "They also fabricated results of blood and urine studies which were never performed on Syntex Corp.'s anti-arthritic drug Naprosyn, according to the indictment."[11] Curiously enough, even though the EPA may have based its decision to register a product or products on falsified laboratory data, this is not considered grounds for removing the product from the market. After receiving permission from the EPA, Mobay, a Pittsburgh-based subsidiary of Bayer AG of West Germany, continued selling Sencor and Nemacur.[12]

Industrial Bio Test Laboratories is bankrupt, its deserted laboratories a mausoleum to bad faith. And yet, in spite of the fact that the EPA has declared many similar tests "worthless," one has to wonder how many products are still on the market because of "data" submitted to the EPA for review by manufacturers who trusted the results of "scientific studies" performed by a "reputable" laboratory.

"You know," Bonnie Hill says, pausing as though she has just remembered a very important and unpleasant fact, "I don't really think they will bring 2,4,5-T back. They will probably just let it remain where it is, that is, not pass a ban, but refuse Dow's request to lift the suspension order. I may be fooling myself, but I can't conceive of them bringing it back after all that has gone on. I think there will be a lot of very angry and very frustrated people if they do. Because the feeling, the level of frustration, is pretty high now because of what they are spraying. You know, Dow loves to say, 'Oh, these people are against anything; they're just against all sprays.' And I sometimes would say, 'That just isn't true, we really are trying to look at these substances one by one and trying to consider each in what we think is a fair manner.' And I think that is still true for a lot of us, but I also think that a lot of people who live here are feeling very frustrated that people are just coming in whenever they feel like it and spraying with helicopters —we don't know what—*very close to our homes.* I think there is a misconception among our Oregon legislators, and maybe people in general, that this is happening in pretty remote areas, but that just isn't true. In fact, just three days ago, just a half mile from Alsea, a helicopter was spraying as people were bringing their children to preschool. There was a helicopter spraying just across the highway, and people were pretty upset about that. We just don't know *when* they are going to spray, and we don't know *who* is spraying, and we don't know *what* they are spraying. And I just think that's a right that we should have. We have a right to know what's going on in our own backyard. They've continued the use of 2,4-D around here, even though a Canadian study has shown it to be carcinogenic; and some of the other things they're using could be equally or even more dangerous than T for all we know. The chemical companies just keep on making products, and we continue to be their guinea pigs.

"Of course, in spite of all the adverse publicity 2,4,5-T has received, there are people who still argue that we—that is, those of us who would like to see it banned for good—are just trying to wreck the economy or some nonsense like that. Right after the EPA's suspension order was announced, the governor of Oregon released a ludicrous report about how many billions of dollars and thousands of jobs would be lost if 2,4,5-T were removed from the market. But you could ask anyone in Alsea, a community that's almost 100 percent dependent on the timber industry, about that. I mean, how many jobs are provided by a helicopter coming in and spraying, and how many jobs would be provided by hiring a crew to go out and cut brush. And believe me, people are willing to go out and do that. You know, these professors at OSU [Oregon State University] say, 'Oh, you'd never get people to do that kind of work,' but that's not true, there are a lot of people around here who would be happy to do almost anything right now—they just want to work. The economic justification for using these substances just really isn't there, and a lot of people think that's one reason why Dow wanted to terminate the EPA suspension hearings—they really didn't want to get into the 'benefit' section of the hearings because they don't have any real evidence that this stuff is really beneficial. They just haven't done the kind of scientific studies they claim to have done to prove that this stuff is really a benefit to our economy.

"And I just want to say another thing. The old-timers around here are opposed to herbicides. First, because they say the forest used to grow back just fine without them, and second, because they say the wildlife has really been affected by herbicides. The bird population, squirrel population, all the little mammals, have just been decimated. And some fishermen say there used to be a lot more trout in some of the streams. Of course herbicide users claim this is not because of the herbicides, but because the natural habitat has been destroyed—but that's nonsense. There's lots of natural habitat. And the old-timers will tell you—and of course I couldn't use this in my EPA testimony because it's all 'hearsay' —about all the tumors they've found in deer and elk they've killed around here. Lots of very strange, abnormal-looking growths. And these are people that have lived here all their lives.

"It's interesting, isn't it, that the observations of people who have lived in an area all their lives are considered nothing more than hearsay by those who look for a scientific explanation for everything. I went down to hear Dr. Tung, the scientist from Vietnam, when he was speaking in Eugene, and he said something that really struck me. He said that the people have lived in the same area for generations, even centuries, and that they know when something is wrong in their environment. And they know *just what it is,* and he said that he, as a scientist, just had to trust that the people knew enough about their surroundings to detect even minute changes. It seems to me we ought to be listening to some of the people around here who have lived in this area long, long before herbicides were ever sprayed here."

Bonnie Hill and I shake hands and say goodbye, and I walk to the small parking lot where earlier in the day I had spent nearly an hour watching the extraordinary changes in the Oregon weather. For perhaps fifteen minutes the sun would shine, converting the compact car I had rented in Eugene into a mobile solar greenhouse. And then, abruptly, the sky would glower, great dark clouds would swallow the sun, and it would rain. Fifteen minutes later the clouds would vanish behind the mountains, and the rain would stop.

I had spent the previous evening just twenty miles away, at the home of a Vietnam veteran who explained that he had gotten involved in the controversy over herbicides when he read some material that purported to rationalize the use of 2,4,5-T.

"We used to play tapes from loudspeakers," my host told me, "basically saying that the VC are telling the people that herbicides are making them sick, that the spraying is responsible for their miscarriages and illnesses. And the tapes would say that the VC are lying, they just don't like the sprays because it makes it hard for them to hide, and that the VC are actually poisoning people's water so they will believe it's herbicides that are making them sick. I was young and gung-ho at the time; so I just believed the propaganda we were feeding the people. We heard the Vietnamese complain. They talked about depressions, diarrhea, flus, colds, rashes, spontaneous abortions. But it was a war zone, and we just figured there were a lot of diseases that we had never heard of. Thinking back, I recall being struck by the number of children with cleft palates. And I suffered from the same things over and over, screaming pains in my joints, pains in my gut, blood in my urine, my feet going numb. But the hardest thing to deal with was the sudden depressions that came on you. You just wanted to go out into a field and stick a pistol in your mouth and pull the trigger."

During a lull in our conversation I stepped outside. It was a clear, rather brisk spring night, and as I stood in the darkness I could hear water gushing, gurgling, flowing, churning. And I thought about a comment one American scientist had made about herbicide spraying. "Pinpoint bombing you might be able to do," he said, "but pinpoint spraying is impossible."

In Ashford, Washington, a timber company chemist once told a group of women concerned about miscarriages and stillbirths, which they believed might be related to 2,4,5-T, that "babies are replaceable," and they should "plan their pregnancies around the spray schedule." Bonnie Hill was reluctant to talk about the emotional aspects of losing a baby because, she explained, "the media would have loved to see me crying and screaming, but I don't think that is the way we're really going to win this thing." Although they may be unwilling to cater to the media's more prurient whims, women have begun to express their anger over seeing their children suffer from exposure to herbicides, or over experiencing a miscarriage that might have been avoided.

Testifying at the New York State Temporary Commission on Dioxin Exposure hearings in Farmingdale, Long Island, one woman said, "I just took it for granted, as the doctors did, when my daughters were born, that these things just happened. Then I put together the neighbor on this side of me and a neighbor on that side of me having miscarriages—they had normal children when they lived in other towns, no problems. I have one friend who had had four miscarriages since she moved into my area. All four of them were exactly the same as those experienced by veterans' wives, which is, in the third month, up until the third month, the pregnancy is normal. In the third month through the fifth month, the baby starts to disintegrate and dies. There is nothing in the delivery except blood clots. And she had four of these, and she had four normal children when she lived in a different town, not near the railroad tracks."

And another woman testified: "Our property abuts that of the Long Island Rail Road. My backyard, where my children played and we grew vegetables—we also ate outside—is within twenty feet of the tracks. I am the mother of three living children. During the sixties and seventies, the Long Island Rail Road has been spraying along the right-of-way without ever notifying any residents when they were going to spray or what they were using.

"There have been many miscarriages and problems within my area. My two older children were conceived and born elsewhere. I have had two miscarriages since I moved to this address, one of which was considered rare. My daughter was born with multiple birth defects which are similar in nature to the birth defects suffered by Agent Orange victims of Vietnam. Her defects are clubfeet, dislocation of the left hip, spina bifida, no muscles or ligaments from the knees down, nerve damage in both legs. She has had eleven operations in six years, and must wear braces on both legs . . .

"We know about our daughter, but we don't know about my two older boys, myself, or my husband. Will these boys be able to produce children? And if so, what defects will they have? Do we have cancer now, or will we contact it in the future?

"Both the veterans from Vietnam and the people who live along the right-of-way have been hurt tremendously. We can't correct what has been done, but we must stop it from happening in the future. Our lives depend upon it."

11

VIETNAM VETERANS ARE AMERICA'S FUTURE

A visitor to Ronald Anderson's home might find some of his habits rather odd. Passing a small oval mirror in the living room he seems to avert his face. In the dining room he stands with his back to a rectangular mirror, set, it appears, to reflect a child's drawing on the opposite wall. But it soon becomes clear that he is no more peculiar than anyone else would be in his situation. Anderson* refuses to look in the mirror because he doesn't wish to see that his thick curly black hair (he had been nicknamed "the bear") has fallen out, reappearing in patches that protrude from his skull like tiny white brooms. Nor does he wish to see that his once-handsome face is covered with a rash, or that, during periods of sudden weight loss, his cheeks are sunken and his eyes look like those of a dying cat. At thirty-six Anderson simply doesn't want to see the reflection of an old man.

Avoiding mirrors, of course, does nothing to make his chest pains go away, restore his coordination, stop the recurrent bouts of dizziness, or explain the chronic nausea from which he suffers. At times Anderson's muscles are so weak that he is unable to open a jar of peanut butter for his children; and there are days when he sits for hours, sometimes until long after the sun has set,

*Ronald Anderson is a composite portrait.

waiting for a suicidal depression to pass, struggling to remember that things were not always like this, that once he could walk miles in a full field-pack without tiring, do hours of calisthenics without complaining. He passed through basic training, he wrote friends back home, "with a smile." Once he could easily manipulate the straps of his parachute as he glided toward the ground during training exercises with the 101 Airborne.

Sometimes when he thinks about these things he removes a scrapbook and leafs through the photographic proof that he was not always old before his time; and he sees, squeezed between a snapshot of a Vietnamese bar girl and a fading picture of a buddy who did not survive the war, a photograph that he clearly recalls taking. It is a picture of a C123 spraying not more than half a mile from where he was standing. While staring at the photograph Anderson slowly becomes aware that he is afraid. But it is not, he realizes, simply because it reminds him of the twelve months he spent in the bush. That was a different kind of fear, one that for the most part he has been able to leave behind. The nightmares come less frequently now, and his limbs tremble not because he has flashed to a particularly horrible ambush or firefight. He is afraid because, after three years of tests, consultations, prescriptions, X-rays and hospitalization, doctors are still unable to tell him why he is a physical wreck or what, if anything, can be done to stop the progress of this mysterious disease.

There are times, Anderson admits, when he almost wishes he had cancer. Because then it might be possible to remove the malignant portion of his body and arrest the spread of disease. Or perhaps he would be given chemotherapy and eventually his health would return. Much of the time he feels, Anderson tells visitors, like a house infested with termites. The porch is collapsing, the foundation crumbling, the walls so deteriorated a child could push them over, but the parasites remain hidden and no one can explain why the house is tumbling down. He is afraid, he has discovered, not of dying, but of the unknown.

Looking at a photograph of himself at the age of eighteen, Anderson feels a sense of pride. His boots glisten in the sun and his girlfriend and mother stand on each side of him, staring proudly at the set of jump wings that have just been pinned to his uniform. Vietnam had not been a difficult decision for him. His grandfather had fought in the Argonne Forest, his father had landed at Normandy, an uncle had won a bronze star in Korea, and by 1969, when he arrived at Tan Son Nhut, he had already lost one member of his high school football team to the Tet Offensive.

As he stares at the thirteen-year-old photograph, the former paratrooper feels torn by conflicting emotions. He has not lost his love for America, but the tears in his eyes are those of rage rather than pride. "Ask not what your country can do for you . . ." The words reverberate through the room. He remembers a Pakistani doctor (it seemed to him at the time that most of the physicians at the VA were from foreign countries) explaining in halting English that he could not understand Anderson's questions about Agent Orange, then signing papers ordering that he be held for observation in the hospital's psychiatric ward. He recalls the first check he received from the VA. It amounted to forty-eight dollars and would be sent each month, said the VA, not because they believed he was suffering from exposure to Agent Orange, but to help him cope with his "war-related" neurosis. Anderson smiles. He had taken the check into his backyard and, tearing the "insult" into tiny pieces, scattered it, as he once had his father's ashes, to the winds.

Disappearing into his bedroom Anderson returns with a file drawer from which he removes reports, copies of rejection letters from the VA, and letters he has written to Congress, the VA, scientists, the president. Do I realize, asks Anderson, that there are 125,000 Vietnam era veterans in jails or prisons and another 375,000 on parole, probation, or some other form of supervised release? How many of these men, Anderson wonders, suffer from the sudden mood swings symptomatic of dioxin exposure? How many of the violent rages, which may have resulted in their incarceration, were due to the release of dioxin into their bloodstream during sudden weight losses—quite possibly causing psychological imbalances? More than 25 percent of all the inmates in state and federal penitentaries are Vietnam veterans, but has anyone done a fat biopsy study to determine what percentage of these men might be carrying dangerous levels of TCDD-dioxin in their body fat? Could it be that we are paying millions of dollars each year to imprison several battalions of the first army in human history to be poisoned by its own government?

Holding up a recent edition of his hometown paper, Johnson points to a by-line which reads: "$2 Million for Agent Orange Studies Funded." "The bulk of the reassigned money," Anderson reads, his voice shaking with disgust, "will be used for the controversial epidemiological study the VA was ordered to do by Congress three years ago, as well as other Agent Orange projects the VA has planned." Squinting at the paper, Anderson adds that the VA has decided to do "ten new research projects on Agent Orange." The projects will be completed, according to Robert Nimmo of the VA, in five years. Tearing the article from the paper and folding it into squares, Anderson tosses the bulk of the paper into his woodstove. Then he turns and, with his back to the mirror, addresses me as though I were the only person to have remained for the final act of a very, very long play.

"Five years," he says, "five more years. I think I've got it now. I think we've all got it now. They're just waiting. *They are waiting for us all, every fucking one of us, to die.*"

Are we really just waiting for an army to die? In a number of ways the Agent Orange issue is analogous to a murder trial where during the course of the proceedings the prosecutor produces a corpus delicti, witnesses to the crime, even a confession from the murderer, but all to no avail. The judge, for reasons about which one can only speculate, simply refuses to concede that a crime has been committed, dismissing members of the jury with the rather quaint admonishment that he may be calling on them again "in a few years." If the VA denies that there is scientific evidence of the effects of TCDD-dioxin on human beings, and if its administrators continue to insist that Vietnam veterans cannot prove they were exposed to toxic chemicals, then how is it possible for veterans to present their case? In spite of the VA's many rhetorical flourishes of concern, the issue, if one accepts the agency's arguments, is a moot point for still another five years.

Perhaps it is time to remove the Agent Orange issue to another jurisdiction. One way to accomplish this would be for Congress to establish an independent board of inquiry comprised of world experts on toxic chemicals, physicians knowledgeable about the health effects of TCDD-dioxin, Vietnam veterans, and members of the legislature. By taking the entire matter out of the hands of the VA, the American taxpayer will save millions of dollars that might otherwise be spent on redundant studies, resolve some of the urgent questions that have gone unanswered for too many years and, most important, convince the men and women who served in Vietnam that their fellow countrymen do not consider them a "throwaway army."

When asked why more hasn't been done to resolve the Agent Orange issue and provide disability to the sick and dying, many veterans reply that the real issue is money. How much, they ask, are Vietnam veterans worth? And the answer is invariably the same: "As little as possible." If the principal manufacturers of herbicides and the federal government agree on anything, it is that neither wants to be stuck with the bill for compensating thousands of veterans for their illnesses. Other veterans see themselves as scapegoats for an unpopular war. In our haste to forget the pain and divisiveness of the Vietnam era, they say, we have chosen to simply forget about them. Finally, there are those who believe that the Agent Orange issue is a puzzle, with some of the pieces still missing. In time, they argue, a memo will surface from Washington and catapult the nation into an "Orangegate." What had seemed for so many years a controversy will turn out to be a conspiracy.

Perhaps all of these explanations are true, but I think the real answer to why this tragedy continues was given me one evening by a Vietnam veteran. "You know," he said, "I don't think they'll ever really settle this thing because there's just too much money involved. It's gonna cost the chemical companies or the American government billions, and people just don't think we're worth that much. But I just want the American people to know something. They can write me and my children off if they want to. They can say we lost the war or we're all crazy or any bullshit they like. But what they don't know right now is that *we are their future*. What has happened to us will happen to them, and they better believe it because when it comes down, when they start to get sick, when *their* kids start to die and are born deformed or dead, they'll wonder why they wouldn't listen to us. I got nothing against anybody. I'm not as gung-ho as I was when I was eighteen, but this is still my country. But I just can't understand why people don't understand that what they dumped on us over there in Nam they'll be dumping right here tomorrow. So when you go back to write your book, just tell people this: I may die, my brothers may die. Maybe we don't really have any future, but if we don't, who the hell really does?"

Could it be that our willingness to ignore the suffering of thousands of Vietnam veterans is an attempt to avoid looking into our own future? Is it possible that in watching a twenty-eight-year old veteran like Paul Reutershan die of cancer we may be witnessing the death of our own son or daughter from the effects of radiation, dioxin, PCBs, or a host of chemicals that inundate our air and water and are contained in the very food we eat? Or that seeing a photograph of Kerry Ryan, born with sixteen birth defects, or Lori Strait, born with the left half of her brain missing, we are experiencing fears that, as future parents, we find unthinkable? But even if we choose to avoid looking at what has happened to Vietnam veterans, the fact remains that 50 percent of all U.S. groundwater is either contaminated or threatened with contamination, that this year more deaths will be due to air pollution than car accidents, and that more children die in the United States each year from cancer than from any other disease.

On July 22, 1980, Christopher H. Johnson, a Vietnam veteran who had lost his right leg and part of his hearing in Vietnam, and whose son died after being born with multiple birth defects, told the Subcommittee on Medical Facilities and Benefits: "Don't you think that it is only right to take care of the American men who supported you first. We are natural-born citizens of the United States of America. We have been reaching out for years for help. Now is the time for you to step forward and take the responsibility and appropriate action. Don't leave us with the only benefit remaining, which is the burial benefit. A lot of Vietnam veterans have already used it much too early in life. The Vietnam veteran never had the chance to enjoy adulthood. Now I can't enjoy growing old. The evidence and facts have been in for years. Agent Orange is a killer."

Christopher H. Johnson is a Vietnam veteran, but his testimony could be that of any American parent or victim of toxic poisoning. Although the Vietnam War has ended, the Vietnamization of America continues unabated. Vietnam veterans are our future, and however painful that may be for us to admit, our future is now.

APPENDIX

The History of 2,4,5-T*

1941–1946
Tests and development as a chemical and biological warfare agent.

1946
Commercial use on weeds and brush.

Late 1961
Introduced in Vietnam as part of U.S. chemical warfare.

June/July 1969
Reports of frequent birth defects in defoliated areas of Vietnam.

April 1970
Pentagon stops using Agent Orange due to worldwide pressure and significant scientific evidence.

April 1970
Surgeon General reports to Hart committee on restrictions of 2,4,5-T: suspension of liquid formulation for home use; suspension of all aquatic uses; intent to cancel registration of nonliquid formulations for use around homes and on all food crops.

May 1970
Dow et al. appeals decision to cancel use on food crops.

*From Northwest Coalition for Alternatives to Pesticides.

Late 1970
Lawsuit by Consumers Union to force Department of Agriculture to suspend rather than cancel use.

1970
Environmental Protection Agency takes over regulation of pesticides.

January 1971
Appeals court orders EPA to reconsider Department of Agriculture refusal to put firmer restrictions on 2,4,5-T.

May 1971
Science advisory panel set up by EPA recommends that ban on use around homes be lifted and other restrictions set aside. Many scientists severely criticize advisory panel.

August 1971
EPA administrator William Ruckelshaus announces EPA would continue to press for cancellation of 2,4,5-T on food crops, and orders hearing on uses causing greatest human exposure.

September 1971
Dow asks and gets an injunction from district court in Arkansas stopping EPA from cancellation hearings.

April 1973
Appeals court reverses district court decision and upholds EPA order for cancellation.

July 1973
EPA plans go-ahead for cancellation hearings, begins pre-hearing conferences with Dow, Department of Agriculture, Consumers Union and Environmental Defense Fund.

May 1974
Dow and Department of Agriculture hold conference on 2,4,5-T.

June 1974
EPA withdraws order of intent to hold hearings scheduled to begin the following month. Also withdraws cancellation order on rice crop use.

1975
President Gerald Ford announces that the United States would make no first use of military herbicides in offensive operations.

1975
U.S. Forest Service prohibited from using 2,4,5-T in Arkansas because of NEPA violations

1976
U.S. Forest Service in Region 6 voluntarily suspends use of 2,4,5-T while court case against Siuslaw National Forest is in process.

1977
U.S. Forest Service found to violate NEPA process regarding Environmental Impact Statement in uses of 2,4,5-T.

April 1978
EPA issues notice of Rebuttal Presumption Against Registration (RPAR) for 2,4,5-T.

February 1979
EPA issues order of emergency suspension for 2,4,5-T and 2,4,5-TP (Silvex). First emergency suspension.
    Suspended products registered for forestry, right-of-way, pasture uses of 2,4,5-T.
    Suspended products registered for forestry, right-of-way, pasture, home, aquatic, and recreational area uses of 2,4,5-TP.
    EPA initiates cancellation proceedings for 2,4,5-T and 2,4,5-TP suspended uses.

April 1979
Dow fails to win appeal of emergency suspension.

February 1980
EPA cancellation hearings begin. Dow Chemical Corporation and 54 intervenors on their behalf/EPA and 2 intervenors on their behalf.

March 1981
EPA agrees with Dow-initiated motion for suspending cancellation hearings, and begins closed-door meetings to pursue out-of-hearing settlement.

Employment of Riot Control Agents, Flame, Smoke,
Antiplant Agents, and Personnel Detectors
in Counterguerrilla Operations

Department of the Army Training Circular
TC 3-16 April 1969

———

ANTIPLANT AGENT OPERATIONS

Section I
Technical Aspects

51. General. Antiplant agents are chemical agents which possess a
high offensive potential for destroying or seriously limiting the production of food and defoliating vegetation. These compounds include herbicides that kill or inhibit the growth of plants; plant growth
regulators that either regulate or inhibit plant growth, sometimes
causing plant death; desiccants that dry up plant foliage; and soil
sterilants that prevent or inhibit the growth of vegetation by action
with the soil. Military applications for antiplant agents are based on
denying the enemy food and concealment.

52. Antiplant Agents in Use.

a. ORANGE.

(1) *Description.* Agent ORANGE is the Standard A agent. It is
composed of a 50:50 mixture of the n-butyl esters of 2,4-D and 2,4,5-T
(app D and C1, TM 3-215). ORANGE appears as a dark-brown oily
liquid which is insoluble in water but miscible in oils such as diesel
fuel. It weighs about 10.75 pounds per gallon and becomes quite
viscous as the temperature drops, solidifying at 45° F. It is noncorrosive, of low volatility, and nonexplosive, but deteriorates rubber.

(2) *Rate of application.* The recommended rate of application of
ORANGE is 3 gallons per acre. This may vary depending on the
type of vegetation (app C). In some situations better coverage may
be obtained by diluting ORANGE with diesel fuel oil, which results
in a less viscous solution that is dispersed in smaller droplets. Dilution

may also be required when using dispersion equipment which does not permit the flow rate to be conveniently adjusted to 3 gallons per acre. See discussion of application methods in paragraphs 57 and 58.

(3) *Effect on foliage.* ORANGE penetrates the waxy covering of leaves and is absorbed into the plant system. It affects the growing points of the plant, resulting in its death. Rains occurring within the first hour after spraying will not reduce the effectiveness of OR-ANGE to the extent that they reduce the effectiveness of aqueous solutions. Broadleaf plants are highly susceptible to ORANGE. Some grasses can be controlled but require a much higher dose rate than broadleaf plants. Susceptible plants exhibit varying degrees of susceptibility to ORANGE. Death of a given plant may occur within a week or less, or may require up to several months depending on the plant's age, stage of growth, susceptibility, and the dose rate. See employment considerations in paragraphs 53 through 55.

(4) *Safety precautions and decontamination.* ORANGE is relatively nontoxic to man or animals. No injuries have been reported to personnel exposed to aircraft spray. Personnel subject to splashes from handling the agent need not be alarmed, but should shower and change clothes at a convenient opportunity. ORANGE is noncorrosive to metals but will remove aircraft paint and walkway coatings. Contaminated aircraft should be washed with soapy water to remove the agent. Rubber hoses and other rubber parts of transfer and dissemination equipment will deteriorate and require replacement, since ORANGE softens rubber.

b. BLUE (Phytar 560G).

(1) *Description.* Agent BLUE is an aqueous solution containing about 3 pounds per gallon of the sodium salt of cacodylic acid, the proper amount of surfactant (a substance which increases the effectiveness of the solution), and a neutralizer to prevent corrosion of metal spray apparatus. BLUE is the agent normally used for crop destruction.

(2) *Rate of application.* BLUE may be sprayed as received from the manufacturer without dilution, if desired. The recommended application rate for crop destruction is about 1 to 2 gallons per acre (app C). However, much higher use rates of BLUE are required to kill tall grasses, such as elephant grass or sugarcane, because of the large masses of vegetation. For hand-spray operations, two gallons of

BLUE diluted with water to make 50 gallons will give a solution that can be dispersed by hand at a rate equivalent to approximately 1 to 3 gallons of pure agent per acre.

(3) *Effect on foliage.* Enough BLUE applied to any kind of foliage will cause it to dry and shrivel, but the agent is more effective against grassy plants than broadleaf varieties. Best results are obtained when the plant is thoroughly covered, since the agent kills by absorption of moisture from the leaves. The plants will die within 2 to 4 days or less and can then be burned if permitted to dry sufficiently. BLUE in low dose rates can also prevent grain formation in rice without any apparent external effect. The plant develops normally but does not yield a crop. Spray rates higher than about one-half gallon per acre usually kill the crop. Although BLUE can produce relatively rapid defoliation, regrowth may occur again in about 30 days. Repeated spraying is necessary to provide a high degree of continuous plant kill.

(4) *Safety precautions and decontamination.* Normal sanitary precautions should be followed when handling BLUE. Although it contains a form of arsenic, BLUE is relatively nontoxic. It should not be taken internally, however. Any material that gets on the hands, face, or other parts of the body should be washed off at the first opportunity. Clothes that become wet with a solution of BLUE should be changed. Aircraft used for spraying this solution should be washed well afterward. When WHITE is added to BLUE, a precipitate forms that will clog the system. If the same spray apparatus is to be used for spraying agents WHITE and BLUE, the system must be flushed to assure that all residue of the previous agent is removed.

c. *WHITE (Tordon 101).*

(1) *Description.* The active ingredients of agent WHITE are 20 percent picloram and 80 percent isopropylamine salt of 2,4-D. Active ingredients constitute about 25 percent of the solution. A surfactant is also present. WHITE is soluble in water, noncorrosive, nonflammable, nonvolatile, immiscible in oils, and more viscous than ORANGE at the same temperature.

(2) *Rate of application.* WHITE usually should be applied at a rate of 3 to 5 gallons per acre on broadleaf vegetation. However, the rate may vary depending on the type of flora. Quantities required to control jungle vegetation may vary from 5 to 12 gallons per acre. This

quantity exceeds the spray capability of most aircraft spray systems for a single pass. It is usually unfeasible in large-scale military operations to apply such large volumes. For ground-based spray operations, however, high volumes are necessary. Hand-spray operations cannot evenly cover a whole acre with only 3 gallons of solution. Three gallons of WHITE diluted to a 30-gallon solution can be more easily sprayed over an area of one acre. The manufacturer recommends diluting WHITE with sufficient water to make a 10-gallon solution for each gallon of agent.

(3) *Effect on foliage.* WHITE kills foliage in the same manner as ORANGE, since 80 percent of the active ingredient is 2,4-D. PICLORAM is more effective than 2,4-D, but acts slower. WHITE is effective on many plant species, and equal to or more effective than ORANGE on the more woody species. The material must be absorbed through the leaves. The water solution does not penetrate the waxy covering of leaves as well as oily mixtures and is more easily washed off by rain.

(4) *Safety precautions and decontamination.* WHITE exhibits a low hazard from accidental ingestion. However, it may cause some irritation if splashed into the eyes. Should eye contact occur, flush with plenty of water. Splashes on the skin should be thoroughly washed with soap and water at the first opportunity. Contaminated clothing should be washed before reuse. When WHITE is used in the same equipment as BLUE, all of the WHITE should be removed before using BLUE. The two agents produce a white precipitate that will clog spray systems.

COMPOSITION OF MILITARILY SIGNIFICANT ANTIPLANT AGENTS

Antiplant agent	*Composition*
ORANGE	50% 2,4-D (n-butyl-2,4-dichlorophenoxyacetate) 50% 2,4,5-T (n-butyl-2,4,5-trichlorophenoxyacetate)
WHITE	20% picloram (4-amino-3,5,6-trichloropicolinic acid) 80% 2,4-D (triisopropanolamine)
BLUE (Phytar 560G)	3 pounds per gallon of water of: 65% cacodylic acid (dimethylarsenic acid) 35% inert ingredients: sodium chloride, sodium and calcium sulfates, water

AREA TREATED WITH HERBICIDES
IN SOUTH VIETNAM 1962–1969

Year	Defoliation	Crop Destruction
1962	4,940 *acres*	741 *acres*
1963	24,700	247
1964	83,486	10,374
1965	155,610	65,949
1966	741,247	101,517
1967	1,486,446	221,312
1968	1,267,110	63,726
1969 (January–March)	356,421	4,693
	4,119,960	468,559

SOURCE: *Military Assistance Command Vietnam Reports.*

VA Memo Circulated on May 18, 1978

Directors, VA hospitals, domiciliary, outpatient clinics, and regional offices with outpatient clinics.

Subject: Potential exposures of veterans to chemical defoliants during the Vietnam War.

1. During the Vietnam War, herbicidal war chemicals were utilized for defoliation of vegetation. Recently concern has developed among some scientific and other groups that these chemicals may be capable of producing adverse health effects on individuals who were exposed to these herbicides. Because of their potential impact on a segment of the veteran population, the VA is attempting to develop accurate information on the health-related effects of the defoliants utilized during the Vietnam War.

2. The four defoliants utilized regularly were picloram, cacodylic acid, 2,4-D and 2,4,5-T. These were mixed in variable proportions and placed in color-coded storage drums which were identified as "Agent Orange," "Agent White," "Agent Blue," and "Agent Purple." A large number of studies performed on man and several animal species have demonstrated that the four herbicides have a low level of toxicity, both individually and when mixed. Furthermore they appear to be rapidly absorbed and completely excreted in both the human and the animal.

3. Humans exposed repeatedly to these agents may experience temporary and fully reversible neurological symptoms; however, the only chronic condition definitely associated with such exposure in humans is chloracne. Comprehensive animal studies performed under experimental conditions have demonstrated that very massive doses of these agents produce fatty degeneration of solid organs, gastrointestinal disturbances and thymic atrophy, all of which were reversible after withdrawal of the chemicals.

4. These studies have failed to confirm the suggestion in the Vietnamese medical literature that liver cancer, frequent abortions, and fetal birth defects occur among those exposed to the defoliants. In addition, no confirmation has been obtained for the experimental

studies of one scientist who found that hepatic and pancreatic cancers followed prolonged exposure to one of the chemicals.

5. In contrast to the apparent low toxicity of the four defoliants, evidence has been adduced that a contaminant called dioxin found in some of the storage drums has a significant potential toxicity. Although its concentration of dioxin was variable in different drums, it was always found in minute quantities. Experimental evidence from animal studies indicates that this chemical is eliminated from the body fairly rapidly and that it produces its toxic effects rather promptly. All available data suggests that it is not retained in tissues for prolonged periods of time. Accordingly, the recent suggestion by some observers that dioxin might still be detected in the fat tissues of Vietnam veterans exposed to it appears to be implausible.

6. Despite the generally negative results of human and animal studies of the toxicity potential of the Vietnam defoliants, a great deal of concern has been engendered among veterans and their families by media presentations on these agents. The VA is responding to these concerns by working collaboratively with appropriate experts from the federal and private sectors in order to more adequately define the potential human toxicity of the defoliants for humans. You will be periodically informed concerning the results of these efforts.

7. Meanwhile, we request that all VA staff who are called upon to deal with veterans who are concerned about toxic effects from a possible exposure to the defoliants adhere to the following protocol:

A. Every veteran who alleges defoliant exposure must receive prompt, courteous, compassionate consideration.

B. If the veteran has no objective symptoms or signs, simple reassurance should be offered. The veteran should be told that a record of the medical examination will be kept for future reference, but that if the veteran does not now have symptoms and did not previously experience any, the likelihood of herbicide poisoning is virtually zero.

C. If the veteran presents with symptoms and signs which are not clearly explicable in terms of definable disease, a detailed history should be recorded on the VA form 10-10m, including such details the veteran may remember concerning his exposure to defoliant agents. This information can be checked against military data, if indicated.

D. In view of the remaining uncertainties on the long-term effects of the defoliants, all VA personnel should avoid premature commitment to any diagnosis of defoliant poisoning. Similarly, entries in medical records should not contain statements about the relationship between a veteran's illnesses and defoliant exposure unless unequivocal confirmation of such a connection has been established. Accordingly, veterans in whom defoliant poisoning is suspected should be admitted to a VA hospital for appropriate work-up.

E. If there is evidence suggestive of defoliant agent poisoning, pertinent data must be forwarded to the ADCMD for operations (11), VACO.

F. No veterans other than those referred by DVE should be called in for the express purpose of having them examined for possible defoliant poisoning.

G. All VA forms 10-10m indicating that the veteran or the physician has material concern about the possibility of defoliant poisoning, should be preserved until further notification.

H. A 3 × 5 locator card should be developed by MAS so that VA forms 10-10m can be swiftly retrieved if the need develops. MAS staff have received instructions on how to develop these cards. Significant administrative problems may be reported to VACO MAS (136D).

I. If a patient who already is hospitalized intimates that he or she may have been exposed to defoliants, a statement to this effect should be entered in the medical record. If there are symptoms or signs which cannot be explained in terms of well-known medical entities, these should be appropriately investigated.

J. Many agricultural and horticultural agents contain the same herbicidal chemicals as were incorporated in the Vietnam defoliants. Whenever there is suspicion of chemical poisoning, therefore, inquiry should be directed to other sources of intoxication as well as the allegations concerning the Vietnam episodes. There also are many industrial sources of chemical intoxication whose manifestations are similar to the syndromes ascribed to the defoliants. A careful occupational history therefore is necessary.

K. Staff of field HCF's who may be called upon to make public statements concerning the defoliants should not do so before reviewing their proposed expositions with the ADCMD for professional services, whose staff will provide the needed technical guidance.

8. We trust that the foregoing guidance will be sufficient. If new information indicated a change of policy, additional directives will be issued. Should any problem arise which is not covered by this policy statement additional clarification may be sought by calling VACO Medical Service (Dr. Gerrit Schepers, ext. 389-2550). Any freedom of information request should be coordinated with VACO.

Letter from Gilbert Boger, M.D., to the Editor of the
Journal of the American Medical Association,
November 30, 1979 (Vol. 242, No. 22)

Symptoms in Vietnam Veterans Exposed to Agent Orange

To the Editor.—Agent Orange is an herbicide containing equal parts
of 2,4-dichlorophenoxyacetic acid and 2,4,5-trichlorophenoxyacetic
acid. It was used extensively in Vietnam as a defoliant. A toxic
contaminant is dioxin, 2,3,7,8-tetrachlorodibenzo-*p*-dioxin.

A ten-month study of 78 Vietnam veterans who claimed exposure
to Agent Orange yielded many findings: 85% of the men experienced
a rash that was resistant to treatment. Using immunofluorescence in
one patient, a skin biopsy specimen showed intraepithelial and inter-
cellular IgA, IgG, and IgM. In 53% of the patients, the rash was
aggravated by sunlight.

Joint pain occurred in 71%, stiffness in 59%, and swelling in 45%.
Hypersomnolence occurred in 44% of the men and extreme fatigue
in 80%. Sinus bradycardia and premature ventricular contractions
were not infrequent.

Persistent neurological complaints were tingling (55%), numbness
(60%), dizziness (69%), headache (35%), and autonomic dyscontrol
(18%). Severe psychiatric manifestations were depression (73%), suicidal attempts (8%), and violent rages (45%). An inability to concen-
trate occurred in 17% and bouts of sudden lapses of memory were
seen in 21%. Patients have described fearful episodes of suddenly not
knowing where they were going; it was as if their thoughts had left
them. There was also a loss of libido in 47%. Three patients died of
cancer. Another 10% have been treated for cancer.

The Vietnam veterans demonstrated a large number of gastrointestinal ulcerations. Complaints related to the gastrointestinal tract included anorexia (41%), nausea (59%), vomiting (13%), hematemesis
(8%), diarrhea (51%), constipation (31%), and abdominal pain (24%).
Hepatitis was reported in 10% and jaundice in 5%.

Nineteen percent of our group had children with gross birth defects. One or more miscarriages were experienced in 13% of the wives. There were reports of sterility; semen analysis showed low sperm counts and abnormal forms.

The two most frequent genitourinary findings were brown urine (23%) and hematuria (9%). A kidney biopsy specimen in one patient was pathological, with an unknown etiology. Other as yet unexplained symptoms were blurred vision (54%), dyspnea (8%), gynecomastia (4%), and galactorrhea (5%).

This group of veterans has in general been chronically ill. Patients complained of frequent infections and allergies. The mean age of the group was 31.7 years. Both upper and lower socioeconomic levels were represented.

The aforementioned information is intended to create an awareness of a substance known as dioxin. This chemical may cause a variety of symptoms, and physicians should be aware of its potential.

Sixty-Fourth Annual National Convention of the American Legion Chicago, Illinois, August 24–26, 1982

RESOLUTION: No. 410 (Iowa)
COMMITTEE: Veterans Affairs and Rehabilitation
SUBJECT: The American Legion Policy on Agent Orange

WHEREAS, the chemical herbicide commonly known as Agent Orange was sprayed throughout Vietnam during the years 1962–1971, to defoliate jungle and rice paddies; and

WHEREAS, the total long-range toxic effects of the defoliant, of which in excess of 10.6 million gallons were reportedly expended by American military forces, remain virtually unknown; and

WHEREAS, the chemical mixture of 2,4-D and 2,4,5-T, which contains a certain amount of the chemical dioxin, has been subjected to partial bans by the Environmental Protection Agency following reports of spontaneous abortions and stillbirths in areas where heavily used in the United States; and

WHEREAS, a significant number of service personnel serving in Vietnam were exposed to these toxic chemicals and have subsequently developed cancer, neurological disorders, liver dysfunction, severe depression, and other life-threatening diseases; and

WHEREAS, these veterans are now seeking benefits from the VA, to which they believe they are justly entitled, by reason of disease and disability incurred through exposure to Agent Orange; and

WHEREAS, the American Legion is seriously concerned about the effect of Agent Orange on those veterans who served in Vietnam during the time it was used as a defoliant; and

WHEREAS, the American Legion is strongly supportive of the studies and research being conducted by the Air Force, the Center for Disease Control, the Armed Forces Institute of Pathology, the Veterans Administration, etc., on Agent Orange, and has urged the administrator of veterans affairs, the VA Advisory Committee on Health-Related Effects of Herbicides, and the VA Central Office Ad

Hoc Committee on the Toxic Effects of Herbicides to proceed without delay using all resources available, to ascertain with scientific validity the effects of Agent Orange on veterans who were exposed to it during their active military service; and

WHEREAS, section 307 of the Veterans Health Programs Extension and Improvement Act of 1979 (Public Law 96-151) mandated the Veterans Administration to undertake a scientific study of the effect of dioxin exposure on veterans; and

WHEREAS, the Veterans Administration negotiated a contract with the UCLA School of Public Health on May 1, 1981, for the design of the protocol of the Agent Orange study mandated by Public Law 96-151; and

WHEREAS, the protocol has been designed, has undergone peer review and was revised as a result thereof, and preliminary steps are being taken to proceed with a pilot study; and

WHEREAS, the American Legion feels strongly that the study itself should be conducted by an independent scientific entity rather than by the Veterans Administration as the results thereof would be more readily acceptable by the Vietnam veterans who were exposed, their families, and the scientific community; and

WHEREAS, the American Legion is aggressively assisting and counseling veterans in the filing and development of claims for benefits provided under title 38, United States Code, and referring those individuals claiming exposure to the persons responsible for the Agent Orange examination program at the nearest VA medical center or outpatient clinic for an appropriate examination; and

WHEREAS, because of the fact that very few claims for service connection have been granted, the American Legion has continually called upon the administrator of veterans affairs and the Department of Veterans Benefits to take a more objective approach in the adjudication of claims for benefits for disease and disabilities resulting from exposure to Agent Orange, until such time that conclusive scientific evidence is available, and to resolve all reasonable doubt in favor of veterans, their dependents and survivors, in claims for benefits based on exposure to Agent Orange, but such urging has been to little or no avail; and

WHEREAS, a significant number of Vietnam veterans have expressed displeasure with the manner in which they were attended to during their Agent Orange examination at a VA medical facility; now, therefore, be it

RESOLVED, by the American Legion in National Convention assembled in Chicago, Illinois, August 24, 25, 26, 1982, that the American Legion sponsor and support legislation in the Congress of the United States to amend section 307 of Public Law 96-151 by assigning the responsibility of conducting the epidemiological study of Vietnam veterans who were exposed to any of the class of chemicals known as "the dioxins" produced during the manufacture of the various phenoxy herbicides, including Agent Orange, to an independent scientific agency; and, be it further

RESOLVED, that the American Legion support legislation to amend title 38, United States Code, to establish a mechanism for presumption of service connection for certain disabilities traced to Agent Orange exposure once such presumption is justified by conclusive scientific evidence; and, be it further

RESOLVED, that the American Legion closely monitor the development of all ongoing research of the long-term health effects of Agent Orange exposure and point out to the proper officials any perceived deficiencies or discrepancies in these projects; and, be it further

RESOLVED, that the American Legion disseminate the most current responsible information on Agent Orange to Legionnaires, Vietnam veterans and their families, and the public through all resources available to transmit such information; and, be it finally

RESOLVED, that the American Legion continue to make careful observation of the Veterans Administration's Agent Orange examination program to determine whether or not Vietnam veterans reporting to VA medical care facilities claiming exposure are being appropriately examined, and that the examining physicians demonstrate both compassion and thoroughness in the way they receive, examine and treat all Vietnam veterans who present themselves alleging dioxin exposure.

APPROVED

Veterans Organizations and Individuals Who Will Provide Information on Agent Orange

American Legion National Headquarters
1608 K St. N.W.
Washington, DC 20006
Contact: John Sommer
(202) 861-2753

Agent Orange Victims International
27 Washington Square North
New York, NY 10011
Contact: Frank McCarthy
(212) 460-5770
AOVI sends out information on Agent Orange and lobbies on behalf of Vietnam veterans and other victims of Agent Orange.

Dr. Ronald A. Codario
1427 South Broad St.
Philadelphia, PA 19147
(215) 467-3883
Dr. Codario has done research into the possible effects of dioxin on Vietnam veterans, and is studying a possible method to flush TCDD from the human body.

Disabled American Veterans
National Headquarters
P.O. Box 14301
Cincinnati, OH 45214
Contact: Robert Lenham
(606) 441-7300

National Veterans Law Center
4900 Massachusetts Ave. N.W.
Washington, DC 20016
Contact: Louis Milford
(202) 686-2741
National Veterans Law Center provides valuable background information on the Veterans Administration's reluctance to act in good faith on the Agent Orange issue.

National Veterans Task Force on Agent Orange
National Office
P.O. Box 15972
St. Louis, MO 63114
(314) 968-4180
NVTF is a nonprofit coalition of veteran, religious, legal, social service and environmental groups that have united to seek assistance for the growing number of veterans who are experiencing ill health due to the effects of toxic chemicals.

United Vietnam Veterans Organization
P.O. Box 731
Langhorne, PA 19047
Contact: David Christian
(215) 943-6048
UVVO consists of more than 125 Vietnam veterans organizations and has focused its interests on all veterans' issues, particularly Agent Orange and employment for Vietnam veterans.

Veterans of Foreign Wars of the United States
200 Maryland Ave. N.E.
Washington, DC 20002
(202) 543-2239

Vietnam Veterans of America
329 Eighth St. N.E.
Washington, DC 20002
(202) 546-3700

Victor Yannacone & Associates
P.O. Drawer 109
Patchogue, NY 11772
(516) 654-2299
Veterans interested in joining the class action suit against the manufacturers of Agent Orange should contact Yannacone.

State Dioxin or Agent Orange Commissions

State	Contact Person	Address
California	Ms. Rosemary Malich, Information Officer	State of California Division of Veterans Affairs P.O. Box 1559 Sacramento, CA 95807 (916) 445-9578
Connecticut	Legislation recently passed. Information unavailable at this time.	
Georgia	R. Keith Sykes, D.V.M., M.P.H. Thomas W. McKinley, M.P.H.	Georgia Department of Human Resources Division of Physical Health Epidemiology Program, Room 13-14 47 Trinity Avenue S.W. Atlanta, GA 30334 (404) 656-4764
Hawaii	Will Rellahan, Ph.D.	Hawaii Department of Health Agent Orange Program P.O. Box 3378 Honolulu, HI 96801-9984 (808) 548-8705
Illinois	Senator Karl Berning, Chairman Ms. Mary Muench, Secretary	State Capitol Building Room 218 Springfield, IL 62706 (217) 782-5336

Kansas	Don Wilcox, Bureau of Epidemiology	Kansas Department of Health and Environment Forbes Field Topeka, KS 66620 (913) 862-9360
Maine	J. Tukey, Chairman	Room 213 175 Lancaster St. Portland, ME 04111 (207) 780-3584
Massachusetts	State Senator Francis D. Doris, Chairman Paul Camacho, Executive Director	Commission on Concerns of Vietnam Veterans 100 Cambridge Street 10th Floor, Room 1001 Boston, MA 02202 (617) 727-0110
Minnesota	Jerry Bender, Director	Department of Veterans Affairs State of Minnesota Agent Orange Information and Assistance Section Veterans Service Building St. Paul, MN 55155 (612) 296-2562
New Jersey	Wayne Wilson, Executive Director	Broad Street Bank Building Room 515 143 East State Street Trenton, NJ 08608 (609) 984-7397

New York	Robert D. Santos, Chairman Ruth Leverett, Executive Director	New York State Temporary Commission on Dioxin Exposure 194 Washington Avenue, 5th Floor Albany, NY 12210 (518) 473-1287
Ohio	Thomas Helmrath, M.D., Vice Chancellor for Health Affairs	Ohio Board of Regents* 30 East Broad Street Columbus, OH 43215 (614) 466-6000
Oklahoma	Charles Cameron, M.D., Chief, Preventive Medicine Service	Oklahoma Department of Health P.O. Box 53551 Oklahoma City, OK 73152 (405) 271-4026 (405) 271-2114
Pennsylvania†	Donald Reid, M.D. Henry Albert, Environmental Health Col. Albert J. Brown	P.O. Box 90 Harrisburg, PA 17108 (717) 783-8804 Bureau for Veteran Affairs Fort Indian Town Annville, PA 17003 (717) 783-3401

*Not a commission. Undertaking a study of the impact of dioxin exposure on Vietnam veterans.
†Commission has not met.

Texas	George Anderson, M.D.	Texas Department of Health Occupational Medicine and Toxicology 1100 West 49th Street Austin, TX 78756 (512) 458-7251
West Virginia	Charles Conroy	West Virginia Department of Health Office of Community Health Services 1800 Washington Street East Charleston, WV 25305 (304) 348-3210

BIBLIOGRAPHY

Brown, Michael, *Laying Waste: The Poisoning of America by Toxic Chemicals.* New York: Pantheon, 1980.

Carson, Rachel, *Silent Spring.* New York: Fawcett, 1962.

Dux, John, and P.J. Young, *Agent Orange: The Bitter Harvest.* Sydney: Hodder and Stoughton, 1980.

Ensign, Tod, and Michael Uhl. *GI Guinea Pigs: How the Pentagon Exposed Our Troops to Dangers More Deadly Than War.* New York: Playboy Press, 1980.

Fuller, John G. *The Poison That Fell from the Sky.* New York: Random House, 1977.

Hersh, Seymour M. *Chemical and Biological Warfare: America's Hidden Arsenal.* Indianapolis: Bobbs-Merrill, 1968.

Linedecker, Clifford. *Kerry: Agent Orange and an American Family.* New York: St. Martin's Press, 1982.

Pfeiffer, E.W., Arthur H. Westing et al. *Harvest of Death: Chemical Warfare in Vietnam and Cambodia.* New York: Free Press, 1971.

Whiteside, Thomas. *The Pendulum and the Toxic Cloud: The Course of Dioxin Contamination.* New Haven and London: Yale University Press, 1979.

————. *The Withering Rain: America's Herbicidal Folly.* New York: Dutton, 1971.

NOTES

INTRODUCTION

1. "Where Is My Country?" *Time*, February 25, 1980.

I KETCHUP AND WATER

No notes.

2 THE DOOMED PLATOON

No notes.

3 SEALS AND RIVER RATS

No notes.

4 A MAIMED GENERATION

1. *Agent Orange: Information for Veterans Who Served in Vietnam (Questions and Answers),* Office of Public and Consumer Affairs, Veterans Administration, June 1982.
2. Clifford Linedecker, *Kerry: Agent Orange and an American Family* (New York: St. Martin's Press, 1982), p. 176.

3. Ton That Tung, M.D., Ton Duc Lang, M.D., and Do Duc Van, M.D. (Viet Duc Hospital, Hanoi, Vietnam), "The Problem of Mutagenic Effects on the First Generation after Exposure to Defoliants"; Ton That Tung, Ton Duc Lang, and Do Duc Van, "The Mutagenacity of Dioxin and Its Effects on Reproduction among Exposed War Veterans," unpublished papers.

4. Ibid.

5. Arthur W. Galston, "Herbicides in Vietnam," *New Republic,* November 25, 1967.

6. Martin Woollacott, "Agent Orange Still Takes Toll," *The Guardian,* reprinted in U.S. and World Section of the *Boston Globe,* June 4, 1980.

7. Testimony of Maureen Ryan before the Committee on Veterans' Affairs, U.S. Senate, February 21, 1980.

8. Thomas Whiteside, *The Withering Rain: America's Herbicidal Folly* (New York: Dutton, 1971), p. 46.

9. "Vets Told Agent Orange Decision Is Years Away" (AP), *Ithaca Journal,* September 1, 1982.

5 DYING DOWN UNDER

1. Graham Bell, "Agent Orange: 'It Won't Even Hurt Dumb Animals,' " *Grifitti,* student newspaper of Griffith University (Australia).

2. John Dux and P.J. Young, *Agent Orange: The Bitter Harvest* (Sydney: Hodder and Stoughton, 1980), p. 67.

3. Ibid., p. 63.

4. Ibid., p. 131.

6 STONEWALL

1. Statement of the National Veterans Law Center before the Subcommittee on Medical Facilities and Benefits of the Committee on Veterans' Affairs, U.S. House of Representatives, July 22, 1980.

2. Ibid., p. 6.

3. Ibid.

4. Report by the comptroller general of the United States, "Health Effects of Exposure to Herbicide Orange in South Vietnam Should Be Resolved," April 6, 1979, p. 12.

5. Ibid., p. 6.
6. Statement of the National Veterans Law Center, p. 14.
7. Ibid., p. 16.
8. Ibid., pp. 16–18.
9. Testimony of Philip Handler, president, National Academy of Sciences National Research Council, Washington, D.C., before the Subcommittee on Medical Facilities and Benefits of the Committee on Veterans' Affairs, U.S. House of Representatives, September 16, 1980.
10. Ibid.
11. Seymour M. Hersh, *Chemical and Biological Warfare: America's Hidden Arsenal* (Indianapolis: Bobbs-Merrill, 1968), pp. 153–54.
12. Statement of William J. Jacoby, Jr., M.D., deputy chief medical director, Department of Medicine and Surgery, Veterans Administration, before the Subcommittee on Oversight and Investigations, Committee on Veterans' Affairs, U.S. House of Representatives, May 6, 1981, pp. A-3–A-4.
13. Public Hearings, New York State Temporary Commission on Dioxin Exposure, Farmingdale, New York, June 20, 1981.
14. Ibid.
15. Ibid.
16. Statement of Max Cleland, administrator of veterans' affairs, before the Committee on Veterans' Affairs, U.S. Senate, February 21, 1980.
17. Statement of the National Veterans Law Center, p. 22.
18. Ibid., p. 24.
19. *New York Times*, August 18, 1981.
20. *The American Legion*, January 1982, p. 7.
21. Ibid.
22. *Washington Post*, November 19, 1981.
23. "Vets Told Agent Orange Decision Is Years Away," *Ithaca Journal*, September 1, 1982.
24. Ibid.
25. "VA Turns over Agent Orange Study to HHS Unit," *Washington Post*, October 15, 1982.

7   WHEN YOU CAN'T SUE THE GOVERNMENT THAT KILLS YOU

1. Karen J. Payne, "Beyond Vietnam, Beyond Politics, Beyond Causes . . . ," *Barrister*, Spring 1979.
2. Victor J. Yannacone, W. Keith Kavenagh, and Margie T.

Searcy, "Agent Orange Litigation: Cooperation for Victory," *Trial,* February 1982.

3. Ibid.
4. Victor J. Yannacone, W. Keith Kavenagh, and Margie T. Searcy, "Dioxin, Molecule of Death," *Trial,* December 1981.
5. Victor J. Yannacone et al., "Agent Orange Litigation: Cooperation for Victory," *Trial,* February 1982.
6. Ibid.
7. Ibid.

8   CASUALTY REPORT

1. Direct testimony of Dr. Michael L. Gross before the administrator, United States Environmental Protection Agency.
2. Ibid.

9   HUMANS, RATS, AND LESSER BEINGS

1. Matthew Meselson, interview with filmmaker Daniel Keller, February 26, 1981.
2. Federal Register, "Emergency Suspension Order for 2,4,5-T and Silvex," 15874-15920, March 15, 1979.
3. Drs. Ton That Tung, Ton Duc Lang, and Do Duc Van (Viet Duc Hospital, Hanoi, Vietnam), "The Mutagenacity of Dioxin and Its Effects on Reproduction among Exposed War Veterans," unpublished paper.
4. David Kriebel, "The Dioxins' Genetic Risks," Center for the Biology of Natural Systems, Washington University, St. Louis, Missouri, August 1979.
5. Statement of Dr. Steven D. Stellman, assistant vice president for epidemiology, American Cancer Society, before the Subcommittee on Medical Facilities and Benefits of the Committee on Veterans' Affairs, U.S. House of Representatives, July 22, 1980.
6. Testimony of Dr. Samuel S. Epstein, School of Public Health, University of Illinois Medical Center, before the Subcommittee on Medical Facilities and Benefits of the Committee on Veterans' Affairs, U.S. House of Representatives, July 22, 1980.
7. L. Hardell and A. Sandstrom, *British Journal of Cancer,* Vol. 39 (1971), p. 711.
8. O. Axelson et al., *Läkartidningen,* Vol. 76 (1979), p. 3505.

9. M. Eriksson et al., *Läkartidningen*, Vol. 76 (1979), p. 3872.
10. A.M. Thiess and Frentzel-Beyme, "Mortality of Persons Exposed to Dioxin after an Accident Which Occurred in the BASF on 13th November, 1953," Medichemen Congress, University of San Francisco, September 5–9, 1977.
11. M. Eriksson et al., "Soft-Tissue Sarcomas and Exposure to Chemical Substances: A Case-Referent Study," *British Journal of Industrial Medicine*, Vol. 38 (1981), pp. 27–33.
12. Thomas Whiteside, *The Pendulum and the Toxic Cloud: The Course of Dioxin Contamination* (New Haven and London: Yale University Press), 1979, pp. 38–39.
13. Ibid., pp. 116–17.
14. Ibid., p. 120.
15. Ibid., pp. 120–21.
16. Ibid., p. 124.
17. Ibid., pp. 74–75.
18. Statement of Robert O. Muller, executive director, Vietnam Veterans of America, before the Subcommittee on Medical Facilities and Benefits of the Committee on Veterans' Affairs, U.S. House of Representatives, July 22, 1980.
19. Sierra Club presentation, WIXT, June 27, 1980.
20. Statement of Dr. Jeanne M. Stellman, associate professor of public health, Division of Environmental Sciences, Columbia University, before the Subcommittee on Medical Facilities and Benefits of the Committee on Veterans' Affairs, U.S. House of Representatives, July 22, 1980.

10 THE VIETNAMIZATION OF AMERICA

1. "The Globe Incident: 1969–81," *New Times*, June 3–9, 1981.
2. "Herbicide Concerns: A Basic Introduction," Northwest Coalition for Alternatives to Pesticides (NCAP), P.O. Box 375, Eugene, Oregon 97440.
3. Jack Anderson, *Washington Post*, April 24, 1978.
4. Phil Keisling, "The Spraying of Oregon," *Willamette Week*, December 31, 1979.
5. NCAP Staff, "The Saga of 2,4,5-T," *NCAP News*, Fall–Winter 1981–82.
6. *Philadelphia Inquirer*, October 31, 1982.
7. "Herbicide Information Packet," Northwest Coalition for Alternatives to Pesticides (NCAP), p. 65.

8. Ibid., pp. 66–67.
9. Ibid., pp. 67–68.
10. Paul Merrell, "IBT Officials Indicted for Fraud," *NCAP News*, Spring–Summer 1981.
11. Ibid.
12. Ibid.

II   VIETNAM VETERANS ARE AMERICA'S FUTURE

No notes.

INDEX

Agent Blue, xvi*n*, 39, 42, 78
  carcinogenic properties of, 42
  health effects of, 63
Agent Green, 78
Agent Orange:
  amount used in Vietnam, 29
  burning of, 32–33, 38
  chemical content of, xvi
  dioxin levels in, 108
  disposal of, 121*n*
  early testing of, xvi
  exposure to, *see* herbicides, exposure to
  independent board of inquiry needed on, 179
  quantities unaccounted for, 67
  spraying of, *see* herbicides, spraying of
  symptoms from exposure to, *see* symptoms of dioxin poisoning
  teratogenic and carcinogenic effects of, 32
  see also dioxin; 2, 4-D; 2, 4, 5-T
Agent Orange, the Deadly Fog (documentary), 80
"Agent Orange Program Guide" (VA), 84
Agent Orange Victims International, xv, 10

Agent Orange Victims of New York, 18
Agent Pink, 78
Agent White, xvi*n*, 78
Agriculture Department, U.S., 57, 162
Allen, James, 140, 152
Alsea region, Oregon, 151–55, 160–61, 170
American Cancer Society, 8
American Farm Bureau, 161
American Legion, 7
Anderson, Jack, 155
arsenic, 63
A Shau Valley, 49
Augerson, William S., 11–12
Australia:
  investigation of Agent Orange resisted in, 68, 71–74
  media coverage of veterans' problems in, 68
  proposed herbicide study in, 73
  veterans' questionnaire in, 73
  in Vietnam War, 60–78
Australian Repatriation Commission, 65, 78

base camps, spraying around, 4, 26, 67
Bayer AG, 169
Bell, Graham, 63

Berning, Karl, 96
Bionetics Laboratories, 56–57
biopsies, 33–34, 120–23
Bjelke-Petersen, Joh, 71
bladder cancer, 6–15
Bonior, David E., 85
Boston Edison, 147
Boyd, Al, 21
"breathers," 38
Brown, Philip, 23*n*
Bureau of Land Management, U.S.,
    151–55

Cambodia, 36
Canada, 164
Center for Disease Control, U.S., 72,
    96
Chemical and Biological Warfare
    (Hersh), 86–87
chemical companies:
    in lawsuits, 102–11
    VA influenced by, 27–28
    see also specific companies
Chicago Tribune, 101
chloracne, xix, 11, 17, 33, 133*n*
chlorophenols, 137
cholestyramine, 123
Citizen Soldier, 133
Clark, Ray, 5–15
Clark, Mrs. Ray, 7–15
class action lawsuit, *see* lawsuit, class
    action
Cleland, Max, xviii, 51, 81–85, 92, 111–
    12, 138
Codario, Ronald A., 114–25
C123 Provider transports, 3, 26, 66
Congress, U.S., 13, 72, 79, 166, 178–79
    epidemiological study ordered by,
    93
    see also House of Representatives,
    U.S.; Senate, U.S.
Consumer Product Safety Commis-
    sion, U.S., 143*n*
Cranston, Alan, 55, 93

Dak Rosa, 156–58
Dak Siang, 157

Dak Tang Plun, 156–58
Daschle, Thomas A., 85
DeBoer, Linda, 17
DeBoer, Ron, 16–30
Defense Department, Australian, 62,
    66
Defense Department, U.S., 7, 67
    Agent Orange exposure denied
    by, 11–12, 27
    in class action lawsuit, 103–4
    "Defoliation Conference" of, 105*n*
    Dow Chemical suit against, 104
    on exposure delay, 39
    exposure to herbicides unrecord-
    ed by, 83
    widespread exposure denied by, 19
defoliants, *see also* herbicides; *specific
    defoliants*
Defoliation Conference, 105*n*
Delmore, Fred J., 105*n*
DeRock, Eve and Vern, 159–60
DeVictor, Maude, 80, 100
Diamond Shamrock, 27, 107
dioxin, 15
    body absorption of, 37
    diseases caused by, 14
    dispersal of, 29
    DNA and, 37, 131–33
    effects of, 18, 24, 35
    environmental testing for, 164–65
    industrial accidents with, 135–36,
    138–42
    international literature on, 40
    teratogenic and fetotoxic effects
    of, 52
    toxicity of, 29, 127–28
    see also symptoms of dioxin poi-
    soning; treatments for dioxin
    poisoning; *specific chemicals*
"Dioxins' Genetic Risk, The" (Krie-
    bel), 131–32
Dong Tam, 35
Dow Chemical, 18, 27, 29, 39, 56, 99
    107, 143–44, 150, 160
    Defense Department sued by, 104
    in lawsuit against VA, 111–12
    on liability, xviii–xix

McKusick suit against, 150
TCDD carcinogenicity tested by, 135
TCDD in rats studied by, 129
2, 4, 5-T ban challenged by, 160–62, 169–70
2, 4, 5-T dioxin content reduced by, 158
on 2, 4, 5-T toxicity, 105*n*
on VA treatment of veterans, 111–12
DuBridge, Lee, 56
Dux, John, 66, 75*n*

"Effects of Herbicides in South Vietnam, The" (Hickey), 156–58
Environmental Defense Fund, 143–44, 162
Environmental Protection Agency (EPA), U.S., 14, 85, 121*n*, 151, 153–54
Alsea studied by, 160–61
data quality at, 168–69
dioxin-human epidemiology studies on, 85
FEPCA and, 166–69
manufacturer research and, 167–68
Missouri incident and, 166
pesticide reviews by, 166–69
reviewing shortcuts of, 167–69
2, 4-D reregistration and, 168
2, 4, 5-T banned by, 85, 122, 160–62, 169–70
2, 4, 5-T hearings suspended by, 162, 169–70
Epstein, Samuel S., 134–36
Eriksson, M., 117

fatty tissues, 33–34, 120–23, 133–34, 155, 159
Federal Advisory Act, 81
Federal Code of Regulations, Title 8, 91–92
Federal Environmental Pesticide Control Act (FEPCA), 166–69
Federal Food, Drug and Cosmetic Act, 143*n*

Feinberg, Wilfred, 103
Field, Barbara, 52, 72
flamethrower boats ("zippo monitors"), 32–33, 38–39
Food and Drug Administration, U.S., 57
food supplies, Agent Blue and, 39, 42
Foot, Geoffrey, 75*n*
Forest Service, U.S., 147–56
Freedlund, Neddie, 156
Freedom of Information Act, 24, 27, 41, 85
Fukushima, Yoichi, 86

Galston, Arthur W., 53, 57
gas masks, 61–62
General Accounting Office (GAO), U.S., 11*n*, 26–27, 66–67, 83, 96–97
Gibson, Bob, 61–66, 70–71, 75, 78
Goldwater, Barry, 149
Green, John, 4–5
Gross, Michael, 121–22
Guzelian, Philip S., 123

Haber, Paul, 111–12
Handler, Philip, 85–87
Hardell, Lennart, 117
Hardy, Mrs. D. A., 75*n*
Harper, John, 69–71
Hayward, Albert, 105*n*
Health and Human Services Department, U.S., 50
Hematin, 120
herbicides, xv–xxi
Australian spraying of, 61–67
domestic use of, 147–74
economic effects of bans on, 170–71
exposure to, *see* herbicides, exposure to
Japanese study of (1967), 86
NAS study on, 85–87
phenoxy, 35, 77, 106, 137
propaganda concerning, 172
side effects from, 62–63; *see also* symptoms of dioxin poisoning
spraying of, *see* herbicides, spraying of

herbicides (*cont.*)
  wildlife and, 171
  see also specific herbicides
herbicides, exposure to, 4, 9–12,
    88–89
  certainty of, 143–44
  in drinking water, 49, 66
  in food, 66
  herbicide drums and, 39
  histories of, 133
  "markers" for, 133
  multiple route, 138
  official denials of, 11–12, 19, 27, 39
  pesticide spraying and, 67
  after Seveso, Italy, accident, 138–41
  when spraying, 61–63
  from unofficial spraying, 67
  variability of reaction to, 75–76
  on "zippo monitors," 38–39
herbicides, spraying of:
  by Australians, 61–67
  around base camps, 4, 26, 67
  by boats, 67
  buffer zones for, 153–54
  by C123s, 3, 26, 66
  domestic, 147–74
  domestic recordkeeping on, 153
  drift from, 153–54
  by foot soldiers, 61–62, 67
  by Forest Service, 147–56
  by helicopters, 66–67
  from trucks, 67
  unofficial, 67
  weather and, 153–54
HERBS tapes, xvi, 12, 26–27
Hercules, 107
Hersh, Seymour M., 86–87
Hickey, Gerard C., 156–58
Hill, Bonnie, 151–55, 160–63, 169–73
Houk, Vernon, 95
House of Representatives, U.S.:
  Medical Facilities and Benefits
    Subcommittee of, 85–86, 133, 135–
    36, 142–43, 180–81
  Veterans' Affairs Committee of,
    145
Huey helicopters, 4

Industrial Bio-Test Laboratories,
    168–69
"Instructions for Spraying Herbi-
    cides," 62–63
International Paper Company, 159–
    60

Jacoby, William J., Jr., 87
Johnson, Christopher H., 180–81
Justice Department, U.S., 112
Juteau, Ed, 14

Kavenagh, Keith, 104, 110, 112–13
kepone, 123
Kerr, Charles, 72
Kriebel, David, 131–32
Kurtis, Bill, 80

Lang, Ton Duc, 130–31
lawsuit, class action, 28, 98, 100–110
  demands of, 100–101
  dismissal motions in, 102–3, 106
  interest in, 101
  jurisdictional appeals in, 103–4
  liability and damages separated in,
    101
  non-delegable fiduciary obligation
    alleged in, 106–8
  reserve fund in, 100–101
  state vs. federal courts as site for,
    102–4
  task force organized for, 101–2
  "war contractor" defense in,
    104–9
lawsuits, 98–113
  derivative sovereign immunity in,
    104–6
  gross negligence and, 34
  statute of limitations and, 28, 110
  VA Agent Orange Program chal-
    lenged in, 84, 110–12
Lincoln, Abraham, 15
Long Djon, 156–58
Long Island Rail Road, 147, 173–74
Lou Harris and Associates, 23*n*
Lugg, George, 74–75

McCarthy, Frank, 100
McKusick, Bob, 147–50
McMinn, Holt, 69–70
McNulty, Wilbur, 126–30, 133–34, 145–46, 152
MacPhee, Donald, 71–72
malathion, 60
Mayerson, Hy, 116
Mekong Delta, 32
Menzies, Robert, 60
Meselson, Matthew, xxi, 29, 57, 128n
Messner, Anthony, 73–74, 78
Minnesota Multiple Personality Inventory (MMPI), 136
Mississippi Air and Pollution Control Commission, 121n
Missouri incident, 165–66
Mobay, 169
Monsanto Corporation, 27, 107, 168–69
mosquitoes, 60
Moynihan, Daniel Patrick, 8
Muller, Robert O., 142–43
"Mutagenicity of Dioxin and Its Effects on Reproduction among Exposed War Veterans, The" (Tung, Lang, and Van), 130–31

Nader's Raiders, 57
Naples, Charlotte, 33, 36, 42
Naples, Joe, 33–43
Naprosyn, 169
National Academy of Sciences, 85–87, 95
National Association of Concerned Veterans, 81
National Cattlemen's Association, 161
National Forest Products Association, 161
National Health and Medical Research Council (NHMRC), Australian, 71–72
National Veterans Law Center (NVLC), 80–81, 93–94
NCAP News, 162

Nemacur, 168–69
New England Journal of Medicine, 123
New York State, toxic waste task force of, 166
New York State Temporary Commission on Dioxin Exposure, 12, 22, 25–26, 173–74
hearings of, xvii, xix, 25–26, 53, 88–92
members of, 25
New York Times, 94
Nimmo, Robert P., 96, 178
Northeastern Pharmaceutical and Chemical Company, 165–66
Northwest Coalition for Alternatives to Pesticides (NCAP), 162

Office of Technology Assessment, 72, 95
Operation Ranch Hand, 3–4, 23n, 63n, 121n
missions of, 3–4
night flights rejected in, 3
Oregon Regional Primate Research Center, 126–30, 134
Oregon State Board of Forestry, 154
Oregon State University, 153, 170
Owen, Charles, 80

PCBs (polychlorinated biphenyls), 127
PCDDs (polychlorinated dibenzo-p-dioxins), 106
PCDFs (polychlorinated dibenzo furans), 106
Pendulum and the Toxic Cloud: The Course of Dioxin Contamination, The (Whiteside), 138–41
pentachlorophenol, 145
Petryka, Dr., 117–19
phenoxyacetic acid, 35, 77, 106, 137
Phuoc Tuy province, Vietnam, 60–61, 66–67
Plei Jar Tum, 158
Plei Ngol Drong, 158
Plei Ro-O, 157–58
Polei Kleng, 158

Polei Krong, 157–58
Polk County Easter Seals Center, 47–48
Pratt, George C., 103, 106
protective gear, 5, 61–62
punch biopsies, 33–34

Reagan administration, 162
Repatriation Tribunal (Australian), 77
Reutershan, Paul, xv, 99–100
rhesus monkeys, 127–30, 134, 140
Rivkin, Leonard, 41
Rorschach test, 136
Ryan, Maureen, 55

Senate, U.S., Veterans' Affairs Committee of, 11–12, 54–55, 92, 95
Sencor, 168–69
Seveso, Italy, ICMESA plant explosion in, 138–42
Shepard, Barclay, 57–58
Shoecraft, Billie, 149–50
Silvex, 151–54
Simpson, Collin, 76–78
Siuslaw National Forest, 151–55
Sommers, John, 95
Soviet Union, herbicide exposure in, 116
Spivey, Dr., 94
Steiger, Sam, 149
Stellman, Jeanne, 145
Stellman, Steven D., xvii, 132–33
Strait, Heather, 45
Strait, Jerry, 44, 48–51, 56–57
Strait, Lori, 45–48, 51, 55–56
Strait, Sandy, 44–51, 56
Strik, Dr., 119
Supreme Court, U.S., 103–4
Sutton, Bobby, 31–43
Sweden, dioxin exposure in, 135
symptoms of dioxin poisoning, 5, 116–23
    abnormal EEGs, 36, 43
    alcohol intolerance, 21, 37
    birth defects, xvii, 20–21, 37, 45–48, 51–60, 67–73, 130–33, 173–74

blurred vision, 140–41
breathing difficulty, 38
cancers, 13–14, 17–19, 24, 137
chloracne, xix, 11, 17, 33, 133n
coughing blood, 70, 157
diarrhea, 36, 138, 141, 156–57
diminished white-blood-cell counts, 140–41
dizziness, 138, 141
Ehrlich reactions and, 118–19
enlarged prostate gland, 36
eye sensitivity, 36
fevers, 64, 156–57
gastroenteritis, 64
headaches, 36, 48–50, 138, 141
heart problems, 9
hypertension, 21
immune system malfunctioning, 140
insomnia, 65, 138, 156–57
intermediate porphyrin levels, 117–20
liver disease, 114–17, 119–20
loss of balance, 36
lymphoma, 76–78
memory loss, 7, 33
nasal problems, 61, 156–57
neurological disorders, 140
peripheral neuropathies, 36
persistent coughs, 156–57
porphyria cutanea tarda, 117, 119–20
potential delay in, 141–42
premature aging, 88–89, 137–38
rashes, 33–36, 48–50, 61, 64, 70, 141, 156–57
seizures, 46
skin discolorations ("creeping crud"), 16–17
spontaneous abortions, 151–52, 156–61, 172–74
stomach cramps, 138, 156–57, 159
sudden weight loss, xix–xx
trauma as cause of, 73–74, 92–93
in urine samples, 117–19
Vietnamese descriptions of, 156–58
vomiting, 36, 61

weakness, 159
see also treatments for dioxin poisoning
Syntex Corporation, 169

TCC (trichlorocarbanilide), 168–69
TCDD-dioxin, xvi–xvii, 27, 51, 80
  animals tested with, 127–30, 133–34
  carcinogenicity of, 134–37
  in fatty tissues, 120–23, 133–34, 155, 159
  fetotoxicity of, 129
  mutagenic effects of, xvii, 51–52, 129–33
  potency of, xvii
  reactions of different species to, 127, 133
  Seveso, Italy, and, 138–42
  spontaneous abortions from, 139–40
  teratogenic effects of, 129
  2, 4, 5-T in, 72
TCP, 135–36
testicular cancer, 17, 24
Tiernan, Thomas, 121
treatments for dioxin poisoning:
  with cholestyramine, 123
  with Hematine, 120
  psychiatric, 9–10, 37, 50, 53, 91–93, 136, 142, 177
Tung, Ton That, 51–54, 130–31, 171
2, 4-D (n-butyl-2, 4-dichlorophenoxyacetate), xvi, 62, 71, 135, 151–52, 168
2, 4, 5-T (n-butyl-2, 4, 5-trichlorophenoxyacetate), xvi, 14, 18, 52, 56, 62, 71
  birth defects and, 71–73
  carcinogenicity of, 135
  domestic use of, 154–74
  EPA ban on, 85, 122, 160–62, 169–70
  Forest Service use of, 148–50
  marketing of, 144–46
  production levels of, 163
  RPAR scrutiny of, 161
  Seveso, Italy, accident with, 138–42
  TCDD in, 105*n*

teratogenicity of, 56–57
testing for, 164

Uniroyal, 27, 107

Van, Do Duc, 130–31
Verrett, Jacqueline, xvii
veterans, Australian, 68–78
veterans, North Vietnamese, birth defects in children of, 51–53, 130–31
veterans, U.S.:
  bureaucratic indifference to, 8
  family cancer histories of, 13–14
  homecoming receptions for, 6
  pre-Vietnam condition of, 13
  surveillance of, 42
  see also specific persons
Veterans Administration (VA), U.S., 7, 19, 79–97
  Advisory Committee on Health-Related Effects of Herbicides of, 57–58, 81, 85
  Agent Orange disability claims rejected by, 81–82
  Agent Orange-disease connection denied by, xviii, 11, 50–51, 80, 88–89
  Agent Orange Registry of, 87
  Agent Orange Steering Committee of, 85
  birth defect study planned by, 58
  cancer registry numbers destroyed by, 41
  "certain" proof sought by, 143
  chemical company lobbying of, 27–28
  in class action lawsuit, 103–4
  cohort studies not done by, 137
  Dow Chemical on, 111
  effects of dioxin on humans known by, 82–83
  on EPA ban of 2, 4, 5-T, 85
  on EPA studies, 85
  epidemiological study by, *see* Veterans Administration epidemiological study

Veterans Administration (*cont.*)
  exposure denied by, 11, 27
  exposure questionnaire of, 49, 83
  fat biopsy study of, 120–23
  on GAO report, 97
  hospitals of, *see* Veterans Administration hospitals
  ignorance of Agent Orange in (1972), 10–11
  information release denied by, 27
  literature of, 32
  media overreaction alleged by, 54
  money as motive of, 40, 179–80
  names withheld by, 23–24
  new studies planned by, 178
  outreach program rejected by, 54–55, 81–82, 137
  painkilling device of, 36–37
  private decision-making at, 83–85
  Ranch Hand studied by, 23
  rule changes not publicized by, 14
  self-contradiction by, 88
  size of, 79
  strategy of, toward Agent Orange, 80–81
  "study population" needed by, 88
  tumor registry of, 40–41
  victim treatment downplayed by, 82–83
Veterans Administration epidemiological study:
  Center for Disease Control and, 96
  delay of, 54, 57–58, 81, 178
  design rejected for, 72, 95
  ordered by Congress, 93, 178
  "request for proposals" for, 93–94
  scientists restricted from, 94
  true study avoided by, 22–23
Veterans Administration hospitals, 7–10
  Agent Orange examinations at, xix, 10, 49–50, 83–84, 90–91, 121
  biopsy results "lost" by, 34–35
  incompetence at, 37–38
  psychiatric treatment by, xix, 9–10, 37, 50, 53, 91–93, 136, 142, 177
  quality of treatment at, 82–83, 90–91
  secrecy in, 8–9
  staff and facilities lacking in, 12–13
Veterans' Affairs Department, Australian, 73
Vietnam Veterans Action Association (Australian), 69–78
Vietnam Veterans of America, 11*n*
Vulcanus, 121

Wares, Cameron, 59, 67–70, 78
Wares, Jim, 59–61, 64–65, 67–78
water, 4, 49
WBBM (Chicago), 80
Westing, Arthur H., 163–65
Whiteside, Thomas, 56–57, 138–41, 165–66
Williams, Jack, 149

Yannacone, Carol, 99, 112–13
Yannacone, Victor, 18, 20, 34, 96, 98–113, 137
Young, P. J., 66, 75*n*

"zippo monitors" (flamethrower boats), 32–33, 38–39

About the Author

Born in Des Moines, Iowa, FRED A. WILCOX is a graduate of the University of Iowa. He edited, and wrote much of, *Grass Roots: An Anti-Nuclear Source Book*. Mr. Wilcox lives in Ithaca, New York.